EMERIL LAGASSE
POWER AIR FRYER 360
COOK BOOK 1000

Effortless Air Fryer Oven Recipes for Beginners and Busy People to Master Emeril Lagasse Power Air Fryer 360

Byron B. Salo

Copyright© 2021 By Byron B. Salo All Rights Reserved

This book is copyright protected. It is only for personal use. You cannot amend, distribute, sell, use, quote or paraphrase any part of the content within this book, without the consent of the author or publisher.

Under no circumstances will any blame or legal responsibility be held against the publisher, or author, for any damages, reparation, or monetary loss due to the information contained within this book, either directly or indirectly.

Disclaimer Notice:

Please note the information contained within this document is for educational and entertainment purposes only. All effort has been executed to present accurate, up to date, reliable, complete information. No warranties of any kind are declared or implied. Readers acknowledge that the author is not engaged in the rendering of legal, financial, medical or professional advice. The content within this book has been derived from various sources. Please consult a licensed professional before attempting any techniques outlined in this book.

By reading this document, the reader agrees that under no circumstances is the author responsible for any losses, direct or indirect, that are incurred as a result of the use of the information contained within this document, including, but not limited to, errors, omissions, or inaccuracies.

TABLE OF CONTENT

Introduction.. 1	Nut and Seed Muffins...................................14
Chapter 1 Breakfasts.................................. 2	Strawberry Toast... 15
Simple Cinnamon Toasts............................ 2	Spaghetti Squash Fritters............................15
Bacon and Spinach Egg Muffins................ 2	Simple Scotch Eggs...................................... 15
Bourbon Vanilla French Toast................... 2	Vanilla Granola..16
Portobello Eggs Benedict............................ 3	Cajun Breakfast Sausage.............................16
Scotch Eggs.. 3	Breakfast Pita...16
Hearty Cheddar Biscuits............................. 3	Pizza Eggs...17
Double-Dipped Mini Cinnamon Biscuits........... 4	**Chapter 2 Vegetables and Sides**............... 17
Pita and Pepperoni Pizza........................... 5	Easy Potato Croquettes............................... 17
PB&J... 5	Breaded Green Tomatoes...........................17
Egg Muffins... 5	Corn on the Cob.. 18
Sausage Stuffed Poblanos.......................... 6	Grits Casserole...18
Hearty Blueberry Oatmeal........................ 6	Rosemary New Potatoes............................ 18
Sausage Egg Cup... 6	Roasted Sweet Potatoes............................. 18
Denver Omelet...7	Spiced Honey-Walnut Carrots................... 19
Broccoli-Mushroom Frittata...................... 7	Cauliflower Rice Balls.................................19
Potato Bread Rolls...................................... 7	Lemon-Garlic Mushrooms.......................... 19
Three-Berry Dutch Pancake...................... 8	Fried Brussels Sprouts................................20
Coconut Brown Rice Porridge with Dates........ 8	Potato with Creamy Cheese...................... 20
Spinach with Scrambled Eggs................... 8	Blackened Zucchini with Kimchi-Herb Sauce... 20
Two-Cheese Grits.. 9	Indian Eggplant Bharta.............................. 21
Mississippi Spice Muffins.......................... 9	Green Bean Casserole................................ 21
Blueberry Cobbler...................................... 9	Herbed Shiitake Mushrooms..................... 21
Apple Cider Doughnut Holes................... 10	Caesar Whole Cauliflower.......................... 22
Baked Potato Breakfast Boats................. 10	Sesame Carrots and Sugar Snap Peas.......22
Potatoes Lyonnaise................................... 10	Tingly Chili-Roasted Broccoli..................... 22
Maple Granola..11	Indian Chinese Cauliflower........................ 23
Buffalo Egg Cups....................................... 11	Roasted Eggplant..23
Bacon, Egg, and Cheese Roll Ups............11	Easy Rosemary Green Beans..................... 23
Tomato and Mozzarella Bruschetta........12	Garlic-Parmesan Jícama Fries....................23
Meritage Eggs.. 12	Bacon Potatoes and Green Beans............. 24
Nutty Granola.. 12	Buffalo Cauliflower with Blue Cheese...... 24
Pumpkin Donut Holes...............................13	Spiced Butternut Squash........................... 25
Cornflakes Toast Sticks.............................13	Roasted Grape Tomatoes and Asparagus........ 25
Cauliflower Avocado Toast...................... 13	Parmesan-Thyme Butternut Squash........ 25
Chimichanga Breakfast Burrito............... 14	Hawaiian Brown Rice................................. 25
Egg White Cups... 14	Broccoli with Sesame Dressing..................26
Bacon Eggs on the Go............................... 14	Roasted Brussels Sprouts with Orange and

Garlic	26
Five-Spice Roasted Sweet Potatoes	26
Corn and Cilantro Salad	26
Zesty Fried Asparagus	27
Asian-Inspired Roasted Broccoli	27
Radish Chips	27
Cheddar Broccoli with Bacon	28
Mexican Corn in a Cup	28
Sweet and Crispy Roasted Pearl Onions	28
Mediterranean Zucchini Boats	29
Gorgonzola Mushrooms with Horseradish Mayo	29
Garlic-Parmesan Crispy Baby Potatoes	29
Cauliflower with Lime Juice	30
Cauliflower Steaks Gratin	30
Asparagus Fries	30
Parmesan Herb Focaccia Bread	30
Ratatouille	31
Mushrooms with Goat Cheese	31
Spinach and Sweet Pepper Poppers	31
Fried Zucchini Salad	32
Sesame Taj Tofu	32
Citrus-Roasted Broccoli Florets	32
Creamed Asparagus	33

Chapter 3 Poultry 33

Air Fried Chicken Wings with Buffalo Sauce	33
Chicken Strips with Satay Sauce	33
Breaded Turkey Cutlets	34
Chicken Legs with Leeks	34
Hawaiian Chicken Bites	34
French Garlic Chicken	35
Gold Livers	35
Easy Chicken Nachos	35
Wild Rice and Kale Stuffed Chicken Thighs	36
Chicken Drumsticks with Barbecue-Honey Sauce	36
Cracked-Pepper Chicken Wings	36
Lemon-Dijon Boneless Chicken	37
Teriyaki Chicken Legs	37
Korean Flavor Glazed Chicken Wings	37
Golden Chicken Cutlets	38
Chicken Shawarma	38
Chicken with Lettuce	38
Broccoli Cheese Chicken	39
Lemon Chicken	39
Chicken, Zucchini, and Spinach Salad	39
Brazilian Tempero Baiano Chicken Drumsticks	40
Jerk Chicken Kebabs	40
Chicken Parmesan	40
Thai-Style Cornish Game Hens	41
Jalapeño Popper Hasselback Chicken	41
General Tso's Chicken	41
Buffalo Crispy Chicken Strips	42
Lemon-Basil Turkey Breasts	42
Crispy Duck with Cherry Sauce	43
Chicken Manchurian	43
Spinach and Feta Stuffed Chicken Breasts	43
Turkey Meatloaf	44
Crispy Dill Chicken Strips	44
Chicken Wings with Piri Piri Sauce	45
Pecan-Crusted Chicken Tenders	45
Hawaiian Huli Huli Chicken	45
Crunchy Chicken Tenders	46
Taco Chicken	46
Fried Chicken Breasts	47
Tex-Mex Chicken Breasts	47
One-Dish Chicken and Rice	47
Cornish Hens with Honey-Lime Glaze	48
Turkey and Cranberry Quesadillas	48
Israeli Chicken Schnitzel	48
Classic Chicken Kebab	49

Chapter 4 Beef, Pork, and Lamb 49

Five-Spice Pork Belly	49
Jalapeño Popper Pork Chops	50
Mexican-Style Shredded Beef	50
Kielbasa Sausage with Pineapple and Bell Peppers	50
Mushroom in Bacon-Wrapped Filets Mignons	50

Sausage and Pork Meatballs.................................51	
Savory Sausage Cobbler..51	
Chicken Fried Steak with Cream Gravy............52	
Beef Burger..52	
Parmesan-Crusted Steak..52	
Beef and Goat Cheese Stuffed Peppers..............53	
Sichuan Cumin Lamb..53	
Beef Steak Fingers...54	
Panko Pork Chops..54	
Blackened Cajun Pork Roast................................54	
Cinnamon-Beef Kofta...55	
Sweet and Spicy Country-Style Ribs..................55	
Panko Crusted Calf's Liver Strips........................55	
Crescent Dogs...56	
Ground Beef Taco Rolls...56	
Steak with Bell Pepper...56	
Air Fried Beef Satay with Peanut Dipping Sauce..57	
Cheese Pork Chops...57	
Pork and Beef Egg Rolls..58	
Red Curry Flank Steak...58	
Greek-Style Meatloaf..59	
Almond and Caraway Crust Steak......................59	
Peppercorn-Crusted Beef Tenderloin.................59	
Lamb Chops with Horseradish Sauce................59	
Bean and Beef Meatball Taco Pizza....................60	
Pigs in a Blanket..60	
Spicy Lamb Sirloin Chops.....................................60	
Broccoli and Pork Teriyaki....................................61	
Indian Mint and Chile Kebabs.............................61	
Rosemary Roast Beef..62	
Spicy Flank Steak with Zhoug..............................62	
Caraway Crusted Beef Steaks...............................62	
Air Fried Potatoes with Olives.............................63	
Easy Beef Satay..63	
New York Strip with Honey-Mustard Butter....63	
Herb-Crusted Lamb Chops..................................64	
Beefy Poppers...64	
Blackened Steak Nuggets......................................65	
Smoky Pork Tenderloin...65	
Honey-Baked Pork Loin..65	

Chapter 5 Fish and Seafood 66

Tandoori-Spiced Salmon and Potatoes...........66
Salmon with Cauliflower................................66
Tuna Nuggets in Hoisin Sauce........................66
Savory Shrimp...67
Cucumber and Salmon Salad..........................67
Cripsy Shrimp with Cilantro..........................67
Salmon Burgers with Creamy Broccoli Slaw.. 68
Tuna Steak...68
Air Fryer Fish Fry..68
Shrimp Pasta with Basil and Mushrooms 69
Citrus-Soy Salmon with Bok Choy................69
Crawfish Creole Casserole.............................69
Garlicky Cod Fillets...70
Lemon Mahi-Mahi..70
Lemon Pepper Shrimp....................................70
Shrimp and Cherry Tomato Kebabs.............71
Fried Shrimp...71
Blackened Red Snapper..................................71
Teriyaki Salmon...71
Catfish Bites..72
Baked Grouper with Tomatoes and Garlic..... 72
Parmesan Fish Fillets......................................72
Mouthwatering Cod over Creamy Leek Noodles..73
Oregano Tilapia Fingers.................................73
Stuffed Shrimp..73
BBQ Shrimp with Creole Butter Sauce............74
Cayenne Flounder Cutlets..............................74
Tortilla Shrimp Tacos.....................................75
Bang Bang Shrimp...75
Shrimp Kebabs...75
Golden Shrimp...76
Friday Night Fish Fry.....................................76
Quick Shrimp Skewers...................................76
Salmon Spring Rolls.......................................77
Crustless Shrimp Quiche................................77
Tilapia Sandwiches with Tartar Sauce..........77
Crab Cakes with Mango Mayo......................78
Sea Bass with Potato Scales...........................78
Tuna-Stuffed Quinoa Patties.........................79

Trout Amandine with Lemon Butter Sauce..... 79
Baked Tilapia with Garlic Aioli.................. 80
Crab Legs... 80
Tex-Mex Salmon Bowl........................... 80

Chapter 6 Snacks and Appetizers.................. 81

Lemony Endive in Curried Yogurt................ 81
Greek Yogurt Deviled Eggs........................ 81
Homemade Sweet Potato Chips.................. 81
Five-Ingredient Falafel with Garlic-Yogurt Sauce... 81
Pork and Cabbage Egg Rolls...................... 82
Old Bay Chicken Wings........................... 82
Garlic-Roasted Tomatoes and Olives............. 83
Honey-Mustard Chicken Wings................... 83
Egg Roll Pizza Sticks.............................. 83
Cream Cheese Wontons............................ 84
Golden Onion Rings............................... 84
Spinach and Crab Meat Cups..................... 84
Garlic Edamame................................... 85
Artichoke and Olive Pita Flatbread............... 85
Cheesy Steak Fries................................ 85
String Bean Fries.................................. 86
Mexican Potato Skins............................. 86
Cheese Wafers.................................... 86
Asian Five-Spice Wings........................... 87
Asiago Shishito Peppers.......................... 87
Spiced Nuts....................................... 87
Ranch Oyster Snack Crackers.................... 88
Shishito Peppers with Herb Dressing............ 88
Grilled Ham and Cheese on Raisin Bread....... 88
Carrot Chips...................................... 89
Sausage Balls with Cheese....................... 89
Rosemary-Garlic Shoestring Fries................ 89
Dark Chocolate and Cranberry Granola Bars.................................... 90
Onion Pakoras.................................... 90
Kale Chips with Sesame.......................... 90
Garlic-Parmesan Croutons....................... 91
Air Fried Pot Stickers............................. 91
Greek Street Tacos............................... 91
Roasted Mushrooms with Garlic................. 91
Crunchy Basil White Beans...................... 92
Rumaki... 92
Baked Ricotta.................................... 92
Bacon-Wrapped Pickle Spears................... 93
Jalapeño Poppers................................ 93
Italian Rice Balls................................. 93
Stuffed Fried Mushrooms........................ 94
Parmesan French Fries.......................... 94
Garlicky and Cheesy French Fries............... 94
Zucchini Fries with Roasted Garlic Aïoli........ 95
Crispy Chili Chickpeas........................... 95

Chapter 7 Desserts.................................. 95

Cinnamon and Pecan Pie......................... 95
Orange-Anise-Ginger Skillet Cookie............. 96
Indian Toast and Milk............................ 96
Vanilla Pound Cake............................... 97
Pumpkin Cookie with Cream Cheese Frosting 97
Pears with Honey-Lemon Ricotta................ 97
Butter Flax Cookies.............................. 98
Applesauce and Chocolate Brownies............ 98
Jelly Doughnuts.................................. 98
Sweet Potato Donut Holes....................... 99
Crustless Peanut Butter Cheesecake............ 99
Coconut Muffins................................. 99
Apple Dutch Baby................................ 99
Carrot Cake with Cream Cheese Icing.......... 100
Nutty Pear Crumble............................. 100
Double Chocolate Brownies..................... 101
Apple Wedges with Apricots.................... 101
Coconut Mixed Berry Crisp..................... 101
Maple Bacon Moonshine Bread Pudding..... 102
Fried Cheesecake Bites......................... 102
Pecan Butter Cookies........................... 102
Gingerbread..................................... 103
Funnel Cake..................................... 103
Grilled Pineapple Dessert....................... 103
Homemade Mint Pie............................ 104
Fried Oreos..................................... 104
Molten Chocolate Almond Cakes............... 104
Cinnamon Cupcakes with Cream Cheese

Frosting 105
Chocolate Peppermint Cheesecake 105
Simple Pineapple Sticks 105
Mini Peanut Butter Tarts 106
Pumpkin Spice Pecans 106
Gluten-Free Spice Cookies 106
Almond Shortbread 107
Tortilla Fried Pies 107
Zucchini Nut Muffins 107
Mini Cheesecake 108
Lemon Bars 108
Crumbly Coconut-Pecan Cookies 108
Lemon Raspberry Muffins 109
Coconut-Custard Pie 109
Cardamom Custard 109
Shortcut Spiced Apple Butter 110

Chapter 8 Staples, Sauces, Dips, and Dressings 110
Peanut Sauce 110
Tzatziki 110
Peachy Barbecue Sauce 110
Pecan Tartar Sauce 111
Alfredo Sauce 111
Marinara Sauce 111
Pepper Sauce 112
Tomatillo Salsa 112
Gochujang Dip 112
Hot Honey Mustard Dip 112
Cucumber Yogurt Dip 113
Artichoke Dip 113
Italian Dressing 113
Tahini Dressing 113
Apple Cider Dressing 113
Orange Dijon Dressing 114
Miso-Ginger Dressing 114
Blue Cheese Dressing 114
Green Basil Dressing 114
Traditional Caesar Dressing 114
Avocado Dressing 115
Dijon and Balsamic Vinaigrette 115
Hemp Dressing 115

Lemony Tahini 115
Cashew Mayo 115
Mushroom Apple Gravy 116
Homemade Remoulade Sauce 116
Sweet Ginger Teriyaki Sauce 116
Vegan Lentil Dip 116
Lemon Cashew Dip 116
Cauliflower Alfredo Sauce 117
Red Buffalo Sauce 117

Chapter 9 Desserts 117
Cream Cheese Danish 117
Strawberry Pastry Rolls 118
Strawberry Scone Shortcake 118
5-Ingredient Brownies 119
Vanilla and Cardamon Walnuts Tart 119
Ricotta Lemon Poppy Seed Cake 119
Cherry Pie 120
Bourbon Bread Pudding 120
Pumpkin-Spice Bread Pudding 120
Graham Cracker Cheesecake 121
Chocolate Bread Pudding 121
Eggless Farina Cake 122
Mixed Berries with Pecan Streusel Topping 122
Peach Fried Pies 122
Bananas Foster 123
Lemon Poppy Seed Macaroons 123
Butter and Chocolate Chip Cookies 124
Cream-Filled Sandwich Cookies 124
Chocolate Lava Cakes 124
Grilled Peaches 124
Pecan Bars 125
Cream Cheese Shortbread Cookies 125
Baked Peaches with Yogurt and Blueberries 125
Fried Golden Bananas 125
Chocolate Chip-Pecan Biscotti 126
Peanut Butter-Honey-Banana Toast 126
Cinnamon-Sugar Almonds 127
Cream-Filled Sponge Cakes 127
Glazed Cherry Turnovers 127

Crispy Pineapple Rings.................................128
Lime Bars...128
Strawberry Shortcake....................................128
Apple Fries..128
Lemon Curd Pavlova......................................129
Dark Brownies..129
Baked Cheesecake..130
Pumpkin Pudding with Vanilla Wafers......130
Coconut Flour Cake.......................................130
Chocolate and Rum Cupcakes......................131
Baked Apples and Walnuts...........................131
Vanilla Scones..131
Halle Berries-and-Cream Cobbler................131
Chickpea Brownies..132
Blackberry Cobbler..133
Baked Brazilian Pineapple............................133
Olive Oil Cake...133
Maple-Pecan Tart with Sea Salt....................133
Pecan and Cherry Stuffed Apples.................134
Old-Fashioned Fudge Pie..............................134
Rhubarb and Strawberry Crumble...............135
Pecan Brownies..135
Air Fryer Apple Fritters................................135
Almond-Roasted Pears..................................136
Breaded Bananas with Chocolate Topping...136

Chapter 10 Fast and Easy Everyday Favorites....136

Corn Fritters..136
Spinach and Carrot Balls..............................137
Traditional Queso Fundido...........................137
Cheesy Baked Grits..137
Bacon Pinwheels..137
Air Fried Shishito Peppers............................138
Crispy Green Tomatoes Slices......................138
Cheesy Jalapeño Cornbread..........................138
Garlicky Knots with Parsley.........................139
Classic Poutine...139
South Carolina Shrimp and Corn Bake.......139
Honey Bartlett Pears with Lemony Ricotta 140
Air Fried Broccoli..140
Beery and Crunchy Onion Rings.................140
Scalloped Veggie Mix.....................................141
Easy Air Fried Edamame...............................141
Golden Salmon and Carrot Croquettes........141
Rosemary and Orange Roasted Chickpeas 142
Crispy Potato Chips with Lemony Cream Dip..142
Buttery Sweet Potatoes.................................142
Simple Air Fried Crispy Brussels Sprouts..143
Purple Potato Chips with Rosemary............143
Air Fried Tortilla Chips................................143
Lemony and Garlicky Asparagus.................143
Classic Latkes..144
Baked Chorizo Scotch Eggs..........................144
Garlicky Zoodles..144
Beef Bratwursts...145
Simple Cheesy Shrimps.................................145
Frico..145
Air Fried Butternut Squash with Chopped Hazelnuts..145
Simple Baked Green Beans...........................146
Easy Devils on Horseback.............................146
Cheesy Potato Patties....................................146
Crunchy Fried Okra.......................................147
Sweet Corn and Carrot Fritters....................147
Easy Roasted Asparagus...............................147
Baked Cheese Sandwich................................147
Cheesy Chile Toast..148
Spicy Air Fried Old Bay Shrimp...................148
Indian-Style Sweet Potato Fries...................148
Beet Salad with Lemon Vinaigrette.............148
Southwest Corn and Bell Pepper Roast......149
Herb-Roasted Veggies...................................149
Peppery Brown Rice Fritters........................149

Appendix 1 Measurement Conversion Chart & Air Fryer Cooking Chart.................................150

Introduction

We have to wear a lot of hats; we're parents, partners, housekeepers, business professionals, and I'm sure you can think of a few others to add to the list. One massive time waster in my life was waiting around for the convection oven in my kitchen to warm up. I didn't really have the option of making a quick snack when my boys got hunger pangs—the slow building of heat in the oven meant I had to plan ahead.

I decided to clear some counter space for an alternative. Luckily, I already knew what I wanted because I'd been using an air fryer for a while and loved the speed and efficiency. It was a no-brainer to upgrade my air fryer to the Emeril Lagasse Power Air Fryer 360. Why? Because if I wanted roasted potatoes for a snack, all I had to do was pop them in, turn the temperature to 350 degrees Fahrenheit, and cook for 25 minutes—no preheating needed.

What's more, it's versatile. You can bake, broil, fry, toast, and convection cook at the press of a button! If you're familiar with air fryers, you'll know that they also come with these functions; why replace one air fryer with another? The size. The Emeril Lagasse Power Air Fryer 360 has space for nine slices of toast, a 9 in. cake, 5 lb. chicken, or a 12 in. pizza. But, I'm getting ahead of myself. Let's take a step back, and I'll tell you what an air fryer is. Although this appliance has taken America by storm, not all readers may know just how amazing (and healthy) cooking with an air fryer is.

In essence, air-fried food is a healthy option to deep-fried food—you use 95% less oil. You may think that food won't be as delicious as those doused in fat. Believe me: you'll be pleasantly surprised. You'll get the same crisp crunch, golden color, and scrumptious taste. Air fryers are basically countertop convection ovens, and they work on the same premise—ultra-hot air is circulated around food to cook it.

Let's not forget Emeril Lagasse Power Air Fryer 360's toast function! You can donate your stand-alone toaster because the Emeril Lagasse Power Air Fryer 360 version works much better. Furthermore, since this is a mini oven, you'll be able to toast open-faced sandwiches or some English muffins for breakfast. Still, there's more to it; you can warm your leftovers to their former glory. Gone are the days of fried food that turn soggy when reheated—using the Emeril Lagasse Power Air Fryer 360, food will be as crisp as on the day it was made.

Basically, this appliance does what it's supposed to and does it well. The convenience — as well as its health-conscious quality—make it a revolutionary device to have in your kitchen.
I'm glad we outgrew the first air fryer we ever bought. The Emeril Lagasse Power Air Fryer 360 Air Fryer made it possible to take my culinary creativity to a new level. I was somewhat limited by the small size of my previous air fryer. Yes, I still have to cook in batches with the Emeril Lagasse Power Air Fryer 360 when I get guests or want to make a family-favorite like air-fried broccoli with a creamy blue cheese dip. However, where I had to make three or four batches, I can now get away with only two.

If you're worried that the Emeril Lagasse Power Air Fryer 360 isn't big enough—for instance, if it's only you or you and your partner—the appliance is big enough to make a whole meal. For example, air fry some cauliflower for five minutes, add some chicken cubes, air fry for another eight minutes, make a delicious cheese sauce while your Emeril Lagasse Power Air Fryer 360 is working its magic, and there you go: dinner!

You may be asking yourself, "what types of food can I make using the Emeril Lagasse Power Air Fryer Toaster Oven?" The simple answer: anything you'd make in a standard convection oven, but just in a fraction of time.

You will see in this cookbook that I include everything from canapés to desserts. Now, getting to more than 500 recipes that passed the test of family and friends' tastebuds was no easy feat. I wanted to give you only the best tried-and-tested recipes and wanted you to realize that you shouldn't be afraid of experimenting. I've air-fried a variety of foods from avocado to ice cream with huge success—I even baked a granadilla cheesecake in my Emeril Lagasse Power Air Fryer 360. I hope that by trying the recipes in this cookbook, it will spark some ideas, and you'll be brave enough to try your own combinations and concoctions.

If you already have a Emeril Lagasse Power Air Fryer Toaster Oven, it's time to fry, toast, bake, broil, or cook to your heart's content. I'm sure you'll find quite a few recipes you want to try in between the 800 included in this book —although I hope you try and enjoy them all!

For those readers who are still undecided if the Emeril Lagasse Power is the kitchen appliance for them, I suggest you browse through the recipes to see what mouth-watering dishes await you when you use this air fryer, toaster, and oven combo. It'll turn you into a master chef in no time!

Chapter 1 Breakfasts

Simple Cinnamon Toasts

Prep time: 5 minutes | Cook time: 4 minutes | Serves 4

1 tablespoon salted butter
2 teaspoons ground cinnamon
4 tablespoons sugar
½ teaspoon vanilla extract
10 bread slices

1. Select Bake, Air Fry Fan, set temperature to 380°F (193°C) and set time to 4 minutes. Press Start to begin preheating. 2. In a bowl, combine the butter, cinnamon, sugar, and vanilla extract. Spread onto the slices of bread. Transfer the bread to pizza rack. 3. Once preheated, place the rack on the bake position. You may need to work in batches. The bread will be golden brown when done. 4. Serve warm.

Bacon and Spinach Egg Muffins

Prep time: 7 minutes | Cook time: 12 to 14 minutes | Serves 6

6 large eggs
¼ cup heavy (whipping) cream
½ teaspoon sea salt
¼ teaspoon freshly ground black pepper
¼ teaspoon cayenne pepper (optional)
¾ cup frozen chopped spinach, thawed and drained
4 strips cooked bacon, crumbled
2 ounces (57 g) shredded Cheddar cheese

1. Select Bake, Air Fry Fan, set temperature to 300°F (149°C) and set time to 12 to 14 minutes. Press Start to begin preheating. 2. In a large bowl (with a spout if you have one), whisk together the eggs, heavy cream, salt, black pepper, and cayenne pepper (if using). 3. Divide the spinach and bacon among 6 silicone muffin cups. Place the muffin cups on pizza rack. 4. Divide the egg mixture among the muffin cups. Top with the cheese. 5. Once preheated, place the rack on the bake position. It will be done until the eggs are set and cooked through.

Bourbon Vanilla French Toast

Prep time: 15 minutes | Cook time: 6 minutes | Serves 4

2 large eggs
2 tablespoons water
⅔ cup whole or 2% milk
1 tablespoon butter, melted
2 tablespoons bourbon
1 teaspoon vanilla extract
8 (1-inch-thick) French bread slices
Cooking spray

1. Select Bake, Air Fry Fan, set temperature to 320°F (160°C) and set time to 6 minutes. Press Start to begin preheating. Line the pizza rack with parchment paper and spray it with cooking spray. 2. Beat the eggs with the water in a shallow bowl until combined. Add the milk, melted butter, bourbon, and vanilla and stir to mix well. 3. Dredge 4 slices of bread in the batter, turning to coat both sides evenly. Transfer the bread slices onto the parchment paper. 4. Once preheated, place the rack on the bake position. Flip the slices halfway through the cooking time. It will be done until nicely browned. 5. Remove from the oven to a plate and repeat with the remaining 4 slices of bread. 6. Serve warm.

Portobello Eggs Benedict

Prep time: 10 minutes | Cook time: 10 to 14 minutes | Serves 2

1 tablespoon olive oil	2 Roma tomatoes, halved lengthwise	2 tablespoons grated Pecorino Romano cheese
2 cloves garlic, minced	Salt and freshly ground black pepper, to taste	1 tablespoon chopped fresh parsley, for garnish
¼ teaspoon dried thyme	2 large eggs	1 teaspoon truffle oil (optional)
2 portobello mushrooms, stems removed and gills scraped out		

1. Select Air Fry, set temperature to 400°F (204°C) and set time to 10 to 14 minutes. Press Start to begin preheating. 2. In a small bowl, combine the olive oil, garlic, and thyme. Brush the mixture over the mushrooms and tomatoes until thoroughly coated. Season to taste with salt and freshly ground black pepper. 3. Arrange the vegetables, cut side up, on baking pan. Crack an egg into the center of each mushroom and sprinkle with cheese. Once preheated, place the pan on the air fry position. It will be done until the vegetables are tender and the whites are firm. When cool enough to handle, coarsely chop the tomatoes and place on top of the eggs. Scatter parsley on top and drizzle with truffle oil, if desired, just before serving.

Scotch Eggs

Prep time: 10 minutes | Cook time: 20 to 25 minutes | Serves 4

2 tablespoons flour, plus extra for coating	4 hard-boiled eggs, peeled	**Crumb Coating:**
1 pound (454 g) ground breakfast sausage	1 raw egg	¾ cup panko bread crumbs
	1 tablespoon water	¾ cup flour
	Oil for misting or cooking spray	

1. Select Bake, Air Fry Fan, set temperature to 360°F (182°C) and set time to 10 minutes. Press Start to begin preheating. 2. Combine flour with ground sausage and mix thoroughly. 3. Divide into 4 equal portions and mold each around a hard-boiled egg so the sausage completely covers the egg. 4. In a small bowl, beat together the raw egg and water. 5. Dip sausage-covered eggs in the remaining flour, then the egg mixture, then roll in the crumb coating. Transfer the eggs to pizza rack. 6. Once preheated, place the rack on the bake position. 7. Spray eggs, turn, and spray other side. Continue cooking for another 10 to 15 minutes or until sausage is well done.

Hearty Cheddar Biscuits

Prep time: 10 minutes | Cook time: 22 minutes | Makes 8 biscuits

2⅓ cups self-rising flour	minutes	1⅓ cups buttermilk
2 tablespoons sugar	½ cup grated Cheddar cheese, plus more to melt on top	1 cup all-purpose flour, for shaping
½ cup butter (1 stick), frozen for 15		1 tablespoon butter, melted

1. Line a buttered baking pan with parchment paper or a silicone liner. 2. Combine the flour and sugar in a large mixing bowl. Grate the butter into the flour. Add the grated cheese and stir to coat the cheese and butter with flour. Then add the buttermilk and stir just until you can no longer see streaks of flour. The dough should be quite wet. 3. Spread the all-purpose (not self-rising) flour out on a small cookie sheet. With a spoon, scoop 8 evenly sized balls of dough into the flour, making sure they don't touch each other. With floured hands, coat each dough ball with flour and toss them gently from hand to hand to shake off any excess flour. Put each floured dough ball into the prepared pan, right up next to the other. This will help the biscuits rise, rather than spreading out. 4. Select Bake, Air Fry Fan, set temperature to 380°F (193°C) and set time to 20 minutes. Press Start to begin preheating. 5. Once preheated, place the pan on the bake position. Let the ends of the aluminum foil sling hang across the pan before returning to the oven. 6. Check the biscuits twice to make sure they are not getting too brown on top. If they are, re-arrange the aluminum foil strips to cover any brown parts. After 20 minutes, check the biscuits by inserting a toothpick into the center of the biscuits. It should come out clean. If it needs a little more time, continue to bake for two extra minutes. Brush the tops of the biscuits with some melted butter and sprinkle a little more grated cheese on top if desired. Pop the pan back into the air fryer oven for another 2 minutes. 7. Remove the baking pan from the oven. Let the biscuits cool for just a minute or two and then turn them out onto a plate and pull apart. Serve immediately.

Double-Dipped Mini Cinnamon Biscuits

Prep time: 15 minutes | Cook time: 13 minutes | Makes 8 biscuits

2 cups blanched almond flour

½ cup Swerve confectioners'-style sweetener or equivalent amount of liquid or powdered sweetener

1 teaspoon baking powder

½ teaspoon fine sea salt

¼ cup plus 2 tablespoons (¾ stick) very cold unsalted butter

¼ cup unsweetened, unflavored almond milk

1 large egg

1 teaspoon vanilla extract

3 teaspoons ground cinnamon

Glaze:

½ cup Swerve confectioners'-style sweetener or equivalent amount of powdered sweetener

¼ cup heavy cream or unsweetened, unflavored almond milk

1. Select Bake, Air Fry Fan, set temperature to 350°F (177°C) and set time to 10 to 13 minutes. Press Start to begin preheating. Line a baking pan with parchment paper. 2. In a medium-sized bowl, mix together the almond flour, sweetener (if powdered; do not add liquid sweetener), baking powder, and salt. Cut the butter into ½-inch squares, then use a hand mixer to work the butter into the dry ingredients. When you are done, the mixture should still have chunks of butter. 3. In a small bowl, whisk together the almond milk, egg, and vanilla extract (if using liquid sweetener, add it as well) until blended. Using a fork, stir the wet ingredients into the dry ingredients until large clumps form. Add the cinnamon and use your hands to swirl it into the dough. 4. Form the dough into sixteen 1-inch balls and place them on the prepared pan, spacing them about ½ inch apart. (If you're using a smaller air fryer, work in batches if necessary.) Once preheated, place the pan on the bake position. It will be done until golden. Remove from the oven and let cool on the pan for at least 5 minutes. 5. While the biscuits bake, make the glaze: Place the powdered sweetener in a small bowl and slowly stir in the heavy cream with a fork. 6. When the biscuits have cooled somewhat, dip the tops into the glaze, allow it to dry a bit, and then dip again for a thick glaze. 7. Serve warm or at room temperature. Store unglazed biscuits in an airtight container in the refrigerator for up to 3 days or in the freezer for up to a month. Reheat in a preheated 350°F (177°C) air fryer oven for 5 minutes, or until warmed through, and dip in the glaze as instructed above.

Pita and Pepperoni Pizza

Prep time: 10 minutes | Cook time: 6 minutes | Serves 1

1 teaspoon olive oil	6 pepperoni slices	¼ teaspoon dried oregano
1 tablespoon pizza sauce	¼ cup grated Mozzarella cheese	
1 pita bread	¼ teaspoon garlic powder	

1. Select Pizza, Air Fry Fan, set temperature to 350°F (177°C) and set time to 6 minutes. Press Start to begin preheating. Grease the pizza rack with olive oil. 2. Spread the pizza sauce on top of the pita bread. Put the pepperoni slices over the sauce, followed by the Mozzarella cheese. 3. Season with garlic powder and oregano. 4. Transfer pita pizza to the rack. Once preheated, place the rack on the pizza position and bake. 5. Serve.

PB&J

Prep time: 5 minutes | Cook time: 6 minutes | Serves 4

½ cup cornflakes, crushed	6 tablespoons peanut butter	1 egg, beaten
¼ cup shredded coconut	2 medium bananas, cut into ½-inch-thick slices	Cooking spray
8 slices oat nut bread or any whole-grain, oversize bread	6 tablespoons pineapple preserves	

1. Select Air Fry, set temperature to 360°F (182°C) and set time to 6 minutes. Press Start to begin preheating. 2. In a shallow dish, mix the cornflake crumbs and coconut. 3. For each sandwich, spread one bread slice with 1½ tablespoons of peanut butter. Top with banana slices. Spread another bread slice with 1½ tablespoons of preserves. Combine to make a sandwich. 4. Using a pastry brush, brush top of sandwich lightly with beaten egg. Sprinkle with about 1½ tablespoons of crumb coating, pressing it in to make it stick. Spray with cooking spray. 5. Turn sandwich over and repeat to coat and spray the other side. Place the sandwiches on pizza rack. 6. Once preheated, place the rack on the air fry position. The coating will be golden brown and crispy when done. 7. Cut the cooked sandwiches in half and serve warm.

Egg Muffins

Prep time: 10 minutes | Cook time: 11 to 13 minutes | Serves 4

4 eggs	Olive oil	1 cup shredded Colby Jack cheese
Salt and pepper, to taste	4 English muffins, split	4 slices ham or Canadian bacon

1. Select Bake, Air Fry Fan, set temperature to 390°F (199°C) and set time to 2 minutes. Press Start to begin preheating. 2. Beat together eggs and add salt and pepper to taste. Spray a baking pan lightly with oil and add eggs. Once preheated, place the pan on the bake position. Stir, and continue cooking for 3 or 4 minutes, stirring every minute, until eggs are scrambled to your preference. Remove pan from air fryer oven. 3. Place bottom halves of English muffins on pizza rack and place the rack on pizza position. Take half of the shredded cheese and divide it among the muffins. Top each with a slice of ham and one-quarter of the eggs. Sprinkle remaining cheese on top of the eggs. Use a fork to press the cheese into the egg a little so it doesn't slip off before it melts. 4. Select Pizza, Air Fry Fan, set temperature to 360°F (182°C) and set time to 1 minutes. Press Start. Add English muffin tops and cook for 2 to 4 minutes to heat through and toast the muffins.

Sausage Stuffed Poblanos

Prep time: 15 minutes | Cook time: 15 minutes | Serves 4

½ pound (227 g) spicy ground pork breakfast sausage	cheese, softened	8 tablespoons shredded Pepper Jack cheese
4 large eggs	¼ cup canned diced tomatoes and green chiles, drained	½ cup full-fat sour cream
4 ounces (113 g) full-fat cream	4 large poblano peppers	

1. Select Roast, Air Fry Fan, set temperature to 350°F (177°C) and set time to 15 minutes. Press Start to begin preheating. 2. In a medium skillet over medium heat, crumble and brown the ground sausage until no pink remains. Remove sausage and drain the fat from the pan. Crack eggs into the pan, scramble, and cook until no longer runny. 3. Place cooked sausage in a large bowl and fold in cream cheese. Mix in diced tomatoes and chiles. Gently fold in eggs. 4. Cut a 4-inch to 5-inch slit in the top of each poblano, removing the seeds and white membrane with a small knife. Separate the filling into four servings and spoon carefully into each pepper. Top each with 2 tablespoons pepper jack cheese. 5. Place each pepper into the baking pan. 6. Once preheated, place the pan on the roast position. 7. Peppers will be soft and cheese will be browned when ready. Serve immediately with sour cream on top.

Hearty Blueberry Oatmeal

Prep time: 10 minutes | Cook time: 25 minutes | Serves 6

1½ cups quick oats	1 cup unsweetened vanilla almond milk	2 cups blueberries
1¼ teaspoons ground cinnamon, divided	¼ cup honey	Olive oil
½ teaspoon baking powder	1 teaspoon vanilla extract	1½ teaspoons sugar, divided
Pinch salt	1 egg, beaten	6 tablespoons low-fat whipped topping (optional)

1. Select Bake, Air Fry Fan, set temperature to 360°F (182°C) and set time to 20 minutes. Press Start to begin preheating. 2. In a large bowl, mix together the oats, 1 teaspoon of cinnamon, baking powder, and salt. 3. In a medium bowl, whisk together the almond milk, honey, vanilla and egg. 4. Pour the liquid ingredients into the oats mixture and stir to combine. Fold in the blueberries. 5. Lightly spray a baking pan with oil. 6. Add half the blueberry mixture to the pan. 7. Sprinkle ⅛ teaspoon of cinnamon and ½ teaspoon sugar over the top. 8. Once preheated, cover the pan with aluminum foil and place on the bake position. 9. Remove the foil and cook for an additional 5 minutes. Transfer the mixture to a shallow bowl. 10. Repeat with the remaining blueberry mixture, ½ teaspoon of sugar, and ⅛ teaspoon of cinnamon. 11. To serve, spoon into bowls and top with whipped topping.

Sausage Egg Cup

Prep time: 10 minutes | Cook time: 15 minutes | Serves 6

12 ounces (340 g) ground pork breakfast sausage	6 large eggs	¼ teaspoon ground black pepper	½ teaspoon crushed red pepper flakes
	½ teaspoon salt		

1. Select Bake, Air Fry Fan, set temperature to 350°F (177°C) and set time to 15 minutes. Press Start to begin preheating. 2. Place sausage in six 4-inch ramekins (about 2 ounces / 57 g per ramekin) greased with cooking oil. Press sausage down to cover bottom and about ½-inch up the sides of ramekins. Crack one egg into each ramekin and sprinkle evenly with salt, black pepper, and red pepper flakes. 3. Place ramekins on pizza rack. Once preheated, place the basket on the bake position. Egg cups will be done when sausage is fully cooked to at least 145°F (63°C) and

the egg is firm. Serve warm.

Denver Omelet

Prep time: 5 minutes | Cook time: 8 minutes | Serves 1

- 2 large eggs
- ¼ cup unsweetened, unflavored almond milk
- ¼ teaspoon fine sea salt
- ⅛ teaspoon ground black pepper
- ¼ cup diced ham (omit for vegetarian)
- ¼ cup diced green and red bell peppers
- 2 tablespoons diced green onions, plus more for garnish
- ¼ cup shredded Cheddar cheese (about 1 ounce / 28 g) (omit for dairy-free)
- Quartered cherry tomatoes, for serving (optional)

1. Select Bake, Air Fry Fan, set temperature to 350°F (177°C) and set time to 8 minutes. Press Start to begin preheating. Grease a cake pan and set aside. 2. In a small bowl, use a fork to whisk together the eggs, almond milk, salt, and pepper. Add the ham, bell peppers, and green onions. Pour the mixture into the greased pan. Add the cheese on top (if using). 3. Transfer the pan to pizza rack. Once preheated, place the rack on the bake position. It will be done until the eggs are cooked to your liking. 4. Loosen the omelet from the sides of the pan with a spatula and place it on a serving plate. Garnish with green onions and serve with cherry tomatoes, if desired. Best served fresh.

Broccoli-Mushroom Frittata

Prep time: 10 minutes | Cook time: 20 minutes | Serves 2

- 1 tablespoon olive oil
- 1½ cups broccoli florets, finely chopped
- ½ cup sliced brown mushrooms
- ¼ cup finely chopped onion
- ½ teaspoon salt
- ¼ teaspoon freshly ground black pepper
- 6 eggs
- ¼ cup Parmesan cheese

1. Select Bake, Air Fry Fan, set temperature to 400°F (204°C) and set time to 5 minutes. Press Start to begin preheating. 2. In a nonstick cake pan, combine the olive oil, broccoli, mushrooms, onion, salt, and pepper. Stir until the vegetables are thoroughly coated with oil. 3. Once preheated, place the pan on the bake position. It will be done until the vegetables soften. 4. Meanwhile, in a medium bowl, whisk the eggs and Parmesan until thoroughly combined. Pour the egg mixture into the pan and shake gently to distribute the vegetables. Bake for another 15 minutes until the eggs are set. 5. Remove from the oven and let sit for 5 minutes to cool slightly. Use a silicone spatula to gently lift the frittata onto a plate before serving.

Potato Bread Rolls

Prep time: 15 minutes | Cook time: 20 minutes | Serves 5

- 5 large potatoes, boiled and mashed
- Salt and ground black pepper, to taste
- ½ teaspoon mustard seeds
- 1 tablespoon olive oil
- 2 small onions, chopped
- 2 sprigs curry leaves
- ½ teaspoon turmeric powder
- 2 green chilis, seeded and chopped
- 1 bunch coriander, chopped
- 8 slices bread, brown sides discarded

1. Select Air Fry, set temperature to 400°F (204°C) and set time to 15 minutes. Press Start to begin preheating. 2. Put the mashed potatoes in a bowl and sprinkle on salt and pepper. Set to one side. 3. Fry the mustard seeds in olive oil over a medium-low heat in a skillet, stirring continuously, until they sputter. 4. Add the onions and cook until they turn translucent. Add the curry leaves and turmeric powder and stir. Cook for a further 2 minutes until fragrant. 5.

Remove the skillet from the heat and combine with the potatoes. Mix in the green chilies and coriander. 6. Wet the bread slightly and drain of any excess liquid. 7. Spoon a small amount of the potato mixture into the center of the bread and enclose the bread around the filling, sealing it entirely. Continue until the rest of the bread and filling is used up. Brush each bread roll with some oil and transfer to the crisper tray. 8. Once preheated, place the tray on the air fry position and cook, gently shaking the tray at the halfway point to ensure each roll is cooked evenly. 9. Serve immediately.

Three-Berry Dutch Pancake

Prep time: 10 minutes | Cook time: 12 to 16 minutes | Serves 4

2 egg whites
1 egg
½ cup whole-wheat pastry flour
½ cup 2% milk
1 teaspoon pure vanilla extract
1 tablespoon unsalted butter, melted
1 cup sliced fresh strawberries
½ cup fresh blueberries
½ cup fresh raspberries

1. Select Bake, Air Fry Fan, set temperature to 330°F (166°C) and set time to 12 to 16 minutes. Press Start to begin preheating. 2. In a medium bowl, use an eggbeater or hand mixer to quickly mix the egg whites, egg, pastry flour, milk, and vanilla until well combined. 3. Use a pastry brush to grease the bottom of a baking pan with the melted butter. Immediately pour in the batter. Once preheated, place the pan on the bake position. The pancake is puffed and golden brown when done. 4. Remove the pan from the oven; the pancake will fall. Top with the strawberries, blueberries, and raspberries. Serve immediately.

Coconut Brown Rice Porridge with Dates

Prep time: 10 minutes | Cook time: 23 minutes | Serves 1 to 2

1 cup canned coconut milk
½ cup cooked brown rice
¼ cup unsweetened shredded coconut
¼ cup packed dark brown sugar
½ teaspoon kosher salt
¼ teaspoon ground cardamom
4 large Medjool dates, pitted and roughly chopped
Heavy cream, for serving (optional)

1. Select Bake, Air Fry Fan, set temperature to 375°F (191°C) and set time to 23 minutes. Press Start to begin preheating. 2. In a cake pan, stir together the coconut milk, rice, shredded coconut, brown sugar, salt, cardamom, and dates. Once preheated, place the pan on the bake position. It will be done until reduced and thickened and browned on top. Stir halfway through. 3. Remove the pan from the oven and divide the porridge among bowls. Drizzle the porridge with cream, if you like, and serve hot.

Spinach with Scrambled Eggs

Prep time: 10 minutes | Cook time: 10 minutes | Serves 2

2 tablespoons olive oil
4 eggs, whisked
5 ounces (142 g) fresh spinach, chopped
1 medium tomato, chopped
1 teaspoon fresh lemon juice
½ teaspoon coarse salt
½ teaspoon ground black pepper
½ cup of fresh basil, roughly chopped

1. Grease baking pan with the oil, tilting it to spread the oil around. 2. Select Bake, Air Fry Fan, set temperature to 280°F (138°C) and set time to 10 minutes. Press Start to begin preheating. 3. In the pan, mix the remaining ingredients, apart from the basil leaves, whisking well until everything is completely combined. 4. Once preheated,

place the pan on the bake position. 5. Top with fresh basil leaves before serving.

Two-Cheese Grits

Prep time: 10 minutes | Cook time: 10 to 12 minutes | Serves 4

⅔ cup instant grits	¾ cup milk, whole or 2%	1 tablespoon butter, melted
1 teaspoon salt	1 large egg, beaten	1 cup shredded mild Cheddar cheese
1 teaspoon freshly ground black pepper	3 ounces (85 g) cream cheese, at room temperature	1 to 2 tablespoons oil

1. In a large bowl, combine the grits, salt, and pepper. Stir in the milk, egg, cream cheese, and butter until blended. Stir in the Cheddar cheese. 2. Select Air Fry, set temperature to 400°F (204°C) and set time to 5 minutes. Press Start to begin preheating. Spritz a baking pan with oil. 3. Pour the grits mixture into the prepared pan and place it on pizza rack. 4. Once preheated, place the pan on the Air Fry position. Stir the mixture and cook for 5 minutes more for soupy grits or 7 minutes more for firmer grits.

Mississippi Spice Muffins

Prep time: 15 minutes | Cook time: 13 minutes | Makes 12 muffins

4 cups all-purpose flour	1 teaspoon salt	2 cups unsweetened applesauce
1 tablespoon ground cinnamon	1 cup (2 sticks) butter, room temperature	¼ cup chopped pecans
2 teaspoons baking soda		1 to 2 tablespoons oil
2 teaspoons allspice	2 cups sugar	
1 teaspoon ground cloves	2 large eggs, lightly beaten	

1. In a large bowl, whisk the flour, cinnamon, baking soda, allspice, cloves, and salt until blended. 2. In another large bowl, combine the butter and sugar. Using an electric mixer, beat the mixture for 2 to 3 minutes until light and fluffy. Add the beaten eggs and stir until blended. 3. Add the flour mixture and applesauce, alternating between the two and blending after each addition. Stir in the pecans. 4. Select Air Fry, set temperature to 325°F (163°C) and set time to 6 minutes. Press Start to begin preheating. Spritz 12 silicone muffin cups with oil. 5. Pour the batter into the prepared muffin cups, filling each halfway. Transfer the muffins to pizza rack. Once preheated, place the rack on the air fry position. Shake and air fry for 7 minutes more. The muffins are done when a toothpick inserted into the middle comes out clean.

Blueberry Cobbler

Prep time: 5 minutes | Cook time: 15 minutes | Serves 4

⅓ cup whole-wheat pastry flour	½ cup 2% milk	Cooking oil spray
¾ teaspoon baking powder	2 tablespoons pure maple syrup	½ cup fresh blueberries
Dash sea salt	½ teaspoon vanilla extract	¼ cup granola

1. In a medium bowl, whisk the flour, baking powder, and salt. Add the milk, maple syrup, and vanilla and gently whisk, just until thoroughly combined. 2. Select Bake, Air Fry Fan, set temperature to 350°F (177°C) and set time to 15 minutes. Press Start to begin preheating. 3. Spray baking pan with cooking oil and pour the batter into the pan. Top evenly with the blueberries and granola. 4. Once preheated, place the pan on the bake position. 5. When the cooking is complete, the cobbler should be nicely browned and a knife inserted into the middle should come out clean. Enjoy plain or topped with a little vanilla yogurt.

Apple Cider Doughnut Holes

Prep time: 10 minutes | Cook time: 6 minutes | Makes 10 mini doughnuts

Doughnut Holes:
- 1½ cups all-purpose flour
- 2 tablespoons granulated sugar
- 2 teaspoons baking powder
- 1 teaspoon baking soda
- ½ teaspoon kosher salt
- Pinch of freshly grated nutmeg
- ¼ cup plus 2 tablespoons buttermilk, chilled
- 2 tablespoons apple cider (hard or nonalcoholic), chilled
- 1 large egg, lightly beaten
- Vegetable oil, for brushing

Glaze:
- ½ cup powdered sugar
- 2 tablespoons unsweetened applesauce
- ¼ teaspoon vanilla extract
- Pinch of kosher salt

1. Make the doughnut holes: Select Air Fry, set temperature to 350°F (177°C) and set time to 6 minutes. Press Start to begin preheating. 2. In a bowl, whisk together the flour, granulated sugar, baking powder, baking soda, salt, and nutmeg until smooth. Add the buttermilk, cider, and egg and stir with a small rubber spatula or spoon until the dough just comes together. 3. Using a 1-ounce (28-g) ice cream scoop or 2 tablespoons, scoop and drop 10 balls of dough into the crisper tray, spaced evenly apart, and brush the tops lightly with oil. Once preheated, place the tray on the air fry position. It will be done until the doughnut holes are golden brown and fluffy. Allow the doughnut holes to cool completely. 4. Make the glaze: In a small bowl, stir together the powdered sugar, applesauce, vanilla, and salt until smooth. 5. Dip the tops of the doughnuts holes in the glaze, then let stand until the glaze sets before serving. If you're impatient and want warm doughnuts, have the glaze ready to go while the doughnuts cook, then use the glaze as a dipping sauce for the warm doughnuts, fresh out of the oven.

Baked Potato Breakfast Boats

Prep time: 10 minutes | Cook time: 20 minutes | Serves 4

- 2 large russet potatoes, scrubbed
- Olive oil
- Salt and freshly ground black pepper, to taste
- 4 eggs
- 2 tablespoons chopped, cooked bacon
- 1 cup shredded Cheddar cheese

1. Poke holes in the potatoes with a fork and microwave on full power for 5 minutes. 2. Turn potatoes over and cook an additional 3 to 5 minutes, or until the potatoes are fork-tender. 3. Cut the potatoes in half lengthwise and use a spoon to scoop out the inside of the potato. Be careful to leave a layer of potato so that it makes a sturdy "boat." 4. Select Bake, Air Fry Fan, set temperature to 350°F (177°C) and set time to 5 to 10 minutes. (5 to 6 minutes for slightly runny yolk and 7 to 10 minutes for fully cooked yolk). Press Start to begin preheating. 5. Lightly spray the pizza rack with olive oil. Spray the skin side of the potatoes with oil and sprinkle with salt and pepper to taste. 6. Place the potato skins on pizza rack, skin-side down. Crack one egg into each potato skin. 7. Sprinkle ½ tablespoon of bacon pieces and ¼ cup of shredded cheese on top of each egg. Sprinkle with salt and pepper to taste. 8. Once preheated, place the rack on the bake position. 9. Serve warm.

Potatoes Lyonnaise

Prep time: 10 minutes | Cook time: 31 minutes | Serves 4

- 1 Vidalia onion, sliced
- 1 teaspoon butter, melted
- 1 teaspoon brown sugar
- 2 large russet potatoes (about 1 pound / 454 g in total), sliced ½-inch thick
- 1 tablespoon vegetable oil
- Salt and freshly ground black pepper, to taste

1. Select Roast, Air Fry Fan, set temperature to 370°F (188°C) and set time to 8 minutes. Press Start to begin preheating. 2. Toss the sliced onions, melted butter and brown sugar together in the baking pan. Once preheated, place the pan on the roast position. Shake the pan occasionally to help the onions cook evenly. 3. While the onions are cooking, bring a saucepan of salted water to a boil on the stovetop. Par-cook the potatoes in boiling water for 3 minutes. Drain the potatoes and pat them dry with a clean kitchen towel. 4. Add the potatoes to the onions in the baking pan and drizzle with vegetable oil. Toss to coat the potatoes with the oil and season with salt and freshly ground black pepper. 5. Increase the temperature to 400°F (204°C) and roast for 20 minutes, tossing the vegetables a few times during the cooking time to help the potatoes brown evenly. 6. Season with salt and freshly ground black pepper and serve warm.

Maple Granola

Prep time: 5 minutes | Cook time: 40 minutes | Makes 2 cups

1 cup rolled oats	1 tablespoon neutral-flavored oil, such as refined coconut, sunflower, or safflower	¼ teaspoon sea salt
3 tablespoons pure maple syrup		¼ teaspoon ground cinnamon
1 tablespoon sugar		¼ teaspoon vanilla extract

1. Select Bake, Air Fry Fan, set temperature to 250°F (121°C) and set time to 40 minutes. Press Start to begin preheating. 2. In a medium bowl, stir together the oats, maple syrup, sugar, oil, salt, cinnamon, and vanilla until thoroughly combined. Transfer the granola to a baking pan. 3. Once preheated, place the pan into the oven on bake position. 4. After 10 minutes, stir the granola well. Resume cooking, stirring the granola every 10 minutes. The granola will be lightly browned and mostly dry when done. 5. When the cooking is complete, place the granola on a plate to cool. It will become crisp as it cools. Store the completely cooled granola in an airtight container in a cool, dry place for 1 to 2 weeks.

Buffalo Egg Cups

Prep time: 10 minutes | Cook time: 15 minutes | Serves 2

4 large eggs	cheese	½ cup shredded sharp Cheddar cheese
2 ounces (57 g) full-fat cream	2 tablespoons buffalo sauce	

1. Select Bake, Air Fry Fan, set temperature to 320°F (160°C) and set time to 15 minutes. Press Start to begin preheating. Crack eggs into two ramekins. 2. In a small microwave-safe bowl, mix cream cheese, buffalo sauce, and Cheddar. Microwave for 20 seconds and then stir. Place a spoonful into each ramekin on top of the eggs. 3. Once preheated, place the ramekin on the bake position. 4. Serve warm.

Bacon, Egg, and Cheese Roll Ups

Prep time: 15 minutes | Cook time: 15 minutes | Serves 4

2 tablespoons unsalted butter	seeded and chopped	1 cup shredded sharp Cheddar cheese
¼ cup chopped onion	6 large eggs	
½ medium green bell pepper,	12 slices sugar-free bacon	½ cup mild salsa, for dipping

1. In a medium skillet over medium heat, melt butter. Add onion and pepper to the skillet and sauté until fragrant and onions are translucent, about 3 minutes. 2. Whisk eggs in a small bowl and pour into skillet. Scramble eggs with onions and peppers until fluffy and fully cooked, about 5 minutes. Remove from heat and set aside. 3. Select Bake, Air Fry Fan, set temperature to 350°F (177°C) and set time to 15 minutes. Press Start to begin preheating. 4. On work

surface, place three slices of bacon side by side, overlapping about ¼ inch. Place ¼ cup scrambled eggs in a heap on the side closest to you and sprinkle ¼ cup cheese on top of the eggs. 5. Tightly roll the bacon around the eggs and secure the seam with a toothpick if necessary. Place each roll on pizza rack. 6. Once preheated, place the rack on the bake position. Rotate the rolls halfway through the cooking time. 7. Bacon will be brown and crispy when completely cooked. Serve immediately with salsa for dipping.

Tomato and Mozzarella Bruschetta

Prep time: 5 minutes | Cook time: 4 minutes | Serves 1

6 small loaf slices	3 ounces (85 g) Mozzarella cheese, grated	1 tablespoon fresh basil, chopped
½ cup tomatoes, finely chopped		1 tablespoon olive oil

1. Select Bake, Air Fry Fan, set temperature to 350°F (177°C) and set time to 3 minutes. Press Start to begin preheating. 2. Put the loaf slices on pizza rack. Add the tomato, Mozzarella, basil, and olive oil on top. 3. Once preheated, place the rack on the bake position. Bake for an additional minute before serving.

Meritage Eggs

Prep time: 5 minutes | Cook time: 8 minutes | Serves 2

2 teaspoons unsalted butter (or coconut oil for dairy-free), for greasing the ramekins	¼ teaspoon ground black pepper	brand chive cream cheese style spread, softened, for dairy-free)
4 large eggs	2 tablespoons heavy cream (or unsweetened, unflavored almond milk for dairy-free)	Fresh thyme leaves, for garnish (optional)
2 teaspoons chopped fresh thyme	3 tablespoons finely grated Parmesan cheese (or Kite Hill	
½ teaspoon fine sea salt		

1. Select Air Fry, set temperature to 400°F (204°C) and set time to 8 minutes. Press Start to begin preheating. Grease two (4-ounce / 113-g) ramekins with the butter. 2. Crack 2 eggs into each ramekin and divide the thyme, salt, and pepper between the ramekins. Pour 1 tablespoon of the heavy cream into each ramekin. Sprinkle each ramekin with 1½ tablespoons of the Parmesan cheese. 3. Transfer the ramekins to pizza rack. Once preheated, place the pan on the air fry position. 4. Garnish with a sprinkle of ground black pepper and thyme leaves, if desired. Best served fresh.

Nutty Granola

Prep time: 5 minutes | Cook time: 1 hour | Serves 4

½ cup pecans, coarsely chopped	¼ cup ground flaxseed or chia seeds	½ teaspoon ground cinnamon
½ cup walnuts or almonds, coarsely chopped	2 tablespoons sunflower seeds	½ teaspoon vanilla extract
¼ cup unsweetened flaked coconut	2 tablespoons melted butter	¼ teaspoon ground nutmeg
¼ cup almond flour	¼ cup Swerve	¼ teaspoon salt
		2 tablespoons water

1. Select Bake, Air Fry Fan, set temperature to 250°F (121°C) and set time to 60 minutes. Press Start to begin preheating. Cut a piece of parchment paper to fit the baking pan. 2. In a large bowl, toss the nuts, coconut, almond flour, ground flaxseed or chia seeds, sunflower seeds, butter, Swerve, cinnamon, vanilla, nutmeg, salt, and water until thoroughly combined. 3. Spread the granola on the parchment paper and flatten to an even thickness. 4. Once preheated, place the pan on the bake position. It will be done until golden throughout. Remove from the oven and allow to fully cool. Break the granola into bite-size pieces and store in a covered container for up to a week.

Pumpkin Donut Holes

Prep time: 15 minutes | Cook time: 14 minutes | Makes 12 donut holes

- 1 cup whole-wheat pastry flour, plus more as needed
- 3 tablespoons packed brown sugar
- ½ teaspoon ground cinnamon
- 1 teaspoon low-sodium baking powder
- ⅓ cup canned no-salt-added pumpkin purée (not pumpkin pie filling)
- 3 tablespoons 2% milk, plus more as needed
- 2 tablespoons unsalted butter, melted
- 1 egg white
- Powdered sugar (optional)

1. Select Air Fry, set temperature to 360°F (182°C) and set time to 5 to 7 minutes. Press Start to begin preheating. 2. In a medium bowl, mix the pastry flour, brown sugar, -cinnamon, and baking powder. In a small bowl, beat the pumpkin, milk, butter, and egg white until combined. Add the pumpkin mixture to the dry ingredients and mix until combined. You may need to add more flour or milk to form a soft dough. 3. Divide the dough into 12 pieces. With floured hands, form each piece into a ball. 4. Cut a piece of parchment paper or aluminum foil to fit your crisper tray. Poke holes in the paper or foil, leaving some space around each. You may need to work in batches. 5. Once preheated, place the tray on the air fry position. It will be done until the donut holes reach an internal temperature of 200°F (93°C) and are firm and light golden brown. 6. Let cool for 5 minutes. Remove from the basket and roll in powdered sugar, if desired. Repeat with the remaining donut holes and serve.

Cornflakes Toast Sticks

Prep time: 10 minutes | Cook time: 6 minutes | Serves 4

- 2 eggs
- ½ cup milk
- ⅛ teaspoon salt
- ½ teaspoon pure vanilla extract
- ¾ cup crushed cornflakes
- 6 slices sandwich bread, each slice cut into 4 strips
- Maple syrup, for dipping
- Cooking spray

1. Select Air Fry, set temperature to 390°F (199°C) and set time to 6 minutes. Press Start to begin preheating. 2. In a small bowl, beat together the eggs, milk, salt, and vanilla. 3. Put crushed cornflakes on a plate or in a shallow dish. 4. Dip bread strips in egg mixture, shake off excess, and roll in cornflake crumbs. 5. Spray both sides of bread strips with oil. 6. Put bread strips in crisper tray in a single layer. 7. Once preheated, place the tray on the air fry position. It will be done until golden brown. 8. Repeat steps 5 and 6 to AIR CRISP remaining French toast sticks. 9. Serve with maple syrup.

Cauliflower Avocado Toast

Prep time: 15 minutes | Cook time: 8 minutes | Serves 2

- 1 (12-ounce / 340-g) steamer bag cauliflower
- 1 large egg
- ½ cup shredded Mozzarella cheese
- 1 ripe medium avocado
- ½ teaspoon garlic powder
- ¼ teaspoon ground black pepper

1. Select Roast, Air Fry Fan, set temperature to 400°F (204°C) and set time to 8 minutes. Press Start to begin preheating. 2. Cook cauliflower according to package instructions. Remove from bag and place into cheesecloth or clean towel to remove excess moisture. 3. Place cauliflower into a large bowl and mix in egg and Mozzarella. Cut a piece of parchment to fit your baking pan. Separate the cauliflower mixture into two, and place it on the parchment in two mounds. Press out the cauliflower mounds into a ¼-inch-thick rectangle. 4. Once preheated, place the pan on the roast position. 5. Flip the cauliflower halfway through the cooking time. 6. When the timer beeps, remove the

parchment and allow the cauliflower to cool 5 minutes. 7. Cut open the avocado and remove the pit. Scoop out the inside, place it in a medium bowl, and mash it with garlic powder and pepper. Spread onto the cauliflower. Serve immediately.

Chimichanga Breakfast Burrito

Prep time: 10 minutes | Cook time: 10 minutes | Serves 2

2 large (10- to 12-inch) flour tortillas	4 large eggs, cooked scrambled	1 tablespoon vegetable oil
½ cup canned refried beans (pinto or black work equally well)	4 corn tortilla chips, crushed	Guacamole, salsa, and sour cream, for serving (optional)
	½ cup grated Pepper Jack cheese	
	12 pickled jalapeño slices	

1. Select Bake, Air Fry Fan, set temperature to 350°F (177°C) and set time to 10 minutes. Press Start to begin preheating. 2. Place the tortillas on a work surface and divide the refried beans between them, spreading them in a rough rectangle in the center of the tortillas. Top the beans with the scrambled eggs, crushed chips, pepper jack, and jalapeños. Fold one side over the fillings, then fold in each short side and roll up the rest of the way like a burrito. 3. Brush the outside of the burritos with the oil, then transfer to the baking pan, seam-side down. Once preheated, place the pan on the bake position. It will be done until the tortillas are browned and crisp and the filling is warm throughout. 4. Transfer the chimichangas to plates and serve warm with guacamole, salsa, and sour cream, if you like.

Egg White Cups

Prep time: 10 minutes | Cook time: 15 minutes | Serves 4

2 cups 100% liquid egg whites	¼ teaspoon onion powder	½ cup chopped fresh spinach leaves
3 tablespoons salted butter, melted	½ medium Roma tomato, cored and diced	
¼ teaspoon salt		

1. Select Bake, Air Fry Fan, set temperature to 300°F (149°C) and set time to 15 minutes. Press Start to begin preheating. 2. In a large bowl, whisk egg whites with butter, salt, and onion powder. Stir in tomato and spinach, then pour evenly into four ramekins greased with cooking spray. 3. Once preheated, place ramekins on the bake position. Eggs will be fully cooked and firm in the center when done. Serve warm.

Bacon Eggs on the Go

Prep time: 5 minutes | Cook time: 15 minutes | Serves 1

2 eggs	Salt and ground black pepper, to taste
4 ounces (113 g) bacon, cooked	

1. Select Pizza, Air Fry Fan, set temperature to 400°F (204°C) and set time to 15 minutes. Press Start to begin preheating. 2. Crack an egg into each of the cups and add the bacon. Season with some pepper and salt. 3. Transfer cupcake tin to pizza rack. Once preheated, place the pan on the pizza position. It will be done until the eggs are set. Serve warm.

Nut and Seed Muffins

Prep time: 15 minutes | Cook time: 10 minutes | Makes 8 muffins

½ cup whole-wheat flour, plus 2 tablespoons	2 tablespoons flaxseed meal	½ teaspoon baking soda	¼ teaspoon salt
¼ cup oat bran	¼ cup brown sugar	½ teaspoon baking powder	½ teaspoon cinnamon
			½ cup buttermilk

2 tablespoons melted butter
1 egg
½ teaspoon pure vanilla extract
½ cup grated carrots
¼ cup chopped pecans
¼ cup chopped walnuts
1 tablespoon pumpkin seeds
1 tablespoon sunflower seeds
Cooking spray

Special Equipment:
16 foil muffin cups, paper liners removed

1. Select Bake, Air Fry Fan, set temperature to 330°F (166°C) and set time to 10 minutes. Press Start to begin preheating. 2. In a large bowl, stir together the flour, bran, flaxseed meal, sugar, baking soda, baking powder, salt, and cinnamon. 3. In a medium bowl, beat together the buttermilk, butter, egg, and vanilla. Pour into flour mixture and stir just until dry ingredients moisten. Do not beat. 4. Gently stir in carrots, nuts, and seeds. 5. Double up the foil cups so you have 8 total and spritz with cooking spray. 6. Divide half the batter among 4 cups. 7. Once preheated, place the cups on the bake position. It will be done until a toothpick inserted in center comes out clean. 8. Repeat step 6 and 7 to bake remaining 4 muffins. 9. Serve warm.

Strawberry Toast

Prep time: 10 minutes | Cook time: 8 minutes | Makes 4 toasts

4 slices bread, ½-inch thick
Butter-flavored cooking spray
1 cup sliced strawberries
1 teaspoon sugar

1. Select Bake, Air Fry Fan, set temperature to 390°F (199°C) and set time to 8 minutes. Press Start to begin preheating. 2. Spray one side of each bread slice with butter-flavored cooking spray. Lay slices sprayed side down. 3. Divide the strawberries among the bread slices. 4. Sprinkle evenly with the sugar and place on the pizza rack in a single layer. 5. Once preheated, place the rack on the bake position. The bottom should look brown and crisp and the top should look glazed.

Spaghetti Squash Fritters

Prep time: 15 minutes | Cook time: 8 minutes | Serves 4

2 cups cooked spaghetti squash
2 tablespoons unsalted butter, softened
1 large egg
¼ cup blanched finely ground almond flour
2 stalks green onion, sliced
½ teaspoon garlic powder
1 teaspoon dried parsley

1. Select Bake, Air Fry Fan, set temperature to 400°F (204°C) and set time to 8 minutes. Press Start to begin preheating. 2. Remove excess moisture from the squash using a cheesecloth or kitchen towel. 3. Mix all ingredients in a large bowl. Form into four patties. 4. Cut a piece of parchment to fit your baking pan. Place each patty on the parchment. 5. Once preheated, place the pan on the bake position. Flip the patties halfway through the cooking time. 6. Serve warm.

Simple Scotch Eggs

Prep time: 5 minutes | Cook time: 25 minutes | Serves 4

4 large hard boiled eggs
1 (12-ounce / 340-g) package pork sausage
8 slices thick-cut bacon
4 wooden toothpicks, soaked in water for at least 30 minutes

1. Slice the sausage into four parts and place each part into a large circle. 2. Put an egg into each circle and wrap it in the sausage. Put in the refrigerator for 1 hour. 3. Select Air Fry, set temperature to 450°F (235°C) and set time to 25 minutes. Press Start to begin preheating. 4. Make a cross with two pieces of thick-cut bacon. Put a wrapped egg in the

center, fold the bacon over top of the egg, and secure with a toothpick. Transfer to the baking pan. Once preheated, place the pan on the air fry position. 5. Serve immediately.

Vanilla Granola

Prep time: 5 minutes | Cook time: 40 minutes | Serves 4

1 cup rolled oats

3 tablespoons maple syrup

1 tablespoon sunflower oil

1 tablespoon coconut sugar

¼ teaspoon vanilla

¼ teaspoon cinnamon

¼ teaspoon sea salt

1. Select Bake, Air Fry Fan, set temperature to 250°F (121°C) and set time to 40 minutes. Press Start to begin preheating. 2. Mix together the oats, maple syrup, sunflower oil, coconut sugar, vanilla, cinnamon, and sea salt in a medium bowl and stir to combine. Transfer the mixture to a baking pan. 3. Once preheated, place the pan on the bake position. The granola will be mostly dry and lightly browned when done. Stir the granola four times during cooking. 4. Let the granola stand for 5 to 10 minutes before serving.

Cajun Breakfast Sausage

Prep time: 10 minutes | Cook time: 15 to 20 minutes | Serves 8

1½ pounds (680 g) 85% lean ground turkey

3 cloves garlic, finely chopped

¼ onion, grated

1 teaspoon Tabasco sauce

1 teaspoon Creole seasoning

1 teaspoon dried thyme

½ teaspoon paprika

½ teaspoon cayenne

1. Select Bake, Air Fry Fan, set temperature to 370°F (188°C) and set time to 15 to 20 minutes. Press Start to begin preheating. 2. In a large bowl, combine the turkey, garlic, onion, Tabasco, Creole seasoning, thyme, paprika, and cayenne. Mix with clean hands until thoroughly combined. Shape into 16 patties, about ½ inch thick. (Wet your hands slightly if you find the sausage too sticky to handle.) 3. Working in batches if necessary, arrange the patties in a single layer in the baking pan. Once preheated, place the pan on the bake position. Pausing halfway through the cooking time to flip the patties. It will be done until a thermometer inserted into the thickest portion registers 165°F (74°C).

Breakfast Pita

Prep time: 5 minutes | Cook time: 6 minutes | Serves 2

1 whole wheat pita

2 teaspoons olive oil

½ shallot, diced

¼ teaspoon garlic, minced

1 large egg

¼ teaspoon dried oregano

¼ teaspoon dried thyme

⅛ teaspoon salt

2 tablespoons shredded Parmesan cheese

1. Select Bake, Air Fry Fan, set temperature to 380°F (193°C) and set time to 6 minutes. Press Start to begin preheating. 2. Brush the top of the pita with olive oil, then spread the diced shallot and minced garlic over the pita. 3. Crack the egg into a small bowl or ramekin, and season it with oregano, thyme, and salt. 4. Place the pita into the baking pan, and gently pour the egg onto the top of the pita. Sprinkle with cheese over the top. 5. Once preheated, place the pan on the bake position. 6. Allow to cool for 5 minutes before cutting into pieces for serving.

Pizza Eggs

Prep time: 5 minutes | Cook time: 10 minutes | Serves 2

1 cup shredded Mozzarella cheese	¼ teaspoon dried oregano	¼ teaspoon salt
7 slices pepperoni, chopped	¼ teaspoon dried parsley	
1 large egg, whisked	¼ teaspoon garlic powder	

1. Select Bake, Air Fry Fan, set temperature to 330°F (166°C) and set time to 10 minutes. Press Start to begin preheating. 2. Place Mozzarella in a single layer on baking pan. Scatter pepperoni over cheese, then pour egg evenly around pan. 3. Sprinkle with remaining ingredients. 4. Once preheated, place the pan on the bake position. Cheese will be brown and egg will be set when done. 5. Let cool in pan 5 minutes before serving.

Chapter 2 Vegetables and Sides

Easy Potato Croquettes

Prep time: 15 minutes | Cook time: 15 minutes | Serves 10

¼ cup nutritional yeast	1 tablespoon flour	taste
2 cups boiled potatoes, mashed	2 tablespoons chopped chives	2 tablespoons vegetable oil
1 flax egg	Salt and ground black pepper, to	¼ cup bread crumbs

1. Select Air Fry, set temperature to 400°F (204°C) and set time to 15 minutes. Press Start to begin preheating. 2. In a bowl, combine the nutritional yeast, potatoes, flax egg, flour, and chives. Sprinkle with salt and pepper as desired. 3. In a separate bowl, mix the vegetable oil and bread crumbs to achieve a crumbly consistency. 4. Shape the potato mixture into small balls and dip each one into the bread crumb mixture. 5. Put the croquettes on pizza rack and place on air fry position. Ensure the croquettes turn golden brown. 6. Serve immediately.

Breaded Green Tomatoes

Prep time: 15 minutes | Cook time: 30 minutes | Serves 4

½ cup all-purpose flour	1 teaspoon garlic powder	½-inch-thick rounds
2 eggs	Salt and freshly ground black	Cooking oil spray
½ cup yellow cornmeal	pepper, to taste	
½ cup panko bread crumbs	2 green tomatoes, cut into	

1. Place the flour in a small bowl. 2. In another small bowl, beat the eggs. 3. In a third small bowl, stir together the cornmeal, panko, and garlic powder. Season with salt and pepper. 4. Dip each tomato slice into the flour, the egg, and finally the cornmeal mixture to coat. 5. Select Air Fry, set temperature to 400°F (204°C) and set time to 10 minutes. Press Start to begin preheating. 6. Spray the crisper tray with cooking oil. Working in batches, place the tomato slices on the tray in a single layer. Do not stack them. Spray the tomato slices with the cooking oil. 7. Once preheated, place the tray on air fry position. After 5 minutes, Flip the tomatoes. Resume cooking for 4 to 5 minutes, or until crisp. 8. When the cooking is complete, transfer the fried green tomatoes to a plate. Repeat steps 6 and 7 for the remaining tomatoes.

Corn on the Cob

Prep time: 5 minutes | Cook time: 12 to 15 minutes | Serves 4

2 large ears fresh corn
Olive oil for misting
Salt, to taste (optional)

1. Select Air Fry, set temperature to 390°F (199°C) and set time to 12 to 15 minutes. Press Start to begin preheating. 2. Shuck corn, remove silks, and wash. 3. Cut or break each ear in half crosswise. 4. Spray corn with olive oil. Transfer to pizza rack. 5. Once preheated, place the rack on the air fry position. It will be done until browned as much as you like. 6. Serve plain or with coarsely ground salt.

Grits Casserole

Prep time: 5 minutes | Cook time: 28 to 30 minutes | Serves 4

10 fresh asparagus spears, cut into 1-inch pieces
2 cups cooked grits, cooled to room temperature
1 egg, beaten
2 teaspoons Worcestershire sauce
½ teaspoon garlic powder
¼ teaspoon salt
2 slices provolone cheese (about 1½ ounces / 43 g)
Oil for misting or cooking spray

1. Select Bake, Air Fry Fan, set temperature to 390°F (199°C) and set time to 5 minutes. Press Start to begin preheating. 2. Mist asparagus spears on pizza rack with oil. Once preheated, place the rack on the bake position. It will be done until crisp-tender. 3. In a medium bowl, mix together the grits, egg, Worcestershire, garlic powder, and salt. 4. Spoon half of grits mixture into a baking pan and top with asparagus. 5. Tear cheese slices into pieces and layer evenly on top of asparagus. 6. Top with remaining grits. 7. Bake at 360°F (182°C) for 23 to 25 minutes. The casserole will rise a little as it cooks. When done, the top will have browned lightly with just a hint of crispiness.

Rosemary New Potatoes

Prep time: 10 minutes | Cook time: 5 to 6 minutes | Serves 4

3 large red potatoes (enough to make 3 cups sliced)
¼ teaspoon ground rosemary
¼ teaspoon ground thyme
⅛ teaspoon salt
⅛ teaspoon ground black pepper
2 teaspoons extra-light olive oil

1. Select Roast, Air Fry Fan, set temperature to 330°F (166°C) and set time to 4 minutes. Press Start to begin preheating. 2. Place potatoes in large bowl and sprinkle with rosemary, thyme, salt, and pepper. 3. Stir with a spoon to distribute seasonings evenly. 4. Add oil to potatoes and stir again to coat well. 5. Transfer potatoes to pizza rack. Once preheated, place the rack on the roast position. Stir and break apart any that have stuck together. 6. Cook an additional 1 to 2 minutes or until fork-tender.

Roasted Sweet Potatoes

Prep time: 10 minutes | Cook time: 25 minutes | Serves 4

Cooking oil spray
2 sweet potatoes, peeled and cut into 1-inch cubes
1 tablespoon extra-virgin olive oil
Pinch salt
Freshly ground black pepper, to taste
½ teaspoon dried thyme
½ teaspoon dried marjoram
¼ cup grated Parmesan cheese

1. Select Roast, Air Fry Fan, set temperature to 330°F (166°C) and set time to 25 minutes. Press Start to begin preheating. 2. Spray the crisper tray with cooking oil. Put the sweet potato cubes on the tray and drizzle with olive oil.

Toss gently to coat. Sprinkle with the salt, pepper, thyme, and marjoram and toss again. 3. Once preheated, place the tray on the roast position. 4. After 10 minutes, remove the tray and shake the potatoes. Reinsert the tray to resume cooking. After another 10 minutes, remove the tray and shake the potatoes one more time. Sprinkle evenly with the Parmesan cheese. Reinsert the tray to resume cooking. 5. When the cooking is complete, the potatoes should be tender. Serve immediately.

Spiced Honey-Walnut Carrots

Prep time: 5 minutes | Cook time: 12 minutes | Serves 6

1 pound baby carrots

2 tablespoons olive oil

¼ cup raw honey

¼ teaspoon ground cinnamon

¼ cup black walnuts, chopped

1. Select Roast, Air Fry Fan, set temperature to 360°F (182°C) and set time to 6 minutes. Press Start to begin preheating. 2. In a large bowl, toss the baby carrots with olive oil, honey, and cinnamon until well coated. 3. Pour into the baking pan. Once preheated, place the pan on the roast position. Shake the pan, sprinkle the walnuts on top, and roast for 6 minutes more. 4. Remove the carrots from the oven and serve.

Cauliflower Rice Balls

Prep time: 10 minutes | Cook time: 8 minutes | Serves 4

1 (10-ounce / 283-g) steamer bag cauliflower rice, cooked according to package instructions

½ cup shredded Mozzarella cheese

1 large egg

2 ounces (57 g) plain pork rinds,

finely crushed

¼ teaspoon salt

½ teaspoon Italian seasoning

1. Select Roast, Air Fry Fan, set temperature to 400°F (204°C) and set time to 8 minutes. Press Start to begin preheating. Place cauliflower into a large bowl and mix with Mozzarella. 2. Whisk egg in a separate medium bowl. Place pork rinds into another large bowl with salt and Italian seasoning. 3. Separate cauliflower mixture into four equal sections and form each into a ball. Carefully dip a ball into whisked egg, then roll in pork rinds. Repeat with remaining balls. 4. Place cauliflower balls into ungreased baking pan. Once preheated, place the pan on the roast position. Rice balls will be golden when done. 5. Use a spatula to carefully move cauliflower balls to a large dish for serving. Serve warm.

Lemon-Garlic Mushrooms

Prep time: 10 minutes | Cook time: 10 to 15 minutes | Serves 6

12 ounces (340 g) sliced mushrooms

1 tablespoon avocado oil

Sea salt and freshly ground black pepper, to taste

3 tablespoons unsalted butter

1 teaspoon minced garlic

1 teaspoon freshly squeezed lemon juice

½ teaspoon red pepper flakes

2 tablespoons chopped fresh parsley

1. Select Roast, Air Fry Fan, set temperature to 375°F (191°C) and set time to 10 to 15 minutes. Press Start to begin preheating. 2. Place the mushrooms in a medium bowl and toss with the oil. Season to taste with salt and pepper. 3. Place the mushrooms in a single layer in the baking pan. Once preheated, place the pan on the roast position. The mushrooms will be tender when done. 4. While the mushrooms cook, melt the butter in a small pot or skillet over medium-low heat. Stir in the garlic and cook for 30 seconds. Remove the pot from the heat and stir in the lemon juice and red pepper flakes. 5. Toss the mushrooms with the lemon-garlic butter and garnish with the parsley before serving.

Fried Brussels Sprouts

Prep time: 10 minutes | Cook time: 18 minutes | Serves 4

1 teaspoon plus 1 tablespoon extra-virgin olive oil, divided	2 tablespoons freshly squeezed lemon juice	stems trimmed and any tough leaves removed, rinsed, halved lengthwise, and dried
2 teaspoons minced garlic	2 tablespoons rice vinegar	½ teaspoon salt
2 tablespoons honey	2 tablespoons sriracha	Cooking oil spray
1 tablespoon sugar	1 pound (454 g) Brussels sprouts,	

1. In a small saucepan over low heat, combine 1 teaspoon of olive oil, the garlic, honey, sugar, lemon juice, vinegar, and sriracha. Cook for 2 to 3 minutes, or until slightly thickened. Remove the pan from the heat, cover, and set aside. 2. Place the Brussels sprouts in a resealable bag or small bowl. Add the remaining olive oil and the salt, and toss to coat. 3. Select Air Fry, set temperature to 390°F (199°C) and set time to 15 minutes. Press Start to begin preheating. 4. Spray the crisper tray with cooking oil. Add the Brussels sprouts to the tray. 5. Once preheated, place the tray on the air fry position. 6. After 7 or 8 minutes, remove the tray and shake it to toss the sprouts. Reinsert the tray to resume cooking. 7. When the cooking is complete, the leaves should be crispy and light brown and the sprout centers tender. 8. Place the sprouts in a medium serving bowl and drizzle the sauce over the top. Toss to coat, and serve immediately.

Potato with Creamy Cheese

Prep time: 5 minutes | Cook time: 15 minutes | Serves 2

2 medium potatoes	3 tablespoons sour cream	1½ tablespoons grated Parmesan cheese
1 teaspoon butter	1 teaspoon chives	

1. Select Roast, Air Fry Fan, set temperature to 350°F (177°C) and set time to 15 minutes. Press Start to begin preheating. 2. Pierce the potatoes with a fork and boil them in water until they are cooked. 3. Transfer to the baking pan. Once preheated, place the pan on the roast position. 4. In the meantime, combine the sour cream, cheese and chives in a bowl. Cut the potatoes halfway to open them up and fill with the butter and sour cream mixture. 5. Serve immediately.

Blackened Zucchini with Kimchi-Herb Sauce

Prep time: 10 minutes | Cook time: 15 minutes | Serves 2

2 medium zucchini, ends trimmed (about 6 ounces / 170 g each)	¼ cup finely chopped fresh cilantro	2 teaspoons Asian chili-garlic sauce
2 tablespoons olive oil	¼ cup finely chopped fresh flat-leaf parsley, plus more for garnish	1 teaspoon grated fresh ginger
½ cup kimchi, finely chopped	2 tablespoons rice vinegar	Kosher salt and freshly ground black pepper, to taste

1. Select Roast, Air Fry Fan, set temperature to 400°F (204°C) and set time to 15 minutes. Press Start to begin preheating. Brush the zucchini with half of the olive oil, place on pizza rack. Once preheated, place the rack on the roast position. Turn halfway through, until lightly charred on the outside and tender. 2. Meanwhile, in a small bowl, combine the remaining 1 tablespoon olive oil, the kimchi, cilantro, parsley, vinegar, chili-garlic sauce, and ginger. 3. Once the zucchini is finished cooking, transfer it to a colander and let it cool for 5 minutes. Using your fingers, pinch and break the zucchini into bite-size pieces, letting them fall back into the colander. Season the zucchini with salt and pepper, toss to combine, then let sit a further 5 minutes to allow some of its liquid to drain. Pile the zucchini atop the kimchi sauce on a plate and sprinkle with more parsley to serve.

Indian Eggplant Bharta

Prep time: 15 minutes | Cook time: 20 minutes | Serves 4

1 medium eggplant	½ cup finely chopped fresh tomato	cilantro
2 tablespoons vegetable oil	2 tablespoons fresh lemon juice	½ teaspoon kosher salt
½ cup finely minced onion	2 tablespoons chopped fresh	⅛ teaspoon cayenne pepper

1. Select Roast, Air Fry Fan, set temperature to 400°F (204°C) and set time to 20 minutes. Press Start to begin preheating. Rub the eggplant all over on baking pan with the vegetable oil. Once preheated, place the pan on the roast position. The eggplant skin will be blistered and charred when done. 2. Transfer the eggplant to a resealable plastic bag, seal, and set aside for 15 to 20 minutes (the eggplant will finish cooking in the residual heat trapped in the bag). 3. Transfer the eggplant to a large bowl. Peel off and discard the charred skin. Roughly mash the eggplant flesh. Add the onion, tomato, lemon juice, cilantro, salt, and cayenne. Stir to combine.

Green Bean Casserole

Prep time: 10 minutes | Cook time: 20 minutes | Serves 4

1 pound (454 g) fresh green beans, ends trimmed, strings removed, and chopped into 2-inch pieces	½ onion, sliced	pepper
	1 clove garlic, minced	4 ounces (113 g) cream cheese
	1 tablespoon olive oil	½ cup chicken stock
1 (8-ounce / 227-g) package sliced brown mushrooms	½ teaspoon salt	¼ teaspoon ground nutmeg
	¼ teaspoon freshly ground black	½ cup grated Cheddar cheese

1. Select Roast, Air Fry Fan, set temperature to 400°F (204°C) and set time to 10 minutes. Press Start to begin preheating. Coat a casserole dish with olive oil and set aside. 2. In a large bowl, combine the green beans, mushrooms, onion, garlic, olive oil, salt, and pepper. Toss until the vegetables are thoroughly coated with the oil and seasonings. 3. Transfer the mixture to the baking pan. Once preheated, place the pan on the roast position. Pausing halfway through the cooking time to shake the pan. 4. While the vegetables are cooking, in a 2-cup glass measuring cup, warm the cream cheese and chicken stock in the microwave on high for 1 to 2 minutes until the cream cheese is melted. Add the nutmeg and whisk until smooth. 5. Transfer the vegetables to the prepared casserole dish and pour the cream cheese mixture over the top. Top with the Cheddar cheese. Transfer the dish to air fryer oven. Cook for another 10 minutes until the cheese is melted and beginning to brown.

Herbed Shiitake Mushrooms

Prep time: 10 minutes | Cook time: 5 minutes | Serves 4

8 ounces (227 g) shiitake mushrooms, stems removed and caps roughly chopped	½ teaspoon salt	leaves
	Freshly ground black pepper, to taste	1 teaspoon chopped fresh oregano
		1 tablespoon chopped fresh parsley
1 tablespoon olive oil	1 teaspoon chopped fresh thyme	

1. Select Roast, Air Fry Fan, set temperature to 400°F (204°C) and set time to 5 minutes. Press Start to begin preheating. 2. Toss the mushrooms with the olive oil, salt, pepper, thyme and oregano. Transfer to the baking pan. Once preheated, place the pan on the roast position. Shake the pan once or twice during the cooking process. The mushrooms will still be somewhat chewy with a meaty texture. If you'd like them a little more tender, add a couple of minutes to this cooking time. 3. Once cooked, add the parsley to the mushrooms and toss. Season again to taste and

serve.

Caesar Whole Cauliflower

Prep time: 20 minutes | Cook time: 30 minutes | Serves 2 to 4

- 3 tablespoons olive oil
- 2 tablespoons red wine vinegar
- 2 tablespoons Worcestershire sauce
- 2 tablespoons grated Parmesan cheese
- 1 tablespoon Dijon mustard
- 4 garlic cloves, minced
- 4 oil-packed anchovy fillets, drained and finely minced
- Kosher salt and freshly ground black pepper, to taste
- 1 small head cauliflower (about 1 pound / 454 g), green leaves trimmed and stem trimmed flush with the bottom of the head
- 1 tablespoon roughly chopped fresh flat-leaf parsley (optional)

1. In a liquid measuring cup, whisk together the olive oil, vinegar, Worcestershire, Parmesan, mustard, garlic, anchovies, and salt and pepper to taste. Place the cauliflower head upside down on a cutting board and use a paring knife to make an "x" through the full length of the core. Transfer the cauliflower head to a large bowl and pour half the dressing over it. Turn the cauliflower head to coat it in the dressing, then let it rest, stem-side up, in the dressing for at least 10 minutes and up to 30 minutes to allow the dressing to seep into all its nooks and crannies. 2. Select Roast, Air Fry Fan, set temperature to 340°F (171°C) and set time to 25 minutes. Press Start to begin preheating. Transfer the cauliflower head, stem-side down, to the baking pan. Once preheated, place the pan on the roast position. Drizzle the remaining dressing over the cauliflower and cook at 400°F (204°C) until the top of the cauliflower is golden brown and the core is tender, about 5 minutes more. 3. Remove the pan from the oven and transfer the cauliflower to a large plate. Sprinkle with the parsley, if you like, and serve hot.

Sesame Carrots and Sugar Snap Peas

Prep time: 10 minutes | Cook time: 16 minutes | Serves 4

- 1 pound (454 g) carrots, peeled sliced on the bias (½-inch slices)
- 1 teaspoon olive oil
- Salt and freshly ground black pepper, to taste
- ⅓ cup honey
- 1 tablespoon sesame oil
- 1 tablespoon soy sauce
- ½ teaspoon minced fresh ginger
- 4 ounces (113 g) sugar snap peas (about 1 cup)
- 1½ teaspoons sesame seeds

1. Select Roast, Air Fry Fan, set temperature to 360°F (182°C) and set time to 10 minutes. Press Start to begin preheating. 2. Toss the carrots with the olive oil, season with salt and pepper. Transfer to a baking pan. Once preheated, place the pan on the roast position. Shake the pan once or twice during the cooking process. 3. Combine the honey, sesame oil, soy sauce and minced ginger in a large bowl. Add the sugar snap peas and the air-fried carrots to the honey mixture, toss to coat and return everything to the baking pan. 4. Turn up the temperature to 400°F (204°C) and cook for an additional 6 minutes, shaking the pan once during the cooking process. 5. Transfer the carrots and sugar snap peas to a serving bowl. Pour the sauce from the bottom of the cooker over the vegetables and sprinkle sesame seeds over top. Serve immediately.

Tingly Chili-Roasted Broccoli

Prep time: 5 minutes | Cook time: 10 minutes | Serves 2

- 12 ounces (340 g) broccoli florets
- 2 tablespoons Asian hot chili oil
- 1 teaspoon ground Sichuan peppercorns (or black pepper)
- 2 garlic cloves, finely chopped
- 1 (2-inch) piece fresh ginger, peeled and finely chopped
- Kosher salt and freshly ground black pepper, to taste

1. Select Roast, Air Fry Fan, set temperature to 375°F (191°C) and set time to 10 minutes. Press Start to begin preheating. 2. In a bowl, toss together the broccoli, chili oil, Sichuan peppercorns, garlic, ginger, and salt and black pepper to taste. 3. Transfer to the baking pan. Once preheated, place the pan on the roast position. Shake the pan halfway through, until lightly charred and tender. Remove from the oven and serve warm.

Indian Chinese Cauliflower

Prep time: 10 minutes | Cook time: 20 minutes | Serves 4

Cauliflower:
- 4 cups chopped cauliflower
- 1 cup chopped yellow onion
- 1 large bell pepper, chopped
- 2 tablespoons vegetable oil
- 2 teaspoons kosher salt
- 1 teaspoon ground turmeric

Sauce:
- 3 tablespoons ketchup
- 2 tablespoons soy sauce
- 1 tablespoon rice vinegar
- 1 teaspoon minced garlic
- 1 teaspoon minced fresh ginger
- 1 teaspoon Sriracha or other hot sauce

1. For the cauliflower: Select Roast, Air Fry Fan, set temperature to 400°F (204°C) and set time to 20 minutes. Press Start to begin preheating. 2. In a large bowl, combine the cauliflower, onion, and bell pepper. Drizzle with the vegetable oil and sprinkle with the salt and turmeric. Stir until the cauliflower is well coated. 3. Place the cauliflower in the crisper tray. Once preheated, place the rack on the roast position. Stir the cauliflower halfway through the cooking time. 4. Meanwhile, for the sauce: In a small bowl, combine the ketchup, soy sauce, vinegar, garlic, ginger, and Sriracha. 5. Transfer the cauliflower to a large bowl. Pour the sauce over and toss well to combine. Serve immediately.

Roasted Eggplant

Prep time: 15 minutes | Cook time: 15 minutes | Serves 4

- 1 large eggplant
- 2 tablespoons olive oil
- ¼ teaspoon salt
- ½ teaspoon garlic powder

1. Select Roast, Air Fry Fan, set temperature to 390°F (199°C) and set time to 15 minutes. Press Start to begin preheating. 2. Remove top and bottom from eggplant. Slice eggplant into ¼-inch-thick round slices. 3. Brush slices with olive oil. Sprinkle with salt and garlic powder. Place eggplant slices into the crisper tray. 4. Once preheated, place the tray on the roast position. 5. Serve immediately.

Easy Rosemary Green Beans

Prep time: 5 minutes | Cook time: 5 minutes | Serves 1

- 1 tablespoon butter, melted
- 2 tablespoons rosemary
- ½ teaspoon salt
- 3 cloves garlic, minced
- ¾ cup chopped green beans

1. Select Roast, Air Fry Fan, set temperature to 390°F (199°C) and set time to 5 minutes. Press Start to begin preheating. 2. Combine the melted butter with the rosemary, salt, and minced garlic. Toss in the green beans, coating them well. 3. Transfer green beans to baking pan. Once preheated, place the pan on the roast position. 4. Serve immediately.

Garlic-Parmesan Jícama Fries

Prep time: 10 minutes | Cook time: 25 to 35 minutes | Serves 4

- 1 medium jícama, peeled
- 1 tablespoon avocado oil
- ¼ cup (4 tablespoons) unsalted butter
- 1 tablespoon minced garlic
- ¾ teaspoon chopped dried

rosemary

¾ teaspoon sea salt

½ teaspoon freshly ground black pepper

⅓ cup grated Parmesan cheese

Chopped fresh parsley, for garnish

Maldon sea salt, for garnish

1. Using a spiralizer or julienne peeler, cut the jícama into shoestrings, then cut them into 3-inch-long sticks. 2. Bring a large pot of water to boil. Add the jícama and cook for about 10 minutes. 2. Drain and dry on paper towels. Transfer to a medium bowl and toss with the oil. 3. Select Air Fry, set temperature to 400°F (204°C) and set time to 15 to 25 minutes. Press Start to begin preheating. 4. Arrange the jícama in a single layer in the crisper tray, working in batches if necessary. Once preheated, place the tray on the air fry position. Check at intervals, until tender and golden brown. 5. While the fries cook, melt the butter over medium-high heat. Add the garlic, rosemary, salt, and pepper. Cook for about 1 minute. 6. Toss the fries with the garlic butter. Top with the Parmesan cheese, and sprinkle with parsley and Maldon sea salt.

Bacon Potatoes and Green Beans

Prep time: 10 minutes | Cook time: 25 minutes | Serves 4

Oil, for spraying

2 pounds (907 g) medium russet potatoes, quartered

¾ cup bacon bits

10 ounces (283 g) fresh green beans

1 teaspoon salt

½ teaspoon freshly ground black pepper

1. Select Roast, Air Fry Fan, set temperature to 355°F (179°C) and set time to 25 minutes. Press Start to begin preheating. Line the baking pan with parchment and spray lightly with oil. 2. Place the potatoes in the prepared pan. Top with the bacon bits and green beans. Sprinkle with the salt and black pepper and spray liberally with oil. 3. Once preheated, place the pan on the roast position. Stir after 12 minutes and spraying with oil, until the potatoes are easily pierced with a fork.

Buffalo Cauliflower with Blue Cheese

Prep time: 15 minutes | Cook time: 5 to 7 minutes per batch | Serves 6

1 large head cauliflower, rinsed and separated into small florets

1 tablespoon extra-virgin olive oil

½ teaspoon garlic powder

Cooking oil spray

⅓ cup hot wing sauce

⅔ cup nonfat Greek yogurt

¼ cup buttermilk

½ teaspoon hot sauce

1 celery stalk, chopped

2 tablespoons crumbled blue cheese

1. Select Roast, Air Fry Fan, set temperature to 375°F (191°C) and set time to 7 minutes. Press Start to begin preheating. 2. In a large bowl, toss together the cauliflower florets and olive oil. Sprinkle with the garlic powder and toss again to coat. 3. Spray the crisper tray with cooking oil. Put half the cauliflower into the tray. 4. Once preheated, place the tray on the roast position. 5. After 3 minutes, remove the tray and shake the cauliflower. Reinsert the tray to resume cooking. After 2 minutes, check the cauliflower. It is done when it is browned. If not, resume cooking. 6. When the cooking is complete, transfer the cauliflower to a serving bowl and toss with half the hot wing sauce. 7. Repeat steps 4, 5, and 6 with the remaining cauliflower and hot wing sauce. 8. In a small bowl, stir together the yogurt, buttermilk, hot sauce, celery, and blue cheese. Drizzle the sauce over the finished cauliflower and serve.

Spiced Butternut Squash

Prep time: 10 minutes | Cook time: 15 minutes | Serves 4

4 cups 1-inch-cubed butternut squash

2 tablespoons vegetable oil

1 to 2 tablespoons brown sugar

1 teaspoon Chinese five-spice powder

1. Select Roast, Air Fry Fan, set temperature to 400°F (204°C) and set time to 15 minutes. Press Start to begin preheating. 2. In a medium bowl, combine the squash, oil, sugar, and five-spice powder. Toss to coat. Transfer to baking pan. 2. Once preheated, place the pan on the roast position. It will be done until tender.

Roasted Grape Tomatoes and Asparagus

Prep time: 5 minutes | Cook time: 12 minutes | Serves 6

2 cups grape tomatoes

1 bunch asparagus, trimmed

2 tablespoons olive oil

3 garlic cloves, minced

½ teaspoon kosher salt

1. Select Roast, Air Fry Fan, set temperature to 380°F (193°C) and set time to 12 minutes. Press Start to begin preheating. 2. In a large bowl, combine all of the ingredients, tossing until the vegetables are well coated with oil. 3. Pour the vegetable mixture into the baking pan and spread into a single layer. Once preheated, place the pan on the roast position and roast.

Parmesan-Thyme Butternut Squash

Prep time: 15 minutes | Cook time: 20 minutes | Serves 4

2 ½ cups butternut squash, cubed into 1-inch pieces (approximately 1 medium)

2 tablespoons olive oil

¼ teaspoon salt

¼ teaspoon garlic powder

¼ teaspoon black pepper

1 tablespoon fresh thyme

¼ cup grated Parmesan

1. Select Roast, Air Fry Fan, set temperature to 360°F (182°C) and set time to 10 minutes. Press Start to begin preheating. 2. In a large bowl, combine the cubed squash with the olive oil, salt, garlic powder, pepper, and thyme until the squash is well coated. 3. Pour this mixture into the baking pan. Once preheated, place the pan on the roast position and roast. Stir and roast another 8 to 10 minutes more. 4. Remove the squash from the air fryer oven and toss with freshly grated Parmesan before serving.

Hawaiian Brown Rice

Prep time: 10 minutes | Cook time: 12 to 16 minutes | Serves 4 to 6

¼ pound (113 g) ground sausage

1 teaspoon butter

¼ cup minced onion

¼ cup minced bell pepper

2 cups cooked brown rice

1 (8-ounce / 227-g) can crushed pineapple, drained

1. Select Roast, Air Fry Fan, set temperature to 390°F (199°C) and set time to 6 to 8 minutes. Press Start to begin preheating. Shape sausage into 3 or 4 thin patties and transfer to pizza rack. Once preheated, place the rack on the roast position. Remove from oven, drain, and crumble. Set aside. 2. Place butter, onion, and bell pepper in baking pan. Place the pan into oven and roast at 390°F (199°C) for 1 minute and stir. Cook 3 to 4 minutes longer or just until vegetables are tender. 3. Add sausage, rice, and pineapple to vegetables and stir together. 4. Roast for 2 to 3 minutes, until heated through.

Broccoli with Sesame Dressing

Prep time: 5 minutes | Cook time: 10 minutes | Serves 4

6 cups broccoli florets, cut into bite-size pieces

1 tablespoon olive oil

¼ teaspoon salt

2 tablespoons sesame seeds

2 tablespoons rice vinegar

2 tablespoons coconut aminos

2 tablespoons sesame oil

½ teaspoon Swerve

¼ teaspoon red pepper flakes (optional)

1. Select Air Fry, set temperature to 400°F (204°C) and set time to 10 minutes. Press Start to begin preheating. 2. In a large bowl, toss the broccoli with the olive oil and salt until thoroughly coated. 3. Transfer the broccoli to the crisper tray. Once preheated, place the tray on the 10 position. Pausing halfway through the cooking time to shake the tray. It will be done until the stems are tender and the edges are beginning to crisp. 4. Meanwhile, in the same large bowl, whisk together the sesame seeds, vinegar, coconut aminos, sesame oil, Swerve, and red pepper flakes (if using). 5. Transfer the broccoli to the bowl and toss until thoroughly coated with the seasonings. Serve warm or at room temperature.

Roasted Brussels Sprouts with Orange and Garlic

Prep time: 5 minutes | Cook time: 10 minutes | Serves 4

1 pound Brussels sprouts, quartered

2 garlic cloves, minced

2 tablespoons olive oil

½ teaspoon salt

1 orange, cut into rings

1. Select Roast, Air Fry Fan, set temperature to 360°F (182°C) and set time to 10 minutes. Press Start to begin preheating. 2. In a large bowl, toss the quartered Brussels sprouts with the garlic, olive oil, and salt until well coated. 3. Pour the Brussels sprouts into the baking pan, lay the orange slices on top of them. Once preheated, place the pan on the roast position. 4. Remove from the air fryer oven and set the orange slices aside. Toss the Brussels sprouts before serving.

Five-Spice Roasted Sweet Potatoes

Prep time: 10 minutes | Cook time: 12 minutes | Serves 4

½ teaspoon ground cinnamon

¼ teaspoon ground cumin

¼ teaspoon paprika

1 teaspoon chile powder

⅛ teaspoon turmeric

½ teaspoon salt (optional)

Freshly ground black pepper, to taste

2 large sweet potatoes, peeled and cut into ¾-inch cubes (about 3 cups)

1 tablespoon olive oil

1. Select Roast, Air Fry Fan, set temperature to 390°F (199°C) and set time to 6 minutes. Press Start to begin preheating. 2. In a large bowl, mix together cinnamon, cumin, paprika, chile powder, turmeric, salt, and pepper to taste. Add potatoes and stir well. 3. Drizzle the seasoned potatoes with the olive oil and stir until evenly coated. 4. Once preheated, place seasoned potatoes in a baking pan on roast position. 5. Stop, and stir well. Cook for an additional 6 minutes.

Corn and Cilantro Salad

Prep time: 10 minutes | Cook time: 10 minutes | Serves 2

2 ears of corn, shucked (halved crosswise if too large to fit in your air fryer)

1 tablespoon unsalted butter, at room temperature

1 teaspoon chili powder

¼ teaspoon garlic powder

Kosher salt and freshly ground black pepper, to taste

1 cup lightly packed fresh cilantro leaves
1 tablespoon sour cream
1 tablespoon mayonnaise
1 teaspoon adobo sauce (from a can of chipotle peppers in adobo sauce)
2 tablespoons crumbled queso fresco
Lime wedges, for serving

1. Select Air Fry, set temperature to 400°F (204°C) and set time to 10 minutes. Press Start to begin preheating. 2. Brush the corn all over with the butter, then sprinkle with the chili powder and garlic powder, and season with salt and pepper. Place the corn on pizza rack. Once preheated, place the rack on the air fry position. Turn over halfway through, until the kernels are lightly charred and tender. 3. Transfer the ears to a cutting board, let stand 1 minute, then carefully cut the kernels off the cobs and move them to a bowl. Add the cilantro leaves and toss to combine (the cilantro leaves will wilt slightly). 4. In a small bowl, stir together the sour cream, mayonnaise, and adobo sauce. Divide the corn and cilantro among plates and spoon the adobo dressing over the top. Sprinkle with the queso fresco and serve with lime wedges on the side.

Zesty Fried Asparagus

Prep time: 3 minutes | Cook time: 10 minutes | Serves 4

Oil, for spraying
10 to 12 spears asparagus, trimmed
2 tablespoons olive oil
1 tablespoon granulated garlic
1 teaspoon chili powder
½ teaspoon ground cumin
¼ teaspoon salt

1. Select Roast, Air Fry Fan, set temperature to 390°F (199°C) and set time to 5 minutes. Press Start to begin preheating. Line the baking pan with parchment and spray lightly with oil. 2. If the asparagus are too long to fit easily in the oven, cut them in half. 3. Place the asparagus, olive oil, garlic, chili powder, cumin, and salt in a zip-top plastic bag, seal, and toss until evenly coated. 4. Place the asparagus in the prepared pan. 5. Once preheated, place the pan on the roast position. Flip, and cook for another 5 minutes, or until bright green and firm but tender.

Asian-Inspired Roasted Broccoli

Prep time: 10 minutes | Cook time: 15 minutes | Serves 4

Broccoli:
Oil, for spraying
1 pound (454 g) broccoli florets
2 teaspoons peanut oil
1 tablespoon minced garlic
½ teaspoon salt
Sauce:
2 tablespoons soy sauce
2 teaspoons honey
2 teaspoons Sriracha
1 teaspoon rice vinegar

Make the Broccoli: 1. Select Roast, Air Fry Fan, set temperature to 400°F (204°C) and set time to 15 minutes. Press Start to begin preheating. Line the baking pan with parchment and spray lightly with oil. 2. In a large bowl, toss together the broccoli, peanut oil, garlic, and salt until evenly coated. 3. Spread out the broccoli in an even layer in the prepared pan. 4. Once preheated, place the pan on the roast position. Stir halfway through. **Make the Sauce:** 5. Meanwhile, in a small microwave-safe bowl, combine the soy sauce, honey, Sriracha, and rice vinegar and microwave on high for about 15 seconds. Stir to combine. 6. Transfer the broccoli to a serving bowl and add the sauce. Gently toss until evenly coated and serve immediately.

Radish Chips

Prep time: 10 minutes | Cook time: 5 minutes | Serves 4

2 cups water
1 pound (454 g) radishes
¼ teaspoon onion powder
¼ teaspoon paprika
½ teaspoon garlic powder
2 tablespoons coconut oil, melted

1. Place water in a medium saucepan and bring to a boil on stovetop. 2. Remove the top and bottom from each radish, then use a mandoline to slice each radish thin and uniformly. You may also use the slicing blade in the food processor for this step. 3. Place the radish slices into the boiling water for 5 minutes or until translucent. Remove them from the water and place them into a clean kitchen towel to absorb excess moisture. 4. Select Air Fry, set temperature to 320°F (160°C) and set time to 5 minutes. Press Start to begin preheating. Toss the radish chips in a large bowl with remaining ingredients until fully coated in oil and seasoning. Place radish chips into the crisper tray. 5. Once preheated, place the tray on the air fry position. 6. Shake the tray two or three times during the cooking time. Serve warm.

Cheddar Broccoli with Bacon

Prep time: 10 minutes | Cook time: 10 minutes | Serves 2

3 cups fresh broccoli florets	cheese	and crumbled
1 tablespoon coconut oil	¼ cup full-fat sour cream	1 scallion, sliced on the bias
½ cup shredded sharp Cheddar	4 slices sugar-free bacon, cooked	

1. Select Roast, Air Fry Fan, set temperature to 350°F (177°C) and set time to 10 minutes. Press Start to begin preheating. Place broccoli into the baking pan and drizzle it with coconut oil. 2. Once preheated, place the pan on the roast position. 3. Toss the pan two or three times during cooking to avoid burned spots. 4. When broccoli begins to crisp at ends, remove from oven. Top with shredded cheese, sour cream, and crumbled bacon and garnish with scallion slices.

Mexican Corn in a Cup

Prep time: 5 minutes | Cook time: 10 minutes | Serves 4

4 cups frozen corn kernels (do not thaw)	¼ cup mayonnaise	1 teaspoon chili powder
Vegetable oil spray	¼ cup grated Parmesan cheese (or feta, cotija, or queso fresco)	Chopped fresh green onion (optional)
2 tablespoons butter	2 tablespoons fresh lemon or lime juice	Chopped fresh cilantro (optional)
¼ cup sour cream		

1. Select Bake, Air Fry Fan, set temperature to 350°F (177°C) and set time to 10 minutes. Press Start to begin preheating. Place the corn in the baking pan and spray with vegetable oil spray. Once preheated, place the pan on the bake position. 2. Transfer the corn to a serving bowl. Add the butter and stir until melted. Add the sour cream, mayonnaise, cheese, lemon juice, and chili powder; stir until well combined. Serve immediately with green onion and cilantro (if using).

Sweet and Crispy Roasted Pearl Onions

Prep time: 5 minutes | Cook time: 18 minutes | Serves 3

1 (14½-ounce / 411-g) package frozen pearl onions (do not thaw)	2 tablespoons balsamic vinegar	½ teaspoon kosher salt
2 tablespoons extra-virgin olive oil	2 teaspoons finely chopped fresh rosemary	¼ teaspoon black pepper

1. Select Roast, Air Fry Fan, set temperature to 400°F (204°C) and set time to 18 minutes. Press Start to begin preheating. In a medium bowl, combine the onions, olive oil, vinegar, rosemary, salt, and pepper until well coated. 2. Transfer the onions to the baking pan. Once preheated, place the pan on the roast position. The onions will be tender

and lightly charred when done, stirring once or twice during the cooking time.

Mediterranean Zucchini Boats

Prep time: 5 minutes | Cook time: 10 minutes | Serves 4

1 large zucchini, ends removed, halved lengthwise

6 grape tomatoes, quartered

¼ teaspoon salt

¼ cup feta cheese

1 tablespoon balsamic vinegar

1 tablespoon olive oil

1. Select Roast, Air Fry Fan, set temperature to 350°F (177°C) and set time to 10 minutes. Press Start to begin preheating. 2. Use a spoon to scoop out 2 tablespoons from center of each zucchini half, making just enough space to fill with tomatoes and feta. 3. Place tomatoes evenly in centers of zucchini halves and sprinkle with salt. Place into ungreased pizza rack. Once preheated, place the rack on the roast position. When done, zucchini will be tender. 4. Transfer boats to a serving tray and sprinkle with feta, then drizzle with vinegar and olive oil. Serve warm.

Gorgonzola Mushrooms with Horseradish Mayo

Prep time: 15 minutes | Cook time: 10 minutes | Serves 5

½ cup bread crumbs

2 cloves garlic, pressed

2 tablespoons chopped fresh coriander

⅓ teaspoon kosher salt

½ teaspoon crushed red pepper

flakes

1½ tablespoons olive oil

20 medium mushrooms, stems removed

½ cup grated Gorgonzola cheese

¼ cup low-fat mayonnaise

1 teaspoon prepared horseradish, well-drained

1 tablespoon finely chopped fresh parsley

1. Select Roast, Air Fry Fan, set temperature to 380°F (193°C) and set time to 10 minutes. Press Start to begin preheating. 2. Combine the bread crumbs together with the garlic, coriander, salt, red pepper, and olive oil. 3. Take equal-sized amounts of the bread crumb mixture and use them to stuff the mushroom caps. Add the grated Gorgonzola on top of each. 4. Once put the mushrooms in a baking pan and place the pan on the roast position. Ensure the stuffing is warm throughout. 5. In the meantime, prepare the horseradish mayo. Mix the mayonnaise, horseradish and parsley. 6. When the mushrooms are ready, serve with the mayo.

Garlic-Parmesan Crispy Baby Potatoes

Prep time: 10 minutes | Cook time: 15 minutes | Serves 4

Oil, for spraying

1 pound (454 g) baby potatoes

½ cup grated Parmesan cheese, divided

3 tablespoons olive oil

2 teaspoons granulated garlic

½ teaspoon onion powder

½ teaspoon salt

¼ teaspoon freshly ground black pepper

¼ teaspoon paprika

2 tablespoons chopped fresh parsley, for garnish

1. Select Roast, Air Fry Fan, set temperature to 400°F (204°C) and set time to 15 minutes. Press Start to begin preheating. Line the baking pan with parchment and spray lightly with oil. 2. Rinse the potatoes, pat dry with paper towels, and place in a large bowl. 3. In a small bowl, mix together ¼ cup of Parmesan cheese, the olive oil, garlic, onion powder, salt, black pepper, and paprika. Pour the mixture over the potatoes and toss to coat. 4. Transfer the potatoes to the prepared pan and spread them out in an even layer, taking care to keep them from touching. You may need to work in batches. 5. Once preheated, place the pan on the roast position. Stir after 7 to 8 minutes, or until

easily pierced with a fork. Continue to cook for another 1 to 2 minutes, if needed. 6. Sprinkle with the parsley and the remaining Parmesan cheese and serve.

Cauliflower with Lime Juice

Prep time: 10 minutes | Cook time: 7 minutes | Serves 4

2 cups chopped cauliflower florets	2 teaspoons chili powder	1 medium lime
2 tablespoons coconut oil, melted	½ teaspoon garlic powder	2 tablespoons chopped cilantro

1. Select Roast, Air Fry Fan, set temperature to 350°F (177°C) and set time to 7 minutes. Press Start to begin preheating. 2. In a large bowl, toss cauliflower with coconut oil. Sprinkle with chili powder and garlic powder. Place seasoned cauliflower into the crisper tray. 3. Once preheated, place the tray on the roast position. 4. Cauliflower will be tender and begin to turn golden at the edges. Place into a serving bowl. 5. Cut the lime into quarters and squeeze juice over cauliflower. Garnish with cilantro.

Cauliflower Steaks Gratin

Prep time: 10 minutes | Cook time: 13 minutes | Serves 2

1 head cauliflower	pepper, to taste	3 tablespoons grated
1 tablespoon olive oil	½ teaspoon chopped fresh thyme	Parmigiano-Reggiano cheese
Salt and freshly ground black	leaves	2 tablespoons panko bread crumbs

1. Select Roast, Air Fry Fan, set temperature to 370°F (188°C) and set time to 6 minutes. Press Start to begin preheating. 2. Cut two steaks out of the center of the cauliflower. To do this, cut the cauliflower in half and then cut one slice about 1-inch thick off each half. The rest of the cauliflower will fall apart into florets, which you can roast on their own or save for another meal. 3. Brush both sides of the cauliflower steaks with olive oil and season with salt, freshly ground black pepper and fresh thyme. Place the cauliflower steaks into the baking pan. Once preheated, place the pan on the roast position. Turn the steaks over and cook for another 4 minutes. Combine the Parmesan cheese and panko bread crumbs and sprinkle the mixture over the tops of both steaks and cookve browned. Serve this with some sautéed bitter greens and air-fried blistered tomatoes.

Asparagus Fries

Prep time: 15 minutes | Cook time: 5 to 7 minutes per batch | Serves 4

12 ounces (340 g) fresh asparagus spears with tough ends trimmed off	¼ cup water	plus 2 tablespoons
	¾ cup panko bread crumbs	¼ teaspoon salt
2 egg whites	¼ cup grated Parmesan cheese,	Oil for misting or cooking spray

1. Select Air Fry, set temperature to 390°F (199°C) and set time to 5 minutes. Press Start to begin preheating. 2. In a shallow dish, beat egg whites and water until slightly foamy. 3. In another shallow dish, combine panko, Parmesan, and salt. 4. Dip asparagus spears in egg, then roll in crumbs. Spray with oil or cooking spray. 5. Place a layer of asparagus in crisper tray, leaving just a little space in between each spear. Stack another layer on top, crosswise. Once preheated, place the tray on the air fry position. It will be done until crispy and golden brown. 6. Repeat to cook remaining asparagus.

Parmesan Herb Focaccia Bread

Prep time: 10 minutes | Cook time: 10 minutes | Serves 6

1 cup shredded Mozzarella cheese	1 ounce (28 g) full-fat cream cheese	1 cup blanched finely ground

almond flour

¼ cup ground golden flaxseed

¼ cup grated Parmesan cheese

½ teaspoon baking soda

2 large eggs

½ teaspoon garlic powder

¼ teaspoon dried basil

¼ teaspoon dried rosemary

2 tablespoons salted butter, melted and divided

1. Select Roast, Air Fry Fan, set temperature to 400°F (204°C) and set time to 10 minutes. Press Start to begin preheating. 2. Place Mozzarella, cream cheese, and almond flour into a large microwave-safe bowl and microwave for 1 minute. Add the flaxseed, Parmesan, and baking soda and stir until smooth ball forms. If the mixture cools too much, it will be hard to mix. Return to microwave for 10 to 15 seconds to rewarm if necessary. 3. Stir in eggs. You may need to use your hands to get them fully incorporated. Just keep stirring and they will absorb into the dough. 4. Sprinkle dough with garlic powder, basil, and rosemary and knead into dough. Grease the baking pan with 1 tablespoon melted butter. Press the dough evenly into the pan. 5. Once preheated, place the pan on the roast position. 6. At 7 minutes, cover with foil if bread begins to get too dark. 7. Remove and let cool at least 30 minutes. Drizzle with remaining butter and serve.

Ratatouille

Prep time: 15 minutes | Cook time: 20 minutes | Serves 2 to 3

2 cups ¾-inch cubed peeled eggplant

1 small red, yellow, or orange bell pepper, stemmed, seeded, and diced

1 cup cherry tomatoes

6 to 8 cloves garlic, peeled and halved lengthwise

3 tablespoons olive oil

1 teaspoon dried oregano

½ teaspoon dried thyme

1 teaspoon kosher salt

½ teaspoon black pepper

1. Select Roast, Air Fry Fan, set temperature to 400°F (204°C) and set time to 20 minutes. Press Start to begin preheating. 2. In a medium bowl, combine the eggplant, bell pepper, tomatoes, garlic, oil, oregano, thyme, salt, and pepper. Toss to combine. 3. Place the vegetables on the baking pan. Once preheated, place the pan on the roast position. It will be done until the vegetables are crisp-tender.

Mushrooms with Goat Cheese

Prep time: 10 minutes | Cook time: 10 minutes | Serves 4

3 tablespoons vegetable oil

1 pound (454 g) mixed mushrooms, trimmed and sliced

1 clove garlic, minced

¼ teaspoon dried thyme

½ teaspoon black pepper

4 ounces (113 g) goat cheese, diced

2 teaspoons chopped fresh thyme leaves (optional)

1. Select Roast, Air Fry Fan, set temperature to 400°F (204°C) and set time to 10 minutes. Press Start to begin preheating. 2. In a baking pan, combine the oil, mushrooms, garlic, dried thyme, and pepper. Stir in the goat cheese. 3. Once preheated, place the pan on the roast position. .Stir halfway through the cooking time. 4. Sprinkle with fresh thyme, if desired.

Spinach and Sweet Pepper Poppers

Prep time: 10 minutes | Cook time: 8 minutes | Makes 16 poppers

4 ounces (113 g) cream cheese, softened

1 cup chopped fresh spinach leaves

½ teaspoon garlic powder

8 mini sweet bell peppers, tops removed, seeded, and halved

lengthwise

1. Select Roast, Air Fry Fan, set temperature to 400°F (204°C) and set time to 8 minutes. Press Start to begin preheating. 2. In a medium bowl, mix cream cheese, spinach, and garlic powder. Place 1 tablespoon mixture into each sweet pepper half and press down to smooth. 3. Place poppers into ungreased baking pan. Once preheated, place the pan on the roast position. Poppers will be done when cheese is browned on top and peppers are tender-crisp. Serve warm.

Fried Zucchini Salad

Prep time: 10 minutes | Cook time: 5 to 7 minutes | Serves 4

2 medium zucchini, thinly sliced	2 tablespoons chopped fresh mint	¼ cup crumbled feta cheese
5 tablespoons olive oil, divided	Zest and juice of ½ lemon	Freshly ground black pepper, to taste
¼ cup chopped fresh parsley	1 clove garlic, minced	

1. Select Air Fry, set temperature to 400°F (204°C) and set time to 5 to 7 minutes. Press Start to begin preheating. 2. In a large bowl, toss the zucchini slices with 1 tablespoon of the olive oil. 3. Working in batches if necessary, arrange the zucchini slices in an even layer on the crisper tray. Once preheated, place the tray on the air fry position. Pausing halfway through the cooking time to gently shake the tray. It will be done until soft and lightly browned on each side. 4. Meanwhile, in a small bowl, combine the remaining 4 tablespoons olive oil, parsley, mint, lemon zest, lemon juice, and garlic. 5. Arrange the zucchini on a plate and drizzle with the dressing. Sprinkle the feta and black pepper on top. Serve warm or at room temperature.

Sesame Taj Tofu

Prep time: 5 minutes | Cook time: 25 minutes | Serves 4

1 block firm tofu, pressed and cut into 1-inch thick cubes	2 tablespoons soy sauce	1 teaspoon rice vinegar
	2 teaspoons toasted sesame seeds	1 tablespoon cornstarch

1. Select Air Fry, set temperature to 400°F (204°C) and set time to 25 minutes. Press Start to begin preheating. 2. Add the tofu, soy sauce, sesame seeds, and rice vinegar in a bowl together and mix well to coat the tofu cubes. Then cover the tofu in cornstarch and put it in the crisper tray. 3. Once preheated, place the tray on the air fry position. Give the tray a gentle shake every 5 minutes to ensure the tofu cooks evenly. 4. Serve immediately.

Citrus-Roasted Broccoli Florets

Prep time: 5 minutes | Cook time: 12 minutes | Serves 6

4 cups broccoli florets (approximately 1 large head)	½ teaspoon salt	Orange wedges, for serving (optional)
2 tablespoons olive oil	½ cup orange juice	
	1 tablespoon raw honey	

1. Select Roast, Air Fry Fan, set temperature to 360°F (182°C) and set time to 6 minutes. Press Start to begin preheating. 2. In a large bowl, combine the broccoli, olive oil, salt, orange juice, and honey. Toss the broccoli in the liquid until well coated. 3. Pour the broccoli mixture into the baking pan. Once preheated, place the pan on the roast position. Stir and roast for 6 minutes more. 4. Serve alone or with orange wedges for additional citrus flavor, if desired.

Creamed Asparagus

Prep time: 10 minutes | Cook time: 18 minutes | Serves 4

½ cup heavy whipping cream
½ cup grated Parmesan cheese
2 ounces (57 g) cream cheese, softened
1 pound (454 g) asparagus, ends trimmed, chopped into 1-inch pieces
¼ teaspoon salt
¼ teaspoon ground black pepper

1. Select Roast, Air Fry Fan, set temperature to 350°F (177°C) and set time to 18 minutes. Press Start to begin preheating. 2. In a medium bowl, whisk together heavy cream, Parmesan, and cream cheese until combined. 3. Place asparagus into baking pan. Pour cheese mixture over top and sprinkle with salt and pepper. 4. Once preheated, place the pan on roast position. Asparagus will be tender when done. Serve warm.

Chapter 3 Poultry

Air Fried Chicken Wings with Buffalo Sauce

Prep time: 10 minutes | Cook time: 20 minutes | Serves 6

16 chicken drumettes (party wings)
Chicken seasoning or rub, to taste
1 teaspoon garlic powder
Ground black pepper, to taste
¼ cup buffalo wings sauce
Cooking spray

1. Select Air Fry, set temperature to 400°F (204°C) and set time to 10 minutes. Press Start to begin preheating. Spritz the pizza rack with cooking spray. 2. Rub the chicken wings with chicken seasoning, garlic powder, and ground black pepper on a clean work surface. 3. Arrange the chicken wings on pizza rack. Spritz with cooking spray. Once preheated, place the rack on the air fry position. It will be done until lightly browned. Shake the rack halfway through. 4. Transfer the chicken wings in a large bowl, then pour in the buffalo wings sauce and toss to coat well. 5. Put the wings back to the oven and cook for an additional 7 minutes. 6. Serve immediately.

Chicken Strips with Satay Sauce

Prep time: 15 minutes | Cook time: 10 minutes | Serves 4

4 (6-ounce / 170-g) boneless, skinless chicken breasts, sliced into 16 (1-inch) strips
1 teaspoon fine sea salt
1 teaspoon paprika
Sauce:
¼ cup creamy almond butter (or sunflower seed butter for nut-free)
2 tablespoons chicken broth
1½ tablespoons coconut vinegar or unseasoned rice vinegar
1 clove garlic, minced
1 teaspoon peeled and minced fresh ginger
½ teaspoon hot sauce
⅛ teaspoon stevia glycerite, or 2 to 3 drops liquid stevia
For Garnish/Serving (Optional):
¼ cup chopped cilantro leaves
Red pepper flakes
Sea salt flakes
Thinly sliced red, orange, and yellow bell peppers
Special Equipment:
16 wooden or bamboo skewers, soaked in water for 15 minutes

1. Spray the pizza rack with avocado oil. Select Roast, Air Fry Fan, set temperature to 400°F (204°C) and set time to 5 minutes. Press Start to begin preheating. 2. Thread the chicken strips onto the skewers. Season on all sides with the salt and paprika. Once preheated, place the chicken skewers on rack and place the rack on the roast position. Flip, and cook for another 5 minutes, until the chicken is cooked through and the internal temperature reaches 165°F (74°C). 3. While the chicken skewers cook, make the sauce: In a medium-sized bowl, stir together all the sauce

ingredients until well combined. Taste and adjust the sweetness and heat to your liking. 4. Garnish the chicken with cilantro, red pepper flakes, and salt flakes, if desired, and serve with sliced bell peppers, if desired. Serve the sauce on the side. 5. Store leftovers in an airtight container in the fridge for up to 4 days or in the freezer for up to a month. Reheat in a preheated 350°F (177°C) air fryer oven for 3 minutes per side, or until heated through.

Breaded Turkey Cutlets

Prep time: 5 minutes | Cook time: 8 minutes | Serves 4

½ cup whole wheat bread crumbs	¼ teaspoon black pepper	1 egg
¼ teaspoon paprika	⅛ teaspoon dried sage	4 turkey breast cutlets
¼ teaspoon salt	⅛ teaspoon garlic powder	Chopped fresh parsley, for serving

1. Select Bake, Air Fry Fan, set temperature to 380°F (193°C) and set time to 4 minutes. Press Start to begin preheating. 2. In a medium shallow bowl, whisk together the bread crumbs, paprika, salt, black pepper, sage, and garlic powder. 3. In a separate medium shallow bowl, whisk the egg until frothy. 4. Dip each turkey cutlet into the egg mixture, then into the bread crumb mixture, coating the outside with the crumbs. Place the breaded turkey cutlets in a single layer on baking pan, making sure that they don't touch each other. 5. Once preheated, place the pan on the bake position. Turn the cutlets over, then bake for 4 minutes more, or until the internal temperature reaches 165°F (74°C). Sprinkle on the parsley and serve.

Chicken Legs with Leeks

Prep time: 30 minutes | Cook time: 18 minutes | Serves 6

2 leeks, sliced	3 cloves garlic, minced	6 chicken legs, boneless and skinless	cayenne pepper
2 large-sized tomatoes, chopped	½ teaspoon dried oregano	½ teaspoon smoked	2 tablespoons olive oil
			A freshly ground nutmeg

1. Select Roast, Air Fry Fan, set temperature to 375°F (191°C) and set time to 18 minutes. Press Start to begin preheating. 2. In a mixing dish, thoroughly combine all ingredients, minus the leeks. Place in the refrigerator and let it marinate overnight. 3. Lay the leeks onto the bottom of the baking pan. Top with the chicken legs. Once preheated, place the pan on the roast position. Turn halfway through. Serve with hoisin sauce.

Hawaiian Chicken Bites

Prep time: 1 hour 15 minutes | Cook time: 15 minutes | Serves 4

½ cup pineapple juice	2 garlic cloves, minced	4 chicken breasts, cubed
2 tablespoons apple cider vinegar	½ cup brown sugar	Cooking spray
½ tablespoon minced ginger	2 tablespoons sherry	
½ cup ketchup	½ cup soy sauce	

1. Combine the pineapple juice, cider vinegar, ginger, ketchup, garlic, and sugar in a saucepan. Stir to mix well. Heat over low heat for 5 minutes or until thickened. Fold in the sherry and soy sauce. 2. Dunk the chicken cubes in the mixture. Press to submerge. Wrap the bowl in plastic and refrigerate to marinate for at least an hour. 3. Select Roast, Air Fry Fan, set temperature to 360°F (182°C) and set time to 15 minutes. Press Start to begin preheating. Spritz the crisper tray with cooking spray. 4. Remove the chicken cubes from the marinade. Shake the excess off and put in the prepared pan. Spritz with cooking spray. 5. Once preheated, place the tray on the roast position. The chicken cubes will be glazed and well browned when done. Shake the tray at least three times during the frying. 6. Serve

immediately.

French Garlic Chicken

Prep time: 30 minutes | Cook time: 27 minutes | Serves 4

2 tablespoon extra-virgin olive oil	2 teaspoons herbes de Provence	chicken thighs, halved crosswise
1 tablespoon Dijon mustard	½ teaspoon kosher salt	2 tablespoons butter
1 tablespoon apple cider vinegar	1 teaspoon black pepper	8 cloves garlic, chopped
3 cloves garlic, minced	1 pound (454 g) boneless, skinless	¼ cup heavy whipping cream

1. In a small bowl, combine the olive oil, mustard, vinegar, minced garlic, herbes de Provence, salt, and pepper. Use a wire whisk to emulsify the mixture. 2. Pierce the chicken all over with a fork to allow the marinade to penetrate better. Place the chicken in a resealable plastic bag, pour the marinade over, and seal. Massage until the chicken is well coated. Marinate at room temperature for 30 minutes or in the refrigerator for up to 24 hours. 3. When you are ready to cook, select Air Fry, set temperature to 400°F (204°C) and set time to 5 minutes. Press Start to begin preheating. Place the butter and chopped garlic in a baking pan. Once preheated, place the pan on the air fry position. It will be done until the butter has melted and the garlic is sizzling. 4. Add the chicken and the marinade to the seasoned butter. Set the temperature to 350°F (177°C) for 15 minutes. Use a meat thermometer to ensure the chicken has reached an internal temperature of 165°F (74°C). Transfer the chicken to a plate and cover lightly with foil to keep warm. 5. Add the cream to the pan, stirring to combine with the garlic, butter, and cooking juices. Place the pan back to the oven. Set the temperature to to 350°F (177°C) for 7 minutes. 6. Pour the thickened sauce over the chicken and serve.

Gold Livers

Prep time: 10 minutes | Cook time: 20 minutes | Serves 4

2 eggs	2 cups panko breadcrumbs	20 ounces (567 g) chicken livers
2 tablespoons water	1 teaspoon salt	Cooking spray
¾ cup flour	½ teaspoon ground black pepper	

1. Select Roast, Air Fry Fan, set temperature to 390°F (199°C) and set time to 10 minutes. Press Start to begin preheating. Spritz the crisper tray with cooking spray. 2. Whisk the eggs with water in a large bowl. Pour the flour in a separate bowl. Pour the panko on a shallow dish and sprinkle with salt and pepper. 3. Dredge the chicken livers in the flour. Shake the excess off, then dunk the livers in the whisked eggs, and then roll the livers over the panko to coat well. 4. Arrange the livers in the tray and spritz with cooking spray. Work in batches to avoid overcrowding. 5. Once preheated, place the tray on the roast position. The livers will be golden and crispy. Flip the livers halfway through. Repeat with remaining livers. 6. Serve immediately.

Easy Chicken Nachos

Prep time: 5 minutes | Cook time: 5 minutes | Serves 8

Oil, for spraying	seasoning	⅓ cup bacon bits
3 cups shredded cooked chicken	¼ cup sour cream	1 cup shredded Cheddar cheese
1 (1-ounce / 28-g) package ranch	2 cups corn tortilla chips	1 tablespoon chopped scallions

1. Select Air Fry, set temperature to 400°F (204°C) and set time to 3 to 5 minutes. Press Start to begin preheating. Line the crisper tray with parchment and spray lightly with oil. 2. In a small bowl, mix together the chicken, ranch seasoning, and sour cream. 3. Place the tortilla chips in the prepared tray and top with the chicken mixture. Add the

bacon bits, Cheddar cheese, and scallions. 4. Once preheated, place the tray on the air fry position. It will be done until heated through and the cheese is melted.

Wild Rice and Kale Stuffed Chicken Thighs

Prep time: 10 minutes | Cook time: 22 minutes | Serves 4

4 boneless, skinless chicken thighs	2 garlic cloves, minced	½ cup crumbled feta
1 cup cooked wild rice	1 teaspoon salt	Olive oil cooking spray
½ cup chopped kale	Juice of 1 lemon	1 tablespoon olive oil

1. Select Roast, Air Fry Fan, set temperature to 380°F (193°C) and set time to 15 minutes. Press Start to begin preheating. 2. Place the chicken thighs between two pieces of plastic wrap, and using a meat mallet or a rolling pin, pound them out to about ¼-inch thick. 3. In a medium bowl, combine the rice, kale, garlic, salt, and lemon juice and mix well. 4. Place a quarter of the rice mixture into the middle of each chicken thigh, then sprinkle 2 tablespoons of feta over the filling. 5. Spray the pizza rack with olive oil cooking spray. 6. Fold the sides of the chicken thigh over the filling, and then gently place each of them seam-side down on rack. Brush each stuffed chicken thigh with olive oil. 7. Once preheated, place the rack on the roast position. Turn them over and cook for an additional 10 minutes, or until the internal temperature reaches 165°F (74°C).

Chicken Drumsticks with Barbecue-Honey Sauce

Prep time: 5 minutes | Cook time: 40 minutes | Serves 5

1 tablespoon olive oil	Chicken seasoning or rub,	Salt and ground black	1 cup barbecue sauce
10 chicken drumsticks	to taste	pepper, to taste	¼ cup honey

1. Select Roast, Air Fry Fan, set temperature to 390°F (199°C) and set time to 18 minutes. Press Start to begin preheating. Grease the pizza rackwith olive oil. 2. Rub the chicken drumsticks with chicken seasoning or rub, salt and ground black pepper on a clean work surface. 3. Arrange the chicken drumsticks in a single layer on the rack. Once preheated, place the rack on the roast position. It will be done until lightly browned. Flip the drumsticks halfway through. You may need to work in batches to avoid overcrowding. 4. Meanwhile, combine the barbecue sauce and honey in a small bowl. Stir to mix well. 5. Remove the drumsticks from the air fryer oven and baste with the sauce mixture to serve.

Cracked-Pepper Chicken Wings

Prep time: 15 minutes | Cook time: 20 minutes | Serves 4

1 pound (454 g) chicken wings	½ teaspoon smoked paprika	1½ teaspoons freshly cracked black
3 tablespoons vegetable oil	½ teaspoon garlic powder	pepper
½ cup all-purpose flour	½ teaspoon kosher salt	

1. Select Roast, Air Fry Fan, set temperature to 400°F (204°C) and set time to 20 minutes. Press Start to begin preheating. 2. Place the chicken wings in a large bowl. Drizzle the vegetable oil over wings and toss to coat. 3. In a separate bowl, whisk together the flour, paprika, garlic powder, salt, and pepper until combined. 4. Dredge the wings in the flour mixture one at a time, coating them well, and place in the baking pan. Once preheated, place the pan on the roast position. Turn the wings halfway through the cooking time, until the breading is browned and crunchy.

Lemon-Dijon Boneless Chicken

Prep time: 30 minutes | Cook time: 13 to 16 minutes | Serves 6

½ cup sugar-free mayonnaise
1 tablespoon Dijon mustard
1 tablespoon freshly squeezed lemon juice (optional)
1 tablespoon coconut aminos
1 teaspoon Italian seasoning
1 teaspoon sea salt
½ teaspoon freshly ground black pepper
¼ teaspoon cayenne pepper
1½ pounds (680 g) boneless, skinless chicken breasts or thighs

1. In a small bowl, combine the mayonnaise, mustard, lemon juice (if using), coconut aminos, Italian seasoning, salt, black pepper, and cayenne pepper. 2. Place the chicken in a shallow dish or large zip-top plastic bag. Add the marinade, making sure all the pieces are coated. Cover and refrigerate for at least 30 minutes or up to 4 hours. 3. Select Roast, Air Fry Fan, set temperature to 400°F (204°C) and set time to 7 minutes. Press Start to begin preheating. Arrange the chicken in a single layer in the crisper tray, working in batches if necessary. Once preheated, place the tray on the roast position. Flip the chicken and continue cooking for 6 to 9 minutes more, until an instant-read thermometer reads 160°F (71°C).

Teriyaki Chicken Legs

Prep time: 12 minutes | Cook time: 18 to 20 minutes | Serves 2

4 tablespoons teriyaki sauce
1 tablespoon orange juice
1 teaspoon smoked paprika
4 chicken legs
Cooking spray

1. Select Roast, Air Fry Fan, set temperature to 360°F (182°C) and set time to 6 minutes. Press Start to begin preheating. 2. Mix together the teriyaki sauce, orange juice, and smoked paprika. Brush on all sides of chicken legs. 3. Spray the baking pan with nonstick cooking spray and place chicken in pan. 4. Once preheated, place the pan on the roast position. Turn and baste with sauce. Cook for 6 more minutes, turn and baste. Cook for 6 to 8 minutes more, until juices run clear when chicken is pierced with a fork.

Korean Flavor Glazed Chicken Wings

Prep time: 10 minutes | Cook time: 25 minutes | Serves 4

Wings:
2 pounds (907 g) chicken wings
1 teaspoon salt
1 teaspoon ground black pepper
Sauce:
2 tablespoons gochujang
1 tablespoon mayonnaise
1 tablespoon minced ginger
1 tablespoon minced garlic
1 teaspoon agave nectar
2 packets Splenda
1 tablespoon sesame oil
For Garnish:
2 teaspoons sesame seeds
¼ cup chopped green onions

1. Select Air Fry, set temperature to 400°F (204°C) and set time to 20 minutes. Press Start to begin preheating. 2. On a clean work surface, rub the chicken wings with salt and ground black pepper, then arrange the seasoned wings on the pizza rack. 3. Once preheated, place the rack on the air fry position. Flip the wings halfway through. The wings will be well browned when done. You may need to work in batches to avoid overcrowding. 4. Meanwhile, combine the ingredients for the sauce in a small bowl. Stir to mix well. Reserve half of the sauce in a separate bowl until ready to serve. 5. Remove the air fried chicken wings from the air fryer oven and toss with remaining half of the sauce to coat well. 6. Place the wings back to the oven and air fry for 5 more minutes or until the internal temperature of the wings reaches at least 165°F (74°C). 7. Remove the wings from the oven and place on a large plate. Sprinkle with sesame seeds and green onions. Serve with reserved sauce.

Golden Chicken Cutlets

Prep time: 15 minutes | Cook time: 15 minutes | Serves 4

- 2 tablespoons panko breadcrumbs
- ¼ cup grated Parmesan cheese
- ⅛ tablespoon paprika
- ½ tablespoon garlic powder
- 2 large eggs
- 4 chicken cutlets
- 1 tablespoon parsley
- Salt and ground black pepper, to taste
- Cooking spray

1. Select Roast, Air Fry Fan, set temperature to 400°F (204°C) and set time to 15 minutes. Press Start to begin preheating. Spritz the crisper tray with cooking spray. 2. Combine the breadcrumbs, Parmesan, paprika, garlic powder, salt, and ground black pepper in a large bowl. Stir to mix well. Beat the eggs in a separate bowl. 3. Dredge the chicken cutlets in the beaten eggs, then roll over the breadcrumbs mixture to coat well. Shake the excess off. 4. Transfer the chicken cutlets in the tray and spritz with cooking spray. 5. Once preheated, place the tray on the roast position. It will be done until crispy and golden brown. Flip the cutlets halfway through. 6. Serve with parsley on top.

Chicken Shawarma

Prep time: 30 minutes | Cook time: 15 minutes | Serves 4

Shawarma Spice:
- 2 teaspoons dried oregano
- 1 teaspoon ground cinnamon
- 1 teaspoon ground cumin
- 1 teaspoon ground coriander
- 1 teaspoon kosher salt
- ½ teaspoon ground allspice
- ½ teaspoon cayenne pepper

Chicken:
- 1 pound (454 g) boneless, skinless chicken thighs, cut into large bite-size chunks
- 2 tablespoons vegetable oil

For Serving:
- Tzatziki
- Pita bread

1. For the shawarma spice: In a small bowl, combine the oregano, cayenne, cumin, coriander, salt, cinnamon, and allspice. 2. For the chicken: In a large bowl, toss together the chicken, vegetable oil, and shawarma spice to coat. Marinate at room temperature for 30 minutes or cover and refrigerate for up to 24 hours. 3. Select Air Fry, set temperature to 350°F (177°C) and set time to 15 minutes. Press Start to begin preheating. Once preheated, place the chicken in the crisper tray on air fry position. It will be done until the chicken reaches an internal temperature of 165°F (74°C). 4. Transfer the chicken to a serving platter. Serve with tzatziki and pita bread.

Chicken with Lettuce

Prep time: 15 minutes | Cook time: 14 minutes | Serves 4

- 1 pound (454 g) chicken breast tenders, chopped into bite-size pieces
- ½ onion, thinly sliced
- ½ red bell pepper, seeded and thinly sliced
- ½ green bell pepper, seeded and thinly sliced
- 1 tablespoon olive oil
- 1 tablespoon fajita seasoning
- 1 teaspoon kosher salt
- Juice of ½ lime
- 8 large lettuce leaves
- 1 cup prepared guacamole

1. Select Roast, Air Fry Fan, set temperature to 400°F (204°C) and set time to 14 minutes. Press Start to begin preheating. 2. In a large bowl, combine the chicken, onion, and peppers. Drizzle with the olive oil and toss until thoroughly coated. Add the fajita seasoning and salt and toss again. 3. Working in batches if necessary, arrange the chicken and vegetables in a single layer on pizza rack. Once preheated, place the rack on the roast position. Pausing halfway through the cooking time to shake the rack. It will be done until the vegetables are tender and a thermometer inserted into the thickest piece of chicken registers 165°F (74°C). 4. Transfer the mixture to a serving platter and

drizzle with the fresh lime juice. Serve with the lettuce leaves and top with the guacamole.

Broccoli Cheese Chicken

Prep time: 10 minutes | Cook time: 19 to 24 minutes | Serves 6

- 1 tablespoon avocado oil
- ¼ cup chopped onion
- ½ cup finely chopped broccoli
- 4 ounces (113 g) cream cheese, at room temperature
- 2 ounces (57 g) Cheddar cheese, shredded
- 1 teaspoon garlic powder
- ½ teaspoon sea salt, plus additional for seasoning, divided
- ¼ freshly ground black pepper, plus additional for seasoning, divided
- 2 pounds (907 g) boneless, skinless chicken breasts
- 1 teaspoon smoked paprika

1. Heat a medium skillet over medium-high heat and pour in the avocado oil. Add the onion and broccoli and cook, stirring occasionally, for 5 to 8 minutes, until the onion is tender. 2. Transfer to a large bowl and stir in the cream cheese, Cheddar cheese, and garlic powder, and season to taste with salt and pepper. 3. Hold a sharp knife parallel to the chicken breast and cut a long pocket into one side. Stuff the chicken pockets with the broccoli mixture, using toothpicks to secure the pockets around the filling. 4. Select Roast, Air Fry Fan, set temperature to 400°F (204°C) and set time to 14 to 16 minutes. Press Start to begin preheating. 5. In a small dish, combine the paprika, ½ teaspoon salt, and ¼ teaspoon pepper. Sprinkle this over the outside of the chicken. 6. Place the chicken in a single layer on the pizza rack, working in batches if necessary. Once preheated, place the rack on the roast position. It will be done until an instant-read thermometer reads 160°F (71°C). Place the chicken on a plate and tent a piece of aluminum foil over the chicken. Allow to rest for 5 to 10 minutes before serving.

Lemon Chicken

Prep time: 5 minutes | Cook time: 20 to 25 minutes | Serves 4

- 8 bone-in chicken thighs, skin on
- 1 tablespoon olive oil
- 1½ teaspoons lemon-pepper seasoning
- ½ teaspoon paprika
- ½ teaspoon garlic powder
- ¼ teaspoon freshly ground black pepper
- Juice of ½ lemon

1. Select Roast, Air Fry Fan, set temperature to 360°F (182°C) and set time to 20 to 25 minutes. Press Start to begin preheating. 2. Place the chicken in a large bowl and drizzle with the olive oil. Top with the lemon-pepper seasoning, paprika, garlic powder, and freshly ground black pepper. Toss until thoroughly coated. 3. Working in batches if necessary, arrange the chicken in a single layer on pizza rack. Once preheated, place the rack on the roast position. Pausing halfway through the cooking time to turn the chicken. It will be done until a thermometer inserted into the thickest piece registers 165°F (74°C). 4. Transfer the chicken to a serving platter and squeeze the lemon juice over the top.

Chicken, Zucchini, and Spinach Salad

Prep time: 10 minutes | Cook time: 20 minutes | Serves 4

- 3 (5-ounce / 142-g) boneless, skinless chicken breasts, cut into 1-inch cubes
- 5 teaspoons extra-virgin olive oil
- ½ teaspoon dried thyme
- 1 medium red onion, sliced
- 1 red bell pepper, sliced
- 1 small zucchini, cut into strips
- 3 tablespoons freshly squeezed lemon juice
- 6 cups fresh baby spinach leaves

1. Select Roast, Air Fry Fan, set temperature to 375°F (191°C) and set time to 20 minutes. Press Start to begin

preheating. 2. In a large bowl, combine the chicken, olive oil, and thyme. Toss to coat. Transfer to a baking pan. 3. Once preheated, place the pan on the roast position. 4. After 8 minutes, add the red onion, red bell pepper, and zucchini to the pan. Resume cooking. After about 6 minutes more, stir the chicken and vegetables. Resume cooking. 5. When the cooking is complete, a food thermometer inserted into the chicken should register at least 165°F (74°C). Remove the pan from the unit and stir in the lemon juice. 6. Put the spinach in a serving bowl and top with the chicken mixture. Toss to combine and serve immediately.

Brazilian Tempero Baiano Chicken Drumsticks

Prep time: 30 minutes | Cook time: 20 minutes | Serves 4

1 teaspoon cumin seeds	½ teaspoon coriander seeds	¼ cup fresh lime juice
1 teaspoon dried oregano	1 teaspoon kosher salt	2 tablespoons olive oil
1 teaspoon dried parsley	½ teaspoon black peppercorns	1½ pounds (680 g) chicken drumsticks
1 teaspoon ground turmeric	½ teaspoon cayenne pepper	

1. In a clean coffee grinder or spice mill, combine the cumin, oregano, parsley, turmeric, coriander seeds, salt, peppercorns, and cayenne. Process until finely ground. 2. In a small bowl, combine the ground spices with the lime juice and oil. Place the chicken in a resealable plastic bag. Add the marinade, seal, and massage until the chicken is well coated. Marinate at room temperature for 30 minutes or in the refrigerator for up to 24 hours. 3. When you are ready to cook, select Roast, Air Fry Fan, set temperature to 400°F (204°C) and set time to 20 to 25 minutes. Press Start to begin preheating. Once preheated, place the drumsticks skin side up in the pizza rack on roast position. Turn the legs halfway through the cooking time. Use a meat thermometer to ensure that the chicken has reached an internal temperature of 165°F (74°C). 4. Serve with plenty of napkins.

Jerk Chicken Kebabs

Prep time: 10 minutes | Cook time: 14 minutes | Serves 4

8 ounces (227 g) boneless, skinless chicken thighs, cut into 1-inch cubes	2 tablespoons coconut oil	cut into 1-inch pieces
	½ medium red bell pepper, seeded and cut into 1-inch pieces	½ teaspoon salt
2 tablespoons jerk seasoning	¼ medium red onion, peeled and	

1. Select Roast, Air Fry Fan, set temperature to 370°F (188°C) and set time to 14 minutes. Press Start to begin preheating. 2. Place chicken in a medium bowl and sprinkle with jerk seasoning and coconut oil. Toss to coat on all sides. 3. Using eight (6-inch) skewers, build skewers by alternating chicken, pepper, and onion pieces, about three repetitions per skewer. 4. Sprinkle salt over skewers and place on pizza rack. Once preheated, place the rack on the roast position. Turn skewers halfway through cooking. Chicken will be golden and have an internal temperature of at least 165°F (74°C) when done. Serve warm.

Chicken Parmesan

Prep time: 15 minutes | Cook time: 10 minutes | Serves 4

Oil, for spraying	1 cup Italian-style bread crumbs	4 tablespoons unsalted butter, melted
2 (8-ounce / 227-g) boneless, skinless chicken breasts	¼ cup grated Parmesan cheese, plus ½ cup shredded	½ cup marinara sauce

1. Select Roast, Air Fry Fan, set temperature to 360°F (182°C) and set time to 6 minutes. Press Start to begin

preheating. Line the crisper tray with parchment and spray lightly with oil. 2. Cut each chicken breast in half through its thickness to make 4 thin cutlets. Using a meat tenderizer, pound each cutlet until it is about ¾ inch thick. 3. On a plate, mix together the bread crumbs and grated Parmesan cheese. 4. Lightly brush the chicken with the melted butter, then dip into the bread crumb mixture. 5. Place the chicken in the prepared tray and spray lightly with oil. You may need to work in batches. 6. Once preheated, place the tray on the roast position. Top the chicken with the marinara and shredded Parmesan cheese, dividing evenly. Cook for another 3 to 4 minutes, or until golden brown, crispy, and the internal temperature reaches 165°F (74°C).

Thai-Style Cornish Game Hens

Prep time: 30 minutes | Cook time: 20 minutes | Serves 4

1 cup chopped fresh cilantro leaves and stems
2 tablespoons sugar
2 tablespoons lemongrass paste
2 teaspoons black pepper
¼ cup fish sauce
1 tablespoon soy sauce
2 teaspoons ground coriander
1 teaspoon kosher salt
1 teaspoon ground turmeric
1 serrano chile, seeded and chopped
8 garlic cloves, smashed
2 Cornish game hens, giblets removed, split in half lengthwise

1. In a blender, combine the cilantro, fish sauce, soy sauce, serrano, garlic, sugar, lemongrass, black pepper, coriander, salt, and turmeric. Blend until smooth. 2. Place the game hen halves in a large bowl. Pour the cilantro mixture over the hen halves and toss to coat. Marinate at room temperature for 30 minutes, or cover and refrigerate for up to 24 hours. 3. Select Roast, Air Fry Fan, set temperature to 400°F (204°C) and set time to 20 minutes. Press Start to begin preheating. Arrange the hen halves in a single layer in the pizza rack on roast position once preheated. Use a meat thermometer to ensure the game hens have reached an internal temperature of 165°F (74°C).

Jalapeño Popper Hasselback Chicken

Prep time: 10 minutes | Cook time: 19 minutes | Serves 2

Oil, for spraying
2 (8-ounce / 227-g) boneless, skinless chicken breasts
2 ounces (57 g) cream cheese, softened
¼ cup bacon bits
¼ cup chopped pickled jalapeños
½ cup shredded Cheddar cheese, divided

1. Select Roast, Air Fry Fan, set temperature to 350°F (177°C) and set time to 14 minutes. Press Start to begin preheating. Line the baking pan with parchment and spray lightly with oil. 2. Make multiple cuts across the top of each chicken breast, cutting only halfway through. 3. In a medium bowl, mix together the cream cheese, bacon bits, jalapeños, and ¼ cup of Cheddar cheese. Spoon some of the mixture into each cut. 4. Place the chicken on the prepared pan. 5. Once preheated, place the pan on the roast position. Scatter the remaining ¼ cup of cheese on top of the chicken and cook for another 2 to 5 minutes, or until the cheese is melted and the internal temperature reaches 165°F (74°C).

General Tso's Chicken

Prep time: 10 minutes | Cook time: 14 minutes | Serves 4

1 tablespoon sesame oil
1 teaspoon minced garlic
½ teaspoon ground ginger
1 cup chicken broth
4 tablespoons soy sauce, divided
½ teaspoon sriracha, plus more for serving
2 tablespoons hoisin sauce
4 tablespoons cornstarch, divided
4 boneless, skinless chicken breasts, cut into 1-inch pieces
Olive oil spray
2 medium scallions, sliced, green parts only
Sesame seeds, for garnish

1. In a small saucepan over low heat, combine the sesame oil, garlic, and ginger and cook for 1 minute. 2. Add the chicken broth, 2 tablespoons of soy sauce, the sriracha, and hoisin. Whisk to combine. 3. Whisk in 2 tablespoons of cornstarch and continue cooking over low heat until the sauce starts to thicken, about 5 minutes. Remove the pan from the heat, cover it, and set aside. 4. Select Bake, Air Fry Fan, set temperature to 400°F (204°C) and set time to 9 minutes. Press Start to begin preheating. 5. In a medium bowl, toss together the chicken, remaining 2 tablespoons of soy sauce, and remaining 2 tablespoons of cornstarch. 6. Spray the crisper tray with olive oil. Place the chicken into the tray and spray it with olive oil. 7. Once preheated, place the tray on the bake position. 8. After 5 minutes, remove the tray, shake, and spray the chicken with more olive oil. Reinsert the tray to resume cooking. 9. When the cooking is complete, a food thermometer inserted into the chicken should register at least 165°F (74°C). Transfer the chicken to a large bowl and toss it with the sauce. Garnish with the scallions and sesame seeds and serve.

Buffalo Crispy Chicken Strips

Prep time: 15 minutes | Cook time: 13 to 17 minutes per batch | Serves 4

¾ cup all-purpose flour

2 eggs

2 tablespoons water

1 cup seasoned panko bread crumbs

2 teaspoons granulated garlic

1 teaspoon salt

1 teaspoon freshly ground black pepper

16 chicken breast strips, or 3 large boneless, skinless chicken breasts, cut into 1-inch strips

Olive oil spray

¼ cup Buffalo sauce, plus more as needed

1. Put the flour in a small bowl. 2. In another small bowl, whisk the eggs and the water. 3. In a third bowl, stir together the panko, granulated garlic, salt, and pepper. 4. Dip each chicken strip in the flour, in the egg, and in the panko mixture to coat. Press the crumbs onto the chicken with your fingers. 5. Select Roast, Air Fry Fan, set temperature to 375°F (191°C) and set time to 17 minutes. Press Start to begin preheating. 6. Once preheated, place a parchment paper liner into the crisper tray. Working in batches if needed, place the chicken strips into the tray. Do not stack unless using a wire rack for the second layer. Spray the top of the chicken with olive oil. 7. Once preheated, place the tray on the roast position. 8. After 10 or 12 minutes, remove the basket, flip the chicken, and spray again with olive oil. Reinsert the tray to resume cooking. 9. When the cooking is complete, the chicken should be golden brown and crispy and a food thermometer inserted into the chicken should register 165°F (74°C). 10. Repeat steps 6, 7, and 8 with any remaining chicken. 11. Transfer the chicken to a large bowl. Drizzle the Buffalo sauce over the top of the cooked chicken, toss to coat, and serve.

Lemon-Basil Turkey Breasts

Prep time: 30 minutes | Cook time: 58 minutes | Serves 4

2 tablespoons olive oil

2 pounds (907 g) turkey breasts, bone-in, skin-on

Coarse sea salt and ground black pepper, to taste

1 teaspoon fresh basil leaves, chopped

2 tablespoons lemon zest, grated

1. Select Air Fry, set temperature to 330°F (166°C) and set time to 30 minutes. Press Start to begin preheating. Rub olive oil on all sides of the turkey breasts; sprinkle with salt, pepper, basil, and lemon zest. 2. Place the turkey breasts skin side up on the parchment-lined pizza rack. 3. Once preheated, place the rack on the air fry position. Turn them over and cook an additional 28 minutes. Serve with lemon wedges, if desired. Bon appétit!

Crispy Duck with Cherry Sauce

Prep time: 10 minutes | Cook time: 33 minutes | Serves 2 to 4

1 whole duck (up to 5 pounds / 2.3 kg), split in half, back and rib bones removed
1 teaspoon olive oil
Salt and freshly ground black pepper, to taste

Cherry Sauce:
1 tablespoon butter
1 shallot, minced
½ cup sherry
¾ cup cherry preserves
1 cup chicken stock

1 teaspoon white wine vinegar
1 teaspoon fresh thyme leaves
Salt and freshly ground black pepper, to taste

1. Select Air Fry, set temperature to 400°F (204°C) and set time to 20 minutes. Press Start to begin preheating. 2. Trim some of the fat from the duck. Rub olive oil on the duck and season with salt and pepper. Place the duck halves in baking pan, breast side up and facing the center of the pan. 3. Once preheated, place the pan on the air fry position. Turn the duck over and air fry for another 6 minutes. 4. While duck is air frying, make the cherry sauce. Melt the butter in a large sauté pan. Add the shallot and sauté until it is just starting to brown, about 2 to 3 minutes. Add the sherry and deglaze the pan by scraping up any brown bits from the bottom of the pan. Simmer the liquid for a few minutes, until it has reduced by half. Add the cherry preserves, chicken stock and white wine vinegar. Whisk well to combine all the ingredients. Simmer the sauce until it thickens and coats the back of a spoon, about 5 to 7 minutes. Season with salt and pepper and stir in the fresh thyme leaves. 5. When the timer goes off, spoon some cherry sauce over the duck and continue to air fry at 400°F (204°C) for 4 more minutes. Then, turn the duck halves back over so that the breast side is facing up. Spoon more cherry sauce over the top of the duck, covering the skin completely. Air fry for 3 more minutes and then remove the duck to a plate to rest for a few minutes. 6. Serve the duck in halves, or cut each piece in half again for a smaller serving. Spoon any additional sauce over the duck or serve it on the side.

Chicken Manchurian

Prep time: 10 minutes | Cook time: 20 minutes | Serves 2

1 pound (454 g) boneless, skinless chicken breasts, cut into 1-inch pieces
¼ cup ketchup
1 tablespoon tomato-based chili sauce, such as Heinz
1 tablespoon soy sauce
1 tablespoon rice vinegar
2 teaspoons vegetable oil
1 teaspoon hot sauce, such as Tabasco
½ teaspoon garlic powder
¼ teaspoon cayenne pepper
2 scallions, thinly sliced
Cooked white rice, for serving

1. Select Roast, Air Fry Fan, set temperature to 350°F (177°C) and set time to 20 minutes. Press Start to begin preheating. 2. In a bowl, combine the chicken, ketchup, chili sauce, soy sauce, vinegar, oil, hot sauce, garlic powder, cayenne, and three-quarters of the scallions and toss until evenly coated. 3. Scrape the chicken and sauce into baking pan. Once preheated, place the pan on the roast position. Flip the chicken pieces halfway through. It will be done until the chicken is cooked through and the sauce is reduced to a thick glaze. 4. Remove the pan from the oven. Spoon the chicken and sauce over rice and top with the remaining scallions. Serve immediately.

Spinach and Feta Stuffed Chicken Breasts

Prep time: 10 minutes | Cook time: 27 minutes | Serves 4

1 (10-ounce / 283-g) package frozen spinach, thawed and drained well
1 cup feta cheese, crumbled
½ teaspoon freshly ground black pepper
4 boneless chicken breasts
Salt and freshly ground black pepper, to taste
1 tablespoon olive oil

1. Prepare the filling. Squeeze out as much liquid as possible from the thawed spinach. Rough chop the spinach and transfer it to a mixing bowl with the feta cheese and the freshly ground black pepper. 2. Prepare the chicken breast. Place the chicken breast on a cutting board and press down on the chicken breast with one hand to keep it stabilized. Make an incision about 1-inch long in the fattest side of the breast. Move the knife up and down inside the chicken breast, without poking through either the top or the bottom, or the other side of the breast. The inside pocket should be about 3-inches long, but the opening should only be about 1-inch wide. If this is too difficult, you can make the incision longer, but you will have to be more careful when cooking the chicken breast since this will expose more of the stuffing. 3. Once you have prepared the chicken breasts, use your fingers to stuff the filling into each pocket, spreading the mixture down as far as you can. 4. Select Roast, Air Fry Fan, set temperature to 380°F (193°C) and set time to 12 minutes. Press Start to begin preheating. 5. Lightly brush or spray the baking pan and the chicken breasts with olive oil. Transfer two of the stuffed chicken breasts to the pan. Once preheated, place the pan on the roast position. Turn the chicken breasts over halfway through the cooking time. Remove the chicken to a resting plate and cook the second two breasts for 12 minutes. Return the first batch of chicken to the oven with the second batch and cook for 3 more minutes. When the chicken is cooked, an instant read thermometer should register 165°F (74°C) in the thickest part of the chicken, as well as in the stuffing. 6. Remove the chicken breasts and let them rest on a cutting board for 2 to 3 minutes. Slice the chicken on the bias and serve with the slices fanned out.

Turkey Meatloaf

Prep time: 10 minutes | Cook time: 50 minutes | Serves 4

8 ounces (227 g) sliced mushrooms

1 small onion, coarsely chopped

2 cloves garlic

1½ pounds (680 g) 85% lean ground turkey

2 eggs, lightly beaten

1 tablespoon tomato paste

¼ cup almond meal

2 tablespoons almond milk

1 tablespoon dried oregano

1 teaspoon salt

½ teaspoon freshly ground black pepper

1 Roma tomato, thinly sliced

1. Select Air Fry, set temperature to 350°F (177°C) and set time to 50 minutes. Press Start to begin preheating. Lightly coat a baking pan with olive oil and set aside. 2. In a food processor fitted with a metal blade, combine the mushrooms, onion, and garlic. Pulse until finely chopped. Transfer the vegetables to a large mixing bowl. 3. Add the turkey, eggs, tomato paste, almond meal, milk, oregano, salt, and black pepper. Mix gently until thoroughly combined. Transfer the mixture to the prepared pan and shape into a loaf. Arrange the tomato slices on top. 4. Once preheated, place the pan on the air fry position. It will be done until the meatloaf is nicely browned and a thermometer inserted into the thickest part registers 165°F (74°C). Remove from the oven and let rest for about 10 minutes before slicing.

Crispy Dill Chicken Strips

Prep time: 30 minutes | Cook time: 10 minutes | Serves 4

2 whole boneless, skinless chicken breasts (about 1 pound / 454 g each), halved lengthwise

1 cup Italian dressing

3 cups finely crushed potato chips

1 tablespoon dried dill weed

1 tablespoon garlic powder

1 large egg, beaten

1 to 2 tablespoons oil

1. In a large resealable bag, combine the chicken and Italian dressing. Seal the bag and refrigerate to marinate at least 1 hour. 2. In a shallow dish, stir together the potato chips, dill, and garlic powder. Place the beaten egg in a second shallow dish. 3. Remove the chicken from the marinade. Roll the chicken pieces in the egg and the potato chip mixture, coating thoroughly. 4. Select Roast, Air Fry Fan, set temperature to 325°F (163°C) and set time to 5 minutes.

Press Start to begin preheating. Line the pizza rack with parchment paper. 5. Place the coated chicken on the parchment and spritz with oil. 6. Once preheated, place the rack on the roast position. Flip the chicken, spritz it with oil, and cook for 5 minutes more until the outsides are crispy and the insides are no longer pink.

Chicken Wings with Piri Piri Sauce

Prep time: 30 minutes | Cook time: 30 minutes | Serves 6

12 chicken wings
1½ ounces (43 g) butter, melted
1 teaspoon onion powder
½ teaspoon cumin powder
1 teaspoon garlic paste

Sauce:
2 ounces (57 g) piri piri peppers, stemmed and chopped
1 tablespoon pimiento, seeded and minced

1 garlic clove, chopped
2 tablespoons fresh lemon juice
⅓ teaspoon sea salt
½ teaspoon tarragon

1. Steam the chicken wings using a steamer basket that is placed over a saucepan with boiling water; reduce the heat. 2. Now, steam the wings for 10 minutes over a moderate heat. Toss the wings with butter, onion powder, cumin powder, and garlic paste. 3. Let the chicken wings cool to room temperature. Then, refrigerate them for 45 to 50 minutes. 4. Select Roast, Air Fry Fan, set temperature to 330°F (166°C) and set time to 25 to 30 minutes. Press Start to begin preheating. 5. Transfer the chicken wings to pizza rack on roast position once preheated. Make sure to flip them halfway through. 5. While the chicken wings are cooking, prepare the sauce by mixing all of the sauce ingredients in a food processor. Toss the wings with prepared Piri Piri Sauce and serve.

Pecan-Crusted Chicken Tenders

Prep time: 10 minutes | Cook time: 12 minutes | Serves 4

2 tablespoons mayonnaise
1 teaspoon Dijon mustard
1 pound (454 g) boneless, skinless

chicken tenders
½ teaspoon salt
¼ teaspoon ground black pepper

½ cup chopped roasted pecans, finely ground

1. Select Roast, Air Fry Fan, set temperature to 375°F (191°C) and set time to 12 minutes. Press Start to begin preheating. 2. In a small bowl, whisk mayonnaise and mustard until combined. Brush mixture onto chicken tenders on both sides, then sprinkle tenders with salt and pepper. 3. Place pecans in a medium bowl and press each tender into pecans to coat each side. 4. Place tenders into ungreased crisper tray in a single layer, working in batches if needed. Once preheated, place the tray on the roast position. Turn tenders halfway through cooking. Tenders will be golden brown and have an internal temperature of at least 165°F (74°C) when done. Serve warm.

Hawaiian Huli Huli Chicken

Prep time: 30 minutes | Cook time: 15 minutes | Serves 4

4 boneless, skinless chicken thighs (about 1½ pounds / 680 g)
1 (8-ounce / 227-g) can

pineapple chunks in juice, drained, ¼ cup juice reserved
¼ cup soy sauce

¼ cup sugar
2 tablespoons ketchup
1 tablespoon minced fresh ginger

1 tablespoon minced garlic
¼ cup chopped scallions

1. Use a fork to pierce the chicken all over to allow the marinade to penetrate better. Place the chicken in a large bowl or large resealable plastic bag. 2. Set the drained pineapple chunks aside. In a small microwave-safe bowl, combine the pineapple juice, soy sauce, sugar, ketchup, ginger, and garlic. Pour half the sauce over the chicken; toss to coat. Reserve the remaining sauce. Marinate the chicken at room temperature for 30 minutes, or cover and refrigerate for

up to 24 hours. 3. Select Roast, Air Fry Fan, set temperature to 350°F (177°C) and set time to 15 minutes. Press Start to begin preheating. Place the chicken on pizza rack. (Discard marinade.) Once preheated, place the rack on the roast position. Turn halfway through the cooking time. 4. Meanwhile, microwave the reserved sauce on high for 45 to 60 seconds, stirring every 15 seconds, until the sauce has the consistency of a thick glaze. 5. At the end of the cooking time, use a meat thermometer to ensure the chicken has reached an internal temperature of 165°F (74°C). 6. Transfer the chicken to a serving platter. Pour the sauce over the chicken. Garnish with the pineapple chunks and scallions.

Crunchy Chicken Tenders

Prep time: 5 minutes | Cook time: 12 minutes | Serves 4

1 egg	½ teaspoon salt	½ teaspoon garlic powder
¼ cup unsweetened almond milk	½ teaspoon black pepper	1 pound chicken tenderloins
¼ cup whole wheat flour	½ teaspoon dried thyme	1 lemon, quartered
¼ cup whole wheat bread crumbs	½ teaspoon dried sage	

1. Select Roast, Air Fry Fan, set temperature to 360°F (182°C) and set time to 6 minutes. Press Start to begin preheating. 2. In a shallow bowl, beat together the egg and almond milk until frothy. 3. In a separate shallow bowl, whisk together the flour, bread crumbs, salt, pepper, thyme, sage, and garlic powder. 4. Dip each chicken tenderloin into the egg mixture, then into the bread crumb mixture, coating the outside with the crumbs. Place the breaded chicken tenderloins on pizza rack in an even layer, making sure that they don't touch each other. 5. Once preheated, place the pan on the roast position. Then turn and cook for an additional 5 to 6 minutes. Serve with lemon slices.

Taco Chicken

Prep time: 10 minutes | Cook time: 23 minutes | Serves 4

2 large eggs	1 teaspoon smoked paprika	cheese (about 4 ounces / 113 g)
1 tablespoon water	4 (5-ounce / 142-g) boneless,	(omit for dairy-free)
Fine sea salt and ground black pepper, to taste	skinless chicken breasts or thighs, pounded to ¼ inch thick	Sprig of fresh cilantro, for garnish (optional)
1 cup pork dust	1 cup salsa	
1 teaspoon ground cumin	1 cup shredded Monterey Jack	

1. Spray the pizza rack with avocado oil. Select Air Fry, set temperature to 400°F (204°C) and set time to 20 minutes. Press Start to begin preheating. 2. Crack the eggs into a shallow baking dish, add the water and a pinch each of salt and pepper, and whisk to combine. In another shallow baking dish, stir together the pork dust, cumin, and paprika until well combined. 3. Season the chicken breasts well on both sides with salt and pepper. Dip 1 chicken breast in the eggs and let any excess drip off, then dredge both sides of the chicken breast in the pork dust mixture. Spray the breast with avocado oil and place it on the rack. Repeat with the remaining 3 chicken breasts. 4. Once preheated, place the pan on the air fry position. It will be done until the internal temperature reaches 165°F (74°C) and the breading is golden brown, flipping halfway through. 5. Dollop each chicken breast with ¼ cup of the salsa and top with ¼ cup of the cheese. Return the breasts to the oven and cook for 3 minutes, or until the cheese is melted. Garnish with cilantro before serving, if desired. 6. Store leftovers in an airtight container in the refrigerator for up to 4 days. Reheat in a preheated 400°F (204°C) air fryer oven for 5 minutes, or until warmed through.

Fried Chicken Breasts

Prep time: 30 minutes | Cook time: 12 to 14 minutes | Serves 4

- 1 pound (454 g) boneless, skinless chicken breasts
- ¾ cup dill pickle juice
- ¾ cup finely ground blanched almond flour
- ¾ cup finely grated Parmesan cheese
- ½ teaspoon sea salt
- ½ teaspoon freshly ground black pepper
- 2 large eggs
- Avocado oil spray

1. Place the chicken breasts in a zip-top bag or between two pieces of plastic wrap. Using a meat mallet or heavy skillet, pound the chicken to a uniform ½-inch thickness. 2. Place the chicken in a large bowl with the pickle juice. Cover and allow to brine in the refrigerator for up to 2 hours. 3. Select Air Fry, set temperature to 400°F (204°C) and set time to 6 to 7 minutes. Press Start to begin preheating. 4. In a shallow dish, combine the almond flour, Parmesan cheese, salt, and pepper. In a separate, shallow bowl, beat the eggs. 5. Drain the chicken and pat it dry with paper towels. Dip in the eggs and then in the flour mixture, making sure to press the coating into the chicken. Spray both sides of the coated breasts with oil. 6. Spray the crisper tray with oil and put the chicken inside. Once preheated, place the tray on the air fry position. Carefully flip the breasts with a spatula. Spray the breasts again with oil and continue cooking for 6 to 7 minutes more, until golden and crispy.

Tex-Mex Chicken Breasts

Prep time: 10 minutes | Cook time: 17 to 20 minutes | Serves 4

- 1 pound (454 g) low-sodium boneless, skinless chicken breasts, cut into 1-inch cubes
- 1 medium onion, chopped
- 1 red bell pepper, chopped
- 1 jalapeño pepper, minced
- 2 teaspoons olive oil
- ⅔ cup canned low-sodium black beans, rinsed and drained
- ½ cup low-sodium salsa
- 2 teaspoons chili powder

1. Select Roast, Air Fry Fan, set temperature to 400°F (204°C) and set time to 10 minutes. Press Start to begin preheating. 2. In a medium metal bowl, mix the chicken, onion, bell pepper, jalapeño, and olive oil. Transfer to the baking pan. Once preheated, place the pan on the roast position. Stir once during cooking. 3. Add the black beans, salsa, and chili powder. Roast for 7 to 10 minutes more, stirring once, until the chicken reaches an internal temperature of 165°F (74°C) on a meat thermometer. Serve immediately.

One-Dish Chicken and Rice

Prep time: 10 minutes | Cook time: 40 minutes | Serves 4

- 1 cup long-grain white rice, rinsed and drained
- 1 cup cut frozen green beans (do not thaw)
- 1 tablespoon minced fresh ginger
- 3 cloves garlic, minced
- 1 tablespoon toasted sesame oil
- 1 teaspoon kosher salt
- 1 teaspoon black pepper
- 1 pound (454 g) chicken wings, preferably drumettes

1. Select Air Fry, set temperature to 375°F (191°C) and set time to 30 minutes. Press Start to begin preheating. 2. In a baking pan, combine the rice, green beans, ginger, garlic, sesame oil, salt, and pepper. Stir to combine. Place the chicken wings on top of the rice mixture. 3. Cover the pan with foil. Make a long slash in the foil to allow the pan to vent steam. Once preheated, place the pan on the air fry position. 4. Remove the foil. Set the temperature to 400°F (204°C) for 10 minutes, or until the wings have browned and rendered fat into the rice and vegetables, turning the wings halfway through the cooking time.

Cornish Hens with Honey-Lime Glaze

Prep time: 15 minutes | Cook time: 25 to 30 minutes | Serves 2 to 3

1 Cornish game hen (1½ to 2 pounds / 680 to 907 g)	1 teaspoon poultry seasoning
1 tablespoon honey	Salt and pepper, to taste
1 tablespoon lime juice	Cooking spray

1. Select Roast, Air Fry Fan, set temperature to 330°F (166°C) and set time to 25 to 30 minutes. Press Start to begin preheating. To split the hen into halves, cut through breast bone and down one side of the backbone. 2. Mix the honey, lime juice, and poultry seasoning together and brush or rub onto all sides of the hen. Season to taste with salt and pepper. 3. Spray the pizza with cooking spray and place hen halves on the rack, skin-side down. 4. Once preheated, place the rack on the roast position. Hen will be done when juices run clear when pierced at leg joint with a fork. Let hen rest for 5 to 10 minutes before cutting.

Turkey and Cranberry Quesadillas

Prep time: 7 minutes | Cook time: 4 to 8 minutes | Serves 4

6 low-sodium whole-wheat tortillas	cheese	sauce	Olive oil spray, for spraying the tortillas
⅓ cup shredded low-sodium low-fat Swiss	¾ cup shredded cooked low-sodium turkey breast	2 tablespoons dried cranberries	
	2 tablespoons cranberry	½ teaspoon dried basil	

1. Select Bake, Air Fry Fan, set temperature to 400°F (204°C) and set time to 4 to 8 minutes. Press Start to begin preheating. 2. Put 3 tortillas on a work surface. 3. Evenly divide the Swiss cheese, turkey, cranberry sauce, and dried cranberries among the tortillas. Sprinkle with the basil and top with the remaining tortillas. 4. Spray the outsides of the tortillas with olive oil spray. 5. Once preheated, place the tortillas in crisper tray on the bake position. It will be done until crisp and the cheese is melted. Cut into quarters and serve.

Israeli Chicken Schnitzel

Prep time: 5 minutes | Cook time: 10 minutes | Serves 4

2 large boneless, skinless chicken breasts, each weighing about 1 pound (454 g)	1 cup all-purpose flour	1 teaspoon black pepper	2 cups panko bread crumbs
	2 teaspoons garlic powder	1 teaspoon paprika	Vegetable oil spray
	2 teaspoons kosher salt	2 eggs beaten with 2 tablespoons water	Lemon juice, for serving

1. Select Roast, Air Fry Fan, set temperature to 375°F (191°C) and set time to 5 minutes. Press Start to begin preheating. 2. Place 1 chicken breast between 2 pieces of plastic wrap. Use a mallet or a rolling pin to pound the chicken until it is ¼ inch thick. Set aside. Repeat with the second breast. Whisk together the flour, garlic powder, salt, pepper, and paprika on a large plate. Place the panko in a separate shallow bowl or pie plate. 3. Dredge 1 chicken breast in the flour, shaking off any excess, then dip it in the egg mixture. Dredge the chicken breast in the panko, making sure to coat it completely. Shake off any excess panko. Place the battered chicken breast on a plate. Repeat with the second chicken breast. 4. Spray the baking pan with oil spray. Place 1 of the battered chicken breasts in the pan and spray the top with oil spray. Once preheated, place the pan on the air fry position. The top will be browned when done. Flip the chicken and spray the second side with oil spray. Air fry until the second side is browned and crispy and the internal temperature reaches 165°F (74°C). Remove the first chicken breast from the air fryer oven and

repeat with the second chicken breast. 5. Serve hot with lemon juice.

Classic Chicken Kebab

Prep time: 35 minutes | Cook time: 25 minutes | Serves 4

- ¼ cup olive oil
- 1 teaspoon garlic powder
- 1 teaspoon onion powder
- 1 teaspoon ground cumin
- ½ teaspoon dried oregano
- ½ teaspoon dried basil
- ¼ cup lemon juice
- 1 tablespoon apple cider vinegar
- Olive oil cooking spray
- 1 pound boneless skinless chicken thighs, cut into 1-inch pieces
- 1 red bell pepper, cut into 1-inch pieces
- 1 red onion, cut into 1-inch pieces
- 1 zucchini, cut into 1-inch pieces
- 12 cherry tomatoes

1. In a large bowl, mix together the olive oil, garlic powder, onion powder, cumin, oregano, basil, lemon juice, and apple cider vinegar. 2. Spray six skewers with olive oil cooking spray. 3. On each skewer, slide on a piece of chicken, then a piece of bell pepper, onion, zucchini, and finally a tomato and then repeat. Each skewer should have at least two pieces of each item. 4. Once all of the skewers are prepared, place them in the baking pan and pour the olive oil marinade over the top of the skewers. Turn each skewer so that all sides of the chicken and vegetables are coated. 5. Cover the pan with plastic wrap and place it in the refrigerator for 30 minutes. 6. After 30 minutes, select Roast, Air Fry Fan, set temperature to 380°F (193°C) and set time to 10 minutes. Select Start/Stop to begin preheating. 7. Remove the skewers from the marinade and lay them in a single layer on pizza rack. 8. Once preheated, place the rack on the roast position. Then cook them for 15 minutes more. 9. Remove the skewers from the air fryer oven and let them rest for 5 minutes before serving.

Chapter 4 Beef, Pork, and Lamb

Five-Spice Pork Belly

Prep time: 10 minutes | Cook time: 17 minutes | Serves 4

- 1 pound (454 g) unsalted pork belly
- 2 teaspoons Chinese five-spice powder

Sauce:
- 1 tablespoon coconut oil
- 1 (1-inch) piece fresh ginger, peeled and grated
- 2 cloves garlic, minced
- ½ cup beef or chicken broth
- ¼ to ½ cup Swerve confectioners'-style sweetener or equivalent amount of liquid or powdered sweetener
- 3 tablespoons wheat-free tamari, or ½ cup coconut aminos
- 1 green onion, sliced, plus more for garnish

1. Spray the crisper tray with avocado oil. Select Roast, Air Fry Fan, set temperature to 400°F (204°C) and set time to 8 minutes. Press Start to begin preheating. 2. Cut the pork belly into ½-inch-thick slices and season well on all sides with the five-spice powder. Place the slices in a single layer in the tray. Once preheated, place the tray on the roast position. It will be done until cooked to your liking, flipping halfway through. 3. While the pork belly cooks, make the sauce: Heat the coconut oil in a small saucepan over medium heat. Add the ginger and garlic and sauté for 1 minute, or until fragrant. Add the broth, sweetener, and tamari and simmer for 10 to 15 minutes, until thickened. Add the green onion and cook for another minute, until the green onion is softened. Taste and adjust the seasoning to your liking. 4. Transfer the pork belly to a large bowl. Pour the sauce over the pork belly and coat well. Place the pork belly slices on a serving platter and garnish with sliced green onions. 5. Best served fresh. Store leftovers in an airtight

container in the fridge for up to 4 days. Reheat in a preheated 400°F (204°C) air fryer oven for 3 minutes, or until heated through.

Jalapeño Popper Pork Chops

Prep time: 15 minutes | Cook time: 6 to 8 minutes | Serves 4

1¾ pounds (794 g) bone-in, center-cut loin pork chops
Sea salt and freshly ground black pepper, to taste
6 ounces (170 g) cream cheese, at room temperature
4 ounces (113 g) sliced bacon, cooked and crumbled
4 ounces (113 g) Cheddar cheese, shredded
1 jalapeño, seeded and diced
1 teaspoon garlic powder

1. Select Air Fry, set temperature to 400°F (204°C) and set time to 3 minutes. Press Start to begin preheating. Cut a pocket into each pork chop, lengthwise along the side, making sure not to cut it all the way through. Season the outside of the chops with salt and pepper. 2. In a small bowl, combine the cream cheese, bacon, Cheddar cheese, jalapeño, and garlic powder. Divide this mixture among the pork chops, stuffing it into the pocket of each chop. 3. Place the pork chops on baking pan in a single layer, working in batches if necessary. Once preheated, place the pan on the air fry position. Flip the chops and cook for 3 to 5 minutes more, until an instant-read thermometer reads 145°F (63°C). 4. Allow the chops to rest for 5 minutes, then serve warm.

Mexican-Style Shredded Beef

Prep time: 5 minutes | Cook time: 35 minutes | Serves 6

1 (2-pound / 907-g) beef chuck roast, cut into 2-inch cubes
1 teaspoon salt
½ teaspoon ground black pepper
½ cup no-sugar-added chipotle sauce

1. Select Air Fry, set temperature to 400°F (204°C) and set time to 30 minutes. Press Start to begin preheating. 2. In a large bowl, sprinkle beef cubes with salt and pepper and toss to coat. Place beef into ungreased crisper tray. Once preheated, place the tray on the air fry position. Shake the tray halfway through cooking. Beef will be done when internal temperature is at least 160°F (71°C). 3. Place cooked beef into a large bowl and shred with two forks. Pour in chipotle sauce and toss to coat. 4. Return beef to air fryer oven for an additional 5 minutes at 400°F (204°C) to crisp with sauce. Serve warm.

Kielbasa Sausage with Pineapple and Bell Peppers

Prep time: 15 minutes | Cook time: 10 minutes | Serves 2 to 4

¾ pound (340 g) kielbasa sausage, cut into ½-inch slices
1 (8-ounce / 227-g) can pineapple chunks in juice, drained
1 cup bell pepper chunks
1 tablespoon barbecue seasoning
1 tablespoon soy sauce
Cooking spray

1. Select Air Fry, set temperature to 390°F (199°C) and set time to 10 minutes. Press Start to begin preheating. Spritz the baking pan with cooking spray. 2. Combine all the ingredients in a large bowl. Toss to mix well. 3. Pour the sausage mixture in the pan. 4. Once preheated, place the pan on the air fry position. It will be done until the sausage is lightly browned and the bell pepper and pineapple are soft. Shake the pan halfway through. Serve immediately.

Mushroom in Bacon-Wrapped Filets Mignons

Prep time: 10 minutes | Cook time: 13 minutes per batch | Serves 8

1 ounce (28 g) dried porcini mushrooms
½ teaspoon granulated white sugar
½ teaspoon salt
½ teaspoon ground white pepper
8 (4-ounce / 113-g) filets mignons

or beef tenderloin steaks

8 thin-cut bacon strips

1. Select Roast, Air Fry Fan, set temperature to 400°F (204°C) and set time to 13 minutes. Press Start to begin preheating. 2. Put the mushrooms, sugar, salt, and white pepper in a spice grinder and grind to combine. 3. On a clean work surface, rub the filets mignons with the mushroom mixture, then wrap each filet with a bacon strip. Secure with toothpicks if necessary. 4. Arrange the bacon-wrapped filets mignons in the baking pan, seam side down. Work in batches to avoid overcrowding. 5. Once preheated, place the pan on the roast position. It will be done until medium rare. Flip the filets halfway through. 6. Serve immediately.

Sausage and Pork Meatballs

Prep time: 15 minutes | Cook time: 8 to 12 minutes | Serves 8

1 large egg

1 teaspoon gelatin

1 pound (454 g) ground pork

½ pound (227 g) Italian sausage, casings removed, crumbled

⅓ cup Parmesan cheese

¼ cup finely diced onion

1 tablespoon tomato paste

1 teaspoon minced garlic

1 teaspoon dried oregano

¼ teaspoon red pepper flakes

Sea salt and freshly ground black pepper, to taste

Keto-friendly marinara sauce, for serving

1. Beat the egg in a small bowl and sprinkle with the gelatin. Allow to sit for 5 minutes. 2. In a large bowl, combine the ground pork, sausage, Parmesan, onion, tomato paste, garlic, oregano, and red pepper flakes. Season with salt and black pepper. 3. Select Roast, Air Fry Fan, set temperature to 400°F (204°C) and set time to 5 minutes. Press Start to begin preheating. Stir the gelatin mixture, then add it to the other ingredients and, using clean hands, mix to ensure that everything is well combined. Form into 1½-inch round meatballs. 4. Place the meatballs on pizza rack in a single layer, cooking in batches as needed. Once preheated, place the pan on the roast position. Flip and cook for 3 to 7 minutes more, or until an instant-read thermometer reads 160°F (71°C).

Savory Sausage Cobbler

Prep time: 15 minutes | Cook time: 34 minutes | Serves 4

Filling:

1 pound (454 g) ground Italian sausage

1 cup sliced mushrooms

1 teaspoon fine sea salt

2 cups marinara sauce

Biscuits:

3 large egg whites

¾ cup blanched almond flour

1 teaspoon baking powder

¼ teaspoon fine sea salt

2½ tablespoons very cold unsalted butter, cut into ¼-inch pieces

Fresh basil leaves, for garnish

1. Select Roast, Air Fry Fan, set temperature to 400°F (204°C) and set time to 5 minutes. Press Start to begin preheating. 2. Place the sausage in a baking pan. Use your hands to break up the sausage and spread it evenly on the bottom of the pan. Once preheated, place the pan on the roast position. 3. Remove the pan from the air fryer oven and use a fork or metal spatula to crumble the sausage more. Season the mushrooms with the salt and add them to the pan. Stir to combine the mushrooms and sausage, then return the pan to the oven and cook for 4 minutes, or until the mushrooms are soft and the sausage is cooked through. 4. Remove the pan from the oven. Add the marinara sauce and stir well. Set aside. 5. Make the biscuits: Place the egg whites in a large mixing bowl or the bowl of a stand mixer. Using a hand mixer or stand mixer, whip the egg whites until stiff peaks form. 6. In a medium-sized bowl, whisk together the almond flour, baking powder, and salt, then cut in the butter. Gently fold the flour mixture into the egg whites with a rubber spatula. 7. Using a large spoon or ice cream scoop, spoon one-quarter of the dough on top of the

sausage mixture, making sure the butter stays in separate clumps. Repeat with the remaining dough, spacing the biscuits about 1 inch apart. 8. Place the pan in the air fryer oven and cook for 5 minutes, then lower the heat to 325°F (163°C) and roast for another 15 to 20 minutes, until the biscuits are golden brown. Serve garnished with fresh basil leaves. 9. Store leftovers in an airtight container in the refrigerator for up to 3 days. Reheat in a preheated 350°F (177°C) air fryer oven for 5 minutes, or until warmed through.

Chicken Fried Steak with Cream Gravy

Prep time: 5 minutes | Cook time: 10 minutes | Serves 4

4 small thin cube steaks (about 1 pound / 454 g)
½ teaspoon salt
½ teaspoon freshly ground black pepper
¼ teaspoon garlic powder

1 egg, lightly beaten
1 cup crushed pork rinds (about 3 ounces / 85 g)
Cream Gravy:
½ cup heavy cream
2 ounces (57 g) cream cheese

¼ cup bacon grease
2 to 3 tablespoons water
2 to 3 dashes Worcestershire sauce
Salt and freshly ground black pepper, to taste

1. Select Air Fry, set temperature to 400°F (204°C) and set time to 10 minutes. Press Start to begin preheating. 2. Working one at a time, place the steak between two sheets of parchment paper and use a meat mallet to pound to an even thickness. 3. In a small bowl, combine the salt, pepper, and garlic power. Season both sides of each steak with the mixture. 4. Place the egg in a small shallow dish and the pork rinds in another small shallow dish. Dip each steak first in the egg wash, followed by the pork rinds, pressing lightly to form an even coating. Working in batches if necessary, arrange the steaks in a single layer in the pizza rack. Once preheated, place the pan on the air fry position. It will be done until crispy and cooked through. 5. To make the cream gravy: In a heavy-bottomed pot, warm the cream, cream cheese, and bacon grease over medium heat, whisking until smooth. Lower the heat if the mixture begins to boil. Continue whisking as you slowly add the water, 1 tablespoon at a time, until the sauce reaches the desired consistency. Season with the Worcestershire sauce and salt and pepper to taste. Serve over the chicken fried steaks.

Beef Burger

Prep time: 20 minutes | Cook time: 12 minutes | Serves 4

1¼ pounds (567 g) lean ground beef
1 tablespoon coconut aminos
1 teaspoon Dijon mustard
A few dashes of liquid smoke

1 teaspoon shallot powder
1 clove garlic, minced
½ teaspoon cumin powder
¼ cup scallions, minced
⅓ teaspoon sea salt flakes

⅓ teaspoon freshly cracked mixed peppercorns
1 teaspoon celery seeds
1 teaspoon parsley flakes

1. Select Air Fry, set temperature to 360°F (182°C) and set time to 12 minutes. Press Start to begin preheating. 2. Mix all of the above ingredients in a bowl; knead until everything is well incorporated. 3. Shape the mixture into four patties. Next, make a shallow dip in the center of each patty to prevent them puffing up during air frying. 4. Spritz the patties on all sides in a baking pan using nonstick cooking spray. Once preheated, place the pan on the air fry position. Check for doneness, an instant-read thermometer should read 160°F (71°C). Bon appétit!

Parmesan-Crusted Steak

Prep time: 30 minutes | Cook time: 12 minutes | Serves 6

½ cup (1 stick) unsalted butter, at room temperature

1 cup finely grated Parmesan cheese
¼ cup finely ground blanched

almond flour
1½ pounds (680 g) New York strip

steak | Sea salt and freshly ground black pepper, to taste

1. Place the butter, Parmesan cheese, and almond flour in a food processor. Process until smooth. Transfer to a sheet of parchment paper and form into a log. Wrap tightly in plastic wrap. Freeze for 45 minutes or refrigerate for at least 4 hours. 2. While the butter is chilling, season the steak liberally with salt and pepper. Let the steak rest at room temperature for about 45 minutes. 3. Select Roast, Air Fry Fan, set temperature to 400°F (204°C) and set time to 4 minutes. Press Start to begin preheating. 4. Working in batches, if necessary, place the steak in the baking pan of air fryer oven on roast position once preheated. Flip and cook for 3 minutes more, until the steak is brown on both sides. 5. Remove the steak from the air fryer oven and arrange an equal amount of the Parmesan butter on top of each steak. Return the steak to the pan and continue cooking for another 5 minutes, until an instant-read thermometer reads 120°F (49°C) for medium-rare and the crust is golden brown (or to your desired doneness). Transfer the cooked steak to a plate; let rest for 10 minutes before serving.

Beef and Goat Cheese Stuffed Peppers

Prep time: 10 minutes | Cook time: 30 minutes | Serves 4

- 1 pound lean ground beef
- ½ cup cooked brown rice
- 2 Roma tomatoes, diced
- 3 garlic cloves, minced
- ½ yellow onion, diced
- 2 tablespoons fresh oregano, chopped
- 1 teaspoon salt
- ½ teaspoon black pepper
- ¼ teaspoon ground allspice
- 2 bell peppers, halved and seeded
- 4 ounces goat cheese
- ¼ cup fresh parsley, chopped

1. Select Bake, Air Fry Fan, set temperature to 360°F (182°C) and set time to 30 minutes. Press Start to begin preheating. 2. In a large bowl, combine the ground beef, rice, tomatoes, garlic, onion, oregano, salt, pepper, and allspice. Mix well. 3. Divide the beef mixture equally into the halved bell peppers and top each with about 1 ounce (a quarter of the total) of the goat cheese. 4. Place the peppers on pizza rack in a single layer, making sure that they don't touch each other. 5. Once preheated, place the rack on the bake position. Remove the peppers from the oven and top with fresh parsley before serving.

Sichuan Cumin Lamb

Prep time: 30 minutes | Cook time: 10 minutes | Serves 4

Lamb:
- 2 tablespoons cumin seeds
- 1 teaspoon Sichuan peppercorns, or ½ teaspoon cayenne pepper
- 1 pound (454 g) lamb (preferably shoulder), cut into ½ by 2-inch pieces
- 2 tablespoons vegetable oil
- 1 tablespoon light soy sauce
- 1 tablespoon minced garlic
- 2 fresh red chiles, chopped
- 1 teaspoon kosher salt
- ¼ teaspoon sugar

For Serving:
- 2 scallions, chopped
- Large handful of chopped fresh cilantro

1. For the lamb: In a dry skillet, toast the cumin seeds and Sichuan peppercorns (if using) over medium heat, stirring frequently, until fragrant, 1 to 2 minutes. Remove from the heat and let cool. Use a mortar and pestle to coarsely grind the toasted spices. 2. Use a fork to pierce the lamb pieces to allow the marinade to penetrate better. In a large bowl or resealable plastic bag, combine the toasted spices, vegetable oil, soy sauce, garlic, chiles, salt, and sugar. Add the lamb to the bag. Seal and massage to coat. Marinate at room temperature for 30 minutes. 3. Select Roast, Air Fry Fan, set temperature to 350°F (177°C) and set time to 10 minutes. Press Start to begin preheating. Place the lamb in a single layer in the baking pan. Once preheated, place the pan on the roast position. Use a meat thermometer to

ensure the lamb has reached an internal temperature of 145°F (63°C) (medium-rare). 4. Transfer the lamb to a serving bowl. Stir in the scallions and cilantro and serve.

Beef Steak Fingers

Prep time: 5 minutes | Cook time: 8 minutes | Serves 4

4 small beef cube steaks

Salt and ground black pepper, to taste

½ cup flour

Cooking spray

1. Select Air Fry, set temperature to 390°F (199°C) and set time to 4 minutes. Press Start to begin preheating. 2. Cut cube steaks into 1-inch-wide strips. 3. Sprinkle lightly with salt and pepper to taste. 4. Roll in flour to coat all sides. 5. Spritz crisper tray with cooking spray. 6. Put steak strips in the tray in a single layer. Spritz top of steak strips with cooking spray. 7. Once preheated, place the tray on the air fry position. 8. Turn strips over, and spritz with cooking spray. Air fry 4 more minutes and test with fork for doneness. Steak fingers should be crispy outside with no red juices inside. 9. Repeat steps 5 through 7 to air fry remaining strips. 10. Serve immediately.

Panko Pork Chops

Prep time: 10 minutes | Cook time: 12 minutes | Serves 4

4 center-cut boneless pork chops, excess fat trimmed

¼ teaspoon salt

2 eggs

1½ cups panko bread crumbs

3 tablespoons grated Parmesan cheese

1½ teaspoons paprika

½ teaspoon granulated garlic

½ teaspoon onion powder

1 teaspoon chili powder

¼ teaspoon freshly ground black pepper

Olive oil spray

1. Sprinkle the pork chops with salt on both sides and let them sit while you prepare the seasonings and egg wash. 2. In a shallow medium bowl, beat the eggs. 3. In another shallow medium bowl, stir together the panko, Parmesan cheese, paprika, granulated garlic, onion powder, chili powder, and pepper. 4. Dip the pork chops in the egg and in the panko mixture to coat. Firmly press the crumbs onto the chops. 5. Select Roast, Air Fry Fan, set temperature to 400°F (204°C) and set time to 12 minutes. Press Start to begin preheating. 6. Spray the crisper tray with olive oil. Place the pork chops into the tray and spray them with olive oil. 7. Once preheated, place the pan on the roast position. 8. After 6 minutes, flip the pork chops and spray them with more olive oil. Resume cooking. 9. When the cooking is complete, the chops should be golden and crispy and a food thermometer should register 145°F (63°C). Serve immediately.

Blackened Cajun Pork Roast

Prep time: 20 minutes | Cook time: 33 minutes | Serves 4

2 pounds (907 g) bone-in pork loin roast

2 tablespoons oil

¼ cup Cajun seasoning

½ cup diced onion

½ cup diced celery

½ cup diced green bell pepper

1 tablespoon minced garlic

1. Cut 5 slits across the pork roast. Spritz it with oil, coating it completely. Evenly sprinkle the Cajun seasoning over the pork roast. 2. In a medium bowl, stir together the onion, celery, green bell pepper, and garlic until combined. Set aside. 3. Select Roast, Air Fry Fan, set temperature to 360°F (182°C) and set time to 5 minutes. Press Start to begin preheating. Line the crisper tray with parchment paper. 4. Place the pork roast on the parchment and spritz with oil. 5. Once preheated, place the tray on the roast position. Flip the roast and cook for 5 minutes more. Continue to flip

and cook in 5-minute increments for a total cook time of 20 minutes. 6. Increase the temperature to 390°F (199°C). 7. Cook the roast for 8 minutes more and flip. Add the vegetable mixture to the basket and cook for a final 5 minutes. Let the roast sit for 5 minutes before serving.

Cinnamon-Beef Kofta

Prep time: 10 minutes | Cook time: 13 minutes per batch | Makes 12 koftas

1½ pounds (680 g) lean ground beef	¾ teaspoon ground dried turmeric	12 (3½- to 4-inch-long) cinnamon sticks
1 teaspoon onion powder	1 teaspoon ground cumin	Cooking spray
¾ teaspoon ground cinnamon	¾ teaspoon salt	
	¼ teaspoon cayenne	

1. Select Air Fry, set temperature to 375°F (191°C) and set time to 13 minutes. Press Start to begin preheating. Spritz the crisper tray with cooking spray. 2. Combine all the ingredients, except for the cinnamon sticks, in a large bowl. Toss to mix well. 3. Divide and shape the mixture into 12 balls, then wrap each ball around each cinnamon stick and leave a quarter of the length uncovered. 4. Arrange the beef-cinnamon sticks in tray and spritz with cooking spray. Work in batches to avoid overcrowding. 5. Once preheated, place the tray on the air fry position. The beef will be browned when done. Flip the sticks halfway through. 6. Serve immediately.

Sweet and Spicy Country-Style Ribs

Prep time: 10 minutes | Cook time: 25 minutes | Serves 4

2 tablespoons brown sugar	1 teaspoon dry mustard	¼ to ½ teaspoon cayenne pepper
2 tablespoons smoked paprika	1 teaspoon ground cumin	1½ pounds (680 g) boneless country-style pork ribs
1 teaspoon garlic powder	1 teaspoon kosher salt	
1 teaspoon onion powder	1 teaspoon black pepper	1 cup barbecue sauce

1. Select Roast, Air Fry Fan, set temperature to 350°F (177°C) and set time to 15 minutes. Press Start to begin preheating. 2. In a small bowl, stir together the brown sugar, paprika, garlic powder, onion powder, dry mustard, cumin, salt, black pepper, and cayenne. Mix until well combined. 3. Pat the ribs dry with a paper towel. Generously sprinkle the rub evenly over both sides of the ribs and rub in with your fingers. 4. Place the ribs in the pizza rack. Once preheated, place the rack on the roast position. Turn the ribs and brush with ½ cup of the barbecue sauce. Cook for an additional 10 minutes. Use a meat thermometer to ensure the pork has reached an internal temperature of 145°F (63°C). 5. Serve with remaining barbecue sauce.

Panko Crusted Calf's Liver Strips

Prep time: 15 minutes | Cook time: 23 to 25 minutes | Serves 4

1 pound (454 g) sliced calf's liver, cut into ½-inch wide strips	2 tablespoons milk	Salt and ground black pepper, to taste
2 eggs	½ cup whole wheat flour	
	2 cups panko breadcrumbs	Cooking spray

1. Select Air Fry, set temperature to 390°F (199°C) and set time to 5 minutes. Press Start to begin preheating. Spritz the crisper tray with cooking spray. 2. Rub the calf's liver strips with salt and ground black pepper on a clean work surface. 3. Whisk the eggs with milk in a large bowl. Pour the flour in a shallow dish. Pour the panko on a separate shallow dish. 4. Dunk the liver strips in the flour, then in the egg mixture. Shake the excess off and roll the strips over the panko to coat well. 5. Arrange half of the liver strips in a single layer in the crisper tray and spritz with cooking

spray. 6. Once preheated, place the tray on the air fry position. It will be done until browned. Flip the strips halfway through. Repeat with the remaining strips. 7. Serve immediately.

Crescent Dogs

Prep time: 15 minutes | Cook time: 8 minutes | Makes 24 crescent dogs

Oil, for spraying
1 (8-ounce / 227-g) can refrigerated crescent rolls
8 slices Cheddar cheese, cut into thirds
24 cocktail sausages or 8 (6-inch) hot dogs, cut into thirds
2 tablespoons unsalted butter, melted
1 tablespoon sea salt flakes

1. Select Air Fry, set temperature to 325°F (163°C) and set time to 3 to 4 minutes. Press Start to begin preheating. Line the crisper tray with parchment and spray lightly with oil. 2. Separate the dough into 8 triangles. Cut each triangle into 3 narrow triangles so you have 24 total triangles. 3. Top each triangle with 1 piece of cheese and 1 cocktail sausage. 4. Roll up each piece of dough, starting at the wide end and rolling toward the point. 5. Place the rolls in the prepared tray in a single layer. You may need to cook in batches. 6. Once preheated, place the pan on the air fry position. Flip, and cook for another 3 to 4 minutes, or until golden brown. 7. Brush with the melted butter and sprinkle with the sea salt flakes before serving.

Ground Beef Taco Rolls

Prep time: 20 minutes | Cook time: 10 minutes | Serves 4

½ pound (227 g) 80/20 ground beef
⅓ cup water
1 tablespoon chili powder
2 teaspoons cumin
½ teaspoon garlic powder
¼ teaspoon dried oregano
¼ cup canned diced tomatoes and chiles, drained
2 tablespoons chopped cilantro
1½ cups shredded Mozzarella cheese
½ cup blanched finely ground almond flour
2 ounces (57 g) full-fat cream cheese
1 large egg

1. In a medium skillet over medium heat, brown the ground beef about 7 to 10 minutes. When meat is fully cooked, drain. 2. Add water to skillet and stir in chili powder, cumin, garlic powder, oregano, and tomatoes with chiles. Add cilantro. Bring to a boil, then reduce heat to simmer for 3 minutes. 3. In a large microwave-safe bowl, place Mozzarella, almond flour, cream cheese, and egg. Microwave for 1 minute. Stir the mixture quickly until smooth ball of dough forms. 4. Cut a piece of parchment for your work surface. Press the dough into a large rectangle on the parchment, wetting your hands to prevent the dough from sticking as necessary. Cut the dough into eight rectangles. 5. On each rectangle place a few spoons of the meat mixture. Fold the short ends of each roll toward the center and roll the length as you would a burrito. 6. Select Bake, Air Fry Fan, set temperature to 360°F (182°C) and set time to 10 minutes. Press Start to begin preheating. Cut a piece of parchment to fit your baking pan. Place taco rolls onto the parchment. 7. Once preheated, place the pan on the bake position. 8. Flip halfway through the cooking time. 9. Allow to cool 10 minutes before serving.

Steak with Bell Pepper

Prep time: 30 minutes | Cook time: 20 to 23 minutes | Serves 6

¼ cup avocado oil
¼ cup freshly squeezed lime juice
2 teaspoons minced garlic
1 tablespoon chili powder
½ teaspoon ground cumin
Sea salt and freshly ground black pepper, to taste
1 pound (454 g) top sirloin steak or flank steak, thinly sliced against the grain
1 red bell pepper, cored, seeded, and cut into ½-inch slices

1 green bell pepper, cored, seeded, and cut into ½-inch slices 1 large onion, sliced

1. In a small bowl or blender, combine the avocado oil, lime juice, garlic, chili powder, cumin, and salt and pepper to taste. 2. Place the sliced steak in a zip-top bag or shallow dish. Place the bell peppers and onion in a separate zip-top bag or dish. Pour half the marinade over the steak and the other half over the vegetables. Seal both bags and let the steak and vegetables marinate in the refrigerator for at least 1 hour or up to 4 hours. 3. Select Roast, Air Fry Fan, set temperature to 400°F (204°C) and set time to 13 minutes. Press Start to begin preheating. Line the baking pan with an aluminum foil. Remove the vegetables from their bag or dish and shake off any excess marinade. Place the vegetables in the pan. Once preheated, place the pan on the roast position and cook. 4. Remove the steak from its bag or dish and shake off any excess marinade. Place the steak on top of the vegetables. and cook for 7 to 10 minutes or until an instant-read thermometer reads 120°F (49°C) for medium-rare (or cook to your desired doneness). 5. Serve with desired fixings, such as keto tortillas, lettuce, sour cream, avocado slices, shredded Cheddar cheese, and cilantro.

Air Fried Beef Satay with Peanut Dipping Sauce

Prep time: 30 minutes | Cook time: 5 to 7 minutes | Serves 4

8 ounces (227 g) London broil, sliced into 8 strips
2 teaspoons curry powder
½ teaspoon kosher salt
Cooking spray
Peanut Dipping sauce:
2 tablespoons creamy peanut butter
1 tablespoon reduced-sodium soy sauce
2 teaspoons rice vinegar
1 teaspoon honey
1 teaspoon grated ginger
Special Equipment:
4 bamboo skewers, cut into halves and soaked in water for 20 minutes to keep them from burning while cooking

1. Select Air Fry, set temperature to 360°F (182°C) and set time to 5 to 7 minutes. Press Start to begin preheating. Spritz the pizza rack with cooking spray. 2. In a bowl, place the London broil strips and sprinkle with the curry powder and kosher salt to season. Thread the strips onto the soaked skewers. 3. Arrange the skewers on the prepared rack and spritz with cooking spray. Once preheated, place the rack on the air fry position. The beef will be well browned when done, turning halfway through. 4. In the meantime, stir together the peanut butter, soy sauce, rice vinegar, honey, and ginger in a bowl to make the dipping sauce. 5. Transfer the beef to the serving dishes and let rest for 5 minutes. Serve with the peanut dipping sauce on the side.

Cheese Pork Chops

Prep time: 15 minutes | Cook time: 9 to 14 minutes | Serves 4

2 large eggs
½ cup finely grated Parmesan cheese
½ cup finely ground blanched almond flour or finely crushed pork rinds
1 teaspoon paprika
½ teaspoon dried oregano
½ teaspoon garlic powder
Salt and freshly ground black pepper, to taste
1¼ pounds (567 g) (1-inch-thick) boneless pork chops
Avocado oil spray

1. Select Rotisserie, Air Fry Fan, set temperature to 400°F (204°C) and set time to 9 to 14 minutes. Press Start to begin preheating. 2. Beat the eggs in a shallow bowl. In a separate bowl, combine the Parmesan cheese, almond flour, paprika, oregano, garlic powder, and salt and pepper to taste. 3. Dip the pork chops into the eggs, then coat them with the Parmesan mixture, gently pressing the coating onto the meat. Spray the breaded pork chops with oil. 4. Push the

chops onto the rotisserie spit. Slide the forks onto both ends of the spit, ensuring the forks are inserted into the chops. Once preheated, place the prepared chops with the rotisserie spit into the oven. Working in batches if necessary. It will be done until an instant-read thermometer reads 145°F (63°C). 5. Allow the pork chops to rest for at least 5 minutes, then serve.

Pork and Beef Egg Rolls

Prep time: 30 minutes | Cook time: 7 to 8 minutes per batch | Makes 8 egg rolls

¼ pound (113 g) very lean ground beef
¼ pound (113 g) lean ground pork
1 tablespoon soy sauce
1 teaspoon olive oil
½ cup grated carrots
2 green onions, chopped
2 cups grated Napa cabbage
¼ cup chopped water chestnuts
¼ teaspoon salt
¼ teaspoon garlic powder
¼ teaspoon black pepper
1 egg
1 tablespoon water
8 egg roll wraps
Oil for misting or cooking spray

1. In a large skillet, brown beef and pork with soy sauce. Remove cooked meat from skillet, drain, and set aside. 2. Pour off any excess grease from skillet. Add olive oil, carrots, and onions. Sauté until barely tender, about 1 minute. 3. Stir in cabbage, cover, and cook for 1 minute or just until cabbage slightly wilts. Remove from heat. 4. In a large bowl, combine the cooked meats and vegetables, water chestnuts, salt, garlic powder, and pepper. Stir well. If needed, add more salt to taste. 5. Select Roast, Air Fry Fan, set temperature to 390°F (199°C) and set time to 4 minutes. Press Start to begin preheating. Beat together egg and water in a small bowl. 6. Fill egg roll wrappers, using about ¼ cup of filling for each wrap. Roll up and brush all over with egg wash to seal. Spray very lightly with olive oil or cooking spray. Place 4 egg rolls in baking pan. 7. Once preheated, place the pan on the roast position. Turn over and cook 3 to 4 more minutes, until golden brown and crispy. 8. Repeat to cook remaining egg rolls.

Red Curry Flank Steak

Prep time: 30 minutes | Cook time: 12 to 18 minutes | Serves 4

23 tablespoons red curry paste
¼ cup olive oil
2 teaspoons grated fresh ginger
2 tablespoons soy sauce
2 tablespoons rice wine vinegar
3 scallions, minced
1½ pounds (680 g) flank steak
Fresh cilantro (or parsley) leaves

1. Mix the red curry paste, olive oil, ginger, soy sauce, rice vinegar and scallions together in a bowl. Place the flank steak in a shallow glass dish and pour half the marinade over the steak. Pierce the steak several times with a fork or meat tenderizer to let the marinade penetrate the meat. Turn the steak over, pour the remaining marinade over the top and pierce the steak several times again. Cover and marinate the steak in the refrigerator for 6 to 8 hours. 2. When you are ready to cook, remove the steak from the refrigerator and let it sit at room temperature for 30 minutes. 3. Select Air Fry, set temperature to 400°F (204°C) and set time to 12 to 18 minutes. Press Start to begin preheating. 4. Cut the flank steak in half and transfer both pieces to the pizza rack. Pour the marinade over the steak. Once preheated, place the rack on the air fry position. Flip the steak over halfway through the cooking time. 5. When your desired degree of doneness has been reached, remove the steak to a cutting board and let it rest for 5 minutes before slicing. Thinly slice the flank steak against the grain of the meat. Transfer the slices to a serving platter, pour any juice from the bottom of the air fryer oven over the sliced flank steak and sprinkle the fresh cilantro on top.

Greek-Style Meatloaf

Prep time: 5 minutes | Cook time: 25 minutes | Serves 6

- 1 pound lean ground beef
- 2 eggs
- 2 Roma tomatoes, diced
- ½ white onion, diced
- ½ cup whole wheat bread crumbs
- 1 teaspoon garlic powder
- 1 teaspoon dried oregano
- 1 teaspoon dried thyme
- 1 teaspoon salt
- 1 teaspoon black pepper
- 2 ounces mozzarella cheese, shredded
- 1 tablespoon olive oil
- Fresh chopped parsley, for garnish

1. Select Roast, Air Fry Fan, set temperature to 380°F (193°C) and set time to 25 minutes. Press Start to begin preheating. 2. In a large bowl, mix together the ground beef, eggs, tomatoes, onion, bread crumbs, garlic powder, oregano, thyme, salt, pepper, and cheese. 3. Form into a loaf, flattening to 1-inch thick. 4. Brush the top with olive oil, then place the meatloaf on pizza rack. 5. Once preheated, place the rack on the roast position. Remove from the oven and allow to rest for 5 minutes, before slicing and serving with a sprinkle of parsley.

Almond and Caraway Crust Steak

Prep time: 16 minutes | Cook time: 10 minutes | Serves 4

- ⅓ cup almond flour
- 2 eggs
- 2 teaspoons caraway seeds
- 4 beef steaks
- 2 teaspoons garlic powder
- 1 tablespoon melted butter
- Fine sea salt and cayenne pepper, to taste

1. Select Roast, Air Fry Fan, set temperature to 355°F (179°C) and set time to 10 minutes. Press Start to begin preheating. Generously coat steaks with garlic powder, caraway seeds, salt, and cayenne pepper. 2. In a mixing dish, thoroughly combine melted butter with seasoned crumbs. In another bowl, beat the eggs until they're well whisked. 3. First, coat steaks with the beaten egg; then, coat beef steaks with the buttered crumb mixture. Place the steaks in baking pan. 4. Once preheated, place the pan on the roast position. Bon appétit!

Peppercorn-Crusted Beef Tenderloin

Prep time: 10 minutes | Cook time: 25 minutes | Serves 6

- 2 tablespoons salted butter, melted
- 2 teaspoons minced roasted garlic
- 3 tablespoons ground 4-peppercorn blend
- 1 (2-pound / 907-g) beef tenderloin, trimmed of visible fat

1. Select Rotisserie, Air Fry Fan, set temperature to 400°F (204°C) and set time to 25 minutes. Press Start to begin preheating. 2. In a small bowl, mix the butter and roasted garlic. Brush it over the beef tenderloin. 3. Place the ground peppercorns onto a plate and roll the tenderloin through them, creating a crust. 4. Push the tenderloin onto the rotisserie spit. Slide the forks onto both ends of the spit, ensuring the forks are inserted into the tenderloin. 5. Once preheated, place the prepared tenderloin with the rotisserie spit into the oven. Allow meat to rest 10 minutes before slicing.

Lamb Chops with Horseradish Sauce

Prep time: 30 minutes | Cook time: 13 minutes | Serves 4

Lamb:
- 4 lamb loin chops
- 2 tablespoons vegetable oil
- 1 clove garlic, minced
- ½ teaspoon kosher salt
- ½ teaspoon black pepper

Horseradish Cream Sauce:
- ½ cup mayonnaise
- 1 tablespoon Dijon mustard
- 1 to 1½ tablespoons prepared horseradish
- 2 teaspoons sugar

Vegetable oil spray

1. For the lamb: Brush the lamb chops with the oil, rub with the garlic, and sprinkle with the salt and pepper. Marinate at room temperature for 30 minutes. 2. Meanwhile, for the sauce: In a medium bowl, combine the mayonnaise, mustard, horseradish, and sugar. Stir until well combined. Set aside half of the sauce for serving. 3. Select Roast, Air Fry Fan, set temperature to 325°F (163°C) and set time to 10 minutes. Press Start to begin preheating. Spray the crisper tray with vegetable oil spray and place the chops in the tray. Once preheated, place the pan on the roast position. Turn the chops halfway through the cooking time. 4. Remove the chops from the air fryer oven and add to the bowl with the horseradish sauce, turning to coat with the sauce. Place the chops back in the oven. Set the temperature to 400°F (204°C) for 3 minutes. Use a meat thermometer to ensure the meat has reached an internal temperature of 145°F (63°C) (for medium-rare). 5. Serve the chops with the reserved horseradish sauce.

Bean and Beef Meatball Taco Pizza

Prep time: 10 minutes | Cook time: 7 to 9 minutes per batch | Serves 4

¾ cup refried beans (from a 16-ounce / 454-g can)
½ cup salsa
10 frozen precooked beef meatballs, thawed and sliced
1 jalapeño pepper, sliced
4 whole-wheat pita breads
1 cup shredded pepper Jack cheese
½ cup shredded Colby cheese
Cooking oil spray
⅓ cup sour cream

1. In a medium bowl, stir together the refried beans, salsa, meatballs, and jalapeño. 2. Select Pizza, Air Fry Fan, set temperature to 375°F (191°C) and set time to 9 minutes. Press Start to begin preheating. 3. Top the pitas with the refried bean mixture and sprinkle with the cheeses. 4. Spray the crisper tray with cooking oil. Working in batches, place the pizzas into the tray. Once preheated, place the tray on the pizza position. 5. After about 7 minutes, check the pizzas. They are done when the cheese is melted and starts to brown. If not ready, resume cooking. 6. When the cooking is complete, top each pizza with a dollop of sour cream and serve warm.

Pigs in a Blanket

Prep time: 10 minutes | Cook time: 7 minutes | Serves 2

½ cup shredded Mozzarella cheese
2 tablespoons blanched finely ground almond flour
1 ounce (28 g) full-fat cream cheese
2 (2-ounce / 57-g) beef smoked sausages
½ teaspoon sesame seeds

1. Select Air Fry, set temperature to 400°F (204°C) and set time to 7 minutes. Press Start to begin preheating. 2. Place Mozzarella, almond flour, and cream cheese in a large microwave-safe bowl. Microwave for 45 seconds and stir until smooth. Roll dough into a ball and cut in half. 3. Press each half out into a 4 × 5-inch rectangle. Roll one sausage up in each dough half and press seams closed. Sprinkle the top with sesame seeds. 4. Place each wrapped sausage into the crisper tray. 5. Once preheated, place the tray on the air fry position. 6. The outside will be golden when completely cooked. Serve immediately.

Spicy Lamb Sirloin Chops

Prep time: 30 minutes | Cook time: 15 minutes | Serves 4

½ yellow onion, coarsely chopped
4 coin-size slices peeled fresh ginger
5 garlic cloves
1 teaspoon garam masala
1 teaspoon ground fennel
1 teaspoon ground cinnamon
1 teaspoon ground turmeric
½ to 1 teaspoon cayenne pepper

½ teaspoon ground cardamom | 1 teaspoon kosher salt | 1 pound (454 g) lamb sirloin chops

1. In a blender, combine the onion, ginger, garlic, garam masala, fennel, cinnamon, turmeric, cayenne, cardamom, and salt. Pulse until the onion is finely minced and the mixture forms a thick paste, 3 to 4 minutes. 2. Place the lamb chops in a large bowl. Slash the meat and fat with a sharp knife several times to allow the marinade to penetrate better. Add the spice paste to the bowl and toss the lamb to coat. Marinate at room temperature for 30 minutes or cover and refrigerate for up to 24 hours. 3. Select Bake, Air Fry Fan, set temperature to 325°F (163°C) and set time to 15 minutes. Press Start to begin preheating. Place the lamb chops in a single layer in the crisper tray on bake position. Turn the chops halfway through the cooking time. Use a meat thermometer to ensure the lamb has reached an internal temperature of 145°F (63°C) (medium-rare).

Broccoli and Pork Teriyaki

Prep time: 10 minutes | Cook time: 13 minutes | Serves 4

1 head broccoli, trimmed into florets	¼ teaspoon sea salt	tenderloin, trimmed and cut into 1-inch pieces	Olive oil spray
1 tablespoon extra-virgin olive oil	¼ teaspoon freshly ground black pepper	½ cup teriyaki sauce, divided	2 cups cooked brown rice
	1 pound (454 g) pork		Sesame seeds, for garnish

1. Select Roast, Air Fry Fan, set temperature to 400°F (204°C) and set time to 13 minutes. Press Start to begin preheating. 2. In a large bowl, toss together the broccoli, olive oil, salt, and pepper. 3. In a medium bowl, toss together the pork and 3 tablespoons of teriyaki sauce to coat the meat. 4. Spray the crisper tray with olive oil. Put the broccoli and pork into the tray. Spray them with olive oil and drizzle with 1 tablespoon of teriyaki sauce. 5. Once preheated, place the tray on the roast position. 6. After 10 to 12 minutes, the broccoli is tender and light golden brown and a food thermometer inserted into the pork should register 145°F (63°C). Remove the tray and drizzle the broccoli and pork with the remaining ¼ cup of teriyaki sauce and toss to coat. Reinsert the tray to resume cooking for 1 minute. 7. When the cooking is complete, serve immediately over the hot cooked rice, if desired, garnished with the sesame seeds.

Indian Mint and Chile Kebabs

Prep time: 30 minutes | Cook time: 15 minutes | Serves 4

1 pound (454 g) ground lamb	1 tablespoon minced garlic	¼ teaspoon ground cinnamon
½ cup finely minced onion	½ teaspoon ground turmeric	1 teaspoon kosher salt
¼ cup chopped fresh mint	½ teaspoon cayenne pepper	
¼ cup chopped fresh cilantro	¼ teaspoon ground cardamom	

1. In the bowl of a stand mixer fitted with the paddle attachment, combine the lamb, onion, mint, cilantro, garlic, turmeric, cayenne, cardamom, cinnamon, and salt. Mix on low speed until you have a sticky mess of spiced meat. If you have time, let the mixture stand at room temperature for 30 minutes (or cover and refrigerate for up to a day or two, until you're ready to make the kebabs). 2. Select Bake, Air Fry Fan, set temperature to 350°F (177°C) and set time to 10 minutes. Press Start to begin preheating. 2. Divide the meat into eight equal portions. Form each into a long sausage shape. Place the kebabs in a single layer on the pizza rack. Once preheated, place the rack on the bake position. 3. Increase the temperature to 400°F (204°C) and cook for 3 to 4 minutes more to brown the kebabs. Use a meat thermometer to ensure the kebabs have reached an internal temperature of 160°F / 71°C (medium).

Rosemary Roast Beef

Prep time: 30 minutes | Cook time: 30 to 35 minutes | Serves 8

1 (2-pound / 907-g) top round beef roast, tied with kitchen string

Sea salt and freshly ground black pepper, to taste

2 teaspoons minced garlic

2 tablespoons finely chopped fresh rosemary

¼ cup avocado oil

1. Season the roast generously with salt and pepper. 2. In a small bowl, whisk together the garlic, rosemary, and avocado oil. Rub this all over the roast. Cover loosely with aluminum foil or plastic wrap and refrigerate for at least 12 hours or up to 2 days. 3. Remove the roast from the refrigerator and allow to sit at room temperature for about 1 hour. 4. Select Rotisserie, Air Fry Fan, set temperature to 325°F (163°C) and set time to 30 to 35 minutes. Press Start to begin preheating. Push the roast onto the rotisserie spit. Slide the forks onto both ends of the spit, ensuring the forks are inserted into the roast. Once preheated, place the prepared roast with the rotisserie spit into the oven and cook. It will be done until the meat is browned and an instant-read thermometer reads 120°F (49°C) at the thickest part (for medium-rare). 5. Transfer the meat to a cutting board, and let it rest for 15 minutes before thinly slicing and serving.

Spicy Flank Steak with Zhoug

Prep time: 30 minutes | Cook time: 8 minutes | Serves 4

Marinade and Steak:

½ cup dark beer or orange juice

¼ cup fresh lemon juice

3 cloves garlic, minced

2 tablespoons extra-virgin olive oil

2 tablespoons Sriracha

2 tablespoons brown sugar

2 teaspoons ground cumin

2 teaspoons smoked paprika

1 tablespoon kosher salt

1 teaspoon black pepper

1½ pounds (680 g) flank steak, trimmed and cut into 3 pieces

Zhoug:

1 cup packed fresh cilantro leaves

2 cloves garlic, peeled

2 jalapeño or serrano chiles, stemmed and coarsely chopped

½ teaspoon ground cumin

¼ teaspoon ground coriander

¼ teaspoon kosher salt

2 to 4 tablespoons extra-virgin olive oil

1. For the marinade and steak: In a small bowl, whisk together the beer, lemon juice, garlic, olive oil, Sriracha, brown sugar, cumin, paprika, salt, and pepper. Place the steak in a large resealable plastic bag. Pour the marinade over the steak, seal the bag, and massage the steak to coat. Marinate in the refrigerator for 1 hour or up to 24 hours, turning the bag occasionally. 2. Meanwhile, for the zhoug: In a food processor, combine the cilantro, garlic, jalapeños, cumin, coriander, and salt. Process until finely chopped. Add 2 tablespoons olive oil and pulse to form a loose paste, adding up to 2 tablespoons more olive oil if needed. Transfer the zhoug to a glass container. Cover and store in the refrigerator until 30 minutes before serving if marinating more than 1 hour. 3. Remove the steak from the marinade and discard the marinade. Select Rotisserie, Air Fry Fan, set temperature to 400°F (204°C) and set time to 8 minutes. Press Start to begin preheating. 4. Push the steak onto the rotisserie spit. Slide the forks onto both ends of the spit, ensuring the forks are inserted into the steak. 5. Once preheated, place the prepared steak with the rotisserie spit into the oven. Use a meat thermometer to ensure the steak has reached an internal temperature of 150°F / 66°C (for medium). 6. Transfer the steak to a cutting board and let rest for 5 minutes. Slice the steak across the grain and serve with the zhoug.

Caraway Crusted Beef Steaks

Prep time: 5 minutes | Cook time: 10 minutes | Serves 4

4 beef steaks

2 teaspoons caraway seeds

2 teaspoons garlic powder

Sea salt and cayenne pepper, to taste

1 tablespoon melted butter

⅓ cup almond flour

2 eggs, beaten

1. Select Rotisserie, Air Fry Fan, set temperature to 355°F (179°C) and set time to 10 minutes. Press Start to begin preheating. 2. Add the beef steaks to a large bowl and toss with the caraway seeds, garlic powder, salt and pepper until well coated. 3. Stir together the melted butter and almond flour in a bowl. Whisk the eggs in a different bowl. 4. Dredge the seasoned steaks in the eggs, then dip in the almond and butter mixture. 5. Push the coated steaks onto the rotisserie spit. Slide the forks onto both ends of the spit, ensuring the forks are inserted into the steaks. Once preheated, place the prepared steaks with the rotisserie spit into the oven. It will be done until the internal temperature of the beef steaks reaches at least 145°F (63°C) on a meat thermometer. 6. Transfer the steaks to plates. Let cool for 5 minutes and serve hot.

Air Fried Potatoes with Olives

Prep time: 15 minutes | Cook time: 40 minutes | Serves 1

1 medium russet potatoes, scrubbed and peeled

1 teaspoon olive oil

¼ teaspoon onion powder

⅛ teaspoon salt

Dollop of butter

Dollop of cream cheese

1 tablespoon Kalamata olives

1 tablespoon chopped chives

1. In a bowl, coat the potatoes with the onion powder, salt, olive oil, and butter. 2. Select Rotisserie, Air Fry Fan, set temperature to 400°F (204°C) and set time to 40 minutes. Press Start to begin preheating. Push the potato onto the rotisserie spit. Slide the forks onto both ends of the spit, ensuring the forks are inserted into the potato. 3. Once preheated, place the prepared potato with the rotisserie spit into the oven. 4. Take care when removing the potatoes from the air fryer oven and serve with the cream cheese, Kalamata olives and chives on top.

Easy Beef Satay

Prep time: 30 minutes | Cook time: 8 minutes | Serves 4

1 pound (454 g) beef flank steak, thinly sliced into long strips

2 tablespoons vegetable oil

1 tablespoon fish sauce

1 tablespoon soy sauce

1 tablespoon minced fresh ginger

1 tablespoon minced garlic

1 tablespoon sugar

1 teaspoon Sriracha or other hot sauce

1 teaspoon ground coriander

½ cup chopped fresh cilantro

¼ cup chopped roasted peanuts

1. Place the beef strips in a large bowl or resealable plastic bag. Add the vegetable oil, fish sauce, soy sauce, ginger, garlic, sugar, Sriracha, coriander, and ¼ cup of the cilantro to the bag. Seal and massage the bag to thoroughly coat and combine. Marinate at room temperature for 30 minutes, or cover and refrigerate for up to 24 hours. 2. Select Air Fry, set temperature to 400°F (204°C) and set time to 8 minutes. Press Start to begin preheating. Using tongs, remove the beef strips from the bag and lay them flat in the crisper tray, minimizing overlap as much as possible; discard the marinade. Once preheated, place the tray on the air fry position. Turn the beef strips halfway through the cooking time. 3. Transfer the meat to a serving platter. Sprinkle with the remaining ¼ cup cilantro and the peanuts. Serve.

New York Strip with Honey-Mustard Butter

Prep time: 5 minutes | Cook time: 14 minutes | Serves 4

2 pounds (907 g) New York Strip

1 teaspoon cayenne pepper

1 tablespoon honey

1 tablespoon Dijon mustard

½ stick butter, softened

Sea salt and freshly ground black

pepper, to taste

Cooking spray

1. Select Air Fry, set temperature to 400°F (204°C) and set time to 14 minutes. Press Start to begin preheating. Spritz with cooking spray. 2. Sprinkle the New York Strip with cayenne pepper, salt, and black pepper on a clean work surface. 3. Arrange the New York Strip in the crisper tray and spritz with cooking spray. 4. Once preheated, place the tray on the air fry position. It will be done until browned and reach your desired doneness. Flip the New York Strip halfway through. 5. Meanwhile, combine the honey, mustard, and butter in a small bowl. Stir to mix well. 6. Transfer the air fried New York Strip onto a plate and baste with the honey-mustard butter before serving.

Herb-Crusted Lamb Chops

Prep time: 10 minutes | Cook time: 5 minutes | Serves 2

1 large egg
2 cloves garlic, minced
¼ cup pork dust
¼ cup powdered Parmesan cheese
1 tablespoon chopped fresh oregano leaves

1 tablespoon chopped fresh rosemary leaves
1 teaspoon chopped fresh thyme leaves
½ teaspoon ground black pepper
4 (1-inch-thick) lamb chops

For Garnish/Serving (Optional):
Sprigs of fresh oregano
Sprigs of fresh rosemary
Sprigs of fresh thyme
Lavender flowers
Lemon slices

1. Spray the crisper tray with avocado oil. Select Air Fry, set temperature to 400°F (204°C) and set time to 5 minutes. Press Start to begin preheating. 2. Beat the egg in a shallow bowl, add the garlic, and stir well to combine. In another shallow bowl, mix together the pork dust, Parmesan, herbs, and pepper. 3. One at a time, dip the lamb chops into the egg mixture, shake off the excess egg, and then dredge them in the Parmesan mixture. Use your hands to coat the chops well in the Parmesan mixture and form a nice crust on all sides; if necessary, dip the chops again in both the egg and the Parmesan mixture. 4. Place the lamb chops in the tray, leaving space between them. Once preheated, place the tray on the air fry position. It will be done until the internal temperature reaches 145°F (63°C) for medium doneness. Allow to rest for 10 minutes before serving. 5. Garnish with sprigs of oregano, rosemary, and thyme, and lavender flowers, if desired. Serve with lemon slices, if desired. 6. Best served fresh. Store leftovers in an airtight container in the fridge for up to 4 days. Serve chilled over a salad, or reheat in a 350°F (177°C) air fryer oven for 3 minutes, or until heated through.

Beefy Poppers

Prep time: 15 minutes | Cook time: 15 minutes | Makes 8 poppers

8 medium jalapeño peppers, stemmed, halved, and seeded
1 (8-ounce / 227-g) package cream cheese (or Kite Hill brand cream

cheese style spread for dairy-free), softened
2 pounds (907 g) ground beef (85% lean)

1 teaspoon fine sea salt
½ teaspoon ground black pepper
8 slices thin-cut bacon
Fresh cilantro leaves, for garnish

1. Spray the baking pan with avocado oil. Select Roast, Air Fry Fan, set temperature to 400°F (204°C) and set time to 15 minutes. Press Start to begin preheating. 2. Stuff each jalapeño half with a few tablespoons of cream cheese. Place the halves back together again to form 8 jalapeños. 3. Season the ground beef with the salt and pepper and mix with your hands to incorporate. Flatten about ¼ pound (113 g) of ground beef in the palm of your hand and place a stuffed jalapeño in the center. Fold the beef around the jalapeño, forming an egg shape. Wrap the beef-covered jalapeño with a slice of bacon and secure it with a toothpick. 4. Place the jalapeños in the baking pan, leaving space between them

(if you're using a smaller air fryer, work in batches if necessary). Once preheated, place the pan on the roast position. It will be done until the beef is cooked through and the bacon is crispy. Garnish with cilantro before serving. 5. Store leftovers in an airtight container in the fridge for 3 days or in the freezer for up to a month. Reheat in a preheated 350°F (177°C) air fryer oven for 4 minutes, or until heated through and the bacon is crispy.

Blackened Steak Nuggets

Prep time: 10 minutes | Cook time: 7 minutes | Serves 2

1 pound (454 g) rib eye steak, cut into 1-inch cubes
2 tablespoons salted butter, melted
½ teaspoon paprika
½ teaspoon salt
¼ teaspoon garlic powder
¼ teaspoon onion powder
¼ teaspoon ground black pepper
⅛ teaspoon cayenne pepper

1. Select Roast, Air Fry Fan, set temperature to 400°F (204°C) and set time to 7 minutes. Press Start to begin preheating. 2. Place steak into a large bowl and pour in butter. Toss to coat. Sprinkle with remaining ingredients. Place bites into ungreased crisper tray. Shake the tray three times during cooking. Steak will be crispy on the outside and browned when done and internal temperature is at least 150°F (66°C) for medium and 180°F (82°C) for well-done. Serve warm.

Smoky Pork Tenderloin

Prep time: 5 minutes | Cook time: 19 to 22 minutes | Serves 6

1½ pounds (680 g) pork tenderloin
1 tablespoon avocado oil
1 teaspoon chili powder
1 teaspoon smoked paprika
1 teaspoon garlic powder
1 teaspoon sea salt
1 teaspoon freshly ground black pepper

1. Pierce the tenderloin all over with a fork and rub the oil all over the meat. 2. In a small dish, stir together the chili powder, smoked paprika, garlic powder, salt, and pepper. Rub the spice mixture all over the tenderloin. 3. Select Rotisserie, Air Fry Fan, set temperature 400°F (204°C) and set time to 19 to 22 minutes. Press Start to begin preheating. 4. Push the tenderloin onto the rotisserie spit. Slide the forks onto both ends of the spit, ensuring the forks are inserted into the tenderloin. 5. Once preheated, place the prepared tenderloin with the rotisserie spit into the oven. It will be done until an instant-read thermometer reads at least 145°F (63°C). 6. Allow the tenderloin to rest for 5 minutes, then slice and serve.

Honey-Baked Pork Loin

Prep time: 30 minutes | Cook time: 22 to 25 minutes | Serves 6

¼ cup honey
¼ cup freshly squeezed lemon juice
2 tablespoons soy sauce
1 teaspoon garlic powder
1 (2-pound / 907-g) pork loin
2 tablespoons vegetable oil

1. In a medium bowl, whisk together the honey, lemon juice, soy sauce, and garlic powder. Reserve half of the mixture for basting during cooking. 2. Cut 5 slits in the pork loin and transfer it to a resealable bag. Add the remaining honey mixture. Seal the bag and refrigerate to marinate for at least 2 hours. 3. Select Rotisserie, Air Fry Fan, set temperature to 400°F (204°C) and set time to 22 to 25 minutes. Press Start to begin preheating. Remove the pork from the marinade. Spritz with oil, then baste with the reserved marinade. 4. Push the pork onto the rotisserie spit. Slide the forks onto both ends of the spit, ensuring the forks are inserted into the pork. Once preheated, place the prepared pork with the rotisserie spit into the oven. Baste with more marinade and spritz with oil again halfway through the cooking time. It will be done until the internal temperature reaches 145°F (63°C). Let rest for 5 minutes before

serving.

Chapter 5 Fish and Seafood

Tandoori-Spiced Salmon and Potatoes

Prep time: 10 minutes | Cook time: 28 minutes | Serves 2

1 pound (454 g) fingerling potatoes	1 teaspoon ground turmeric	¼ teaspoon cayenne pepper
2 tablespoons vegetable oil, divided	1 teaspoon ground cumin	2 (6-ounce / 170-g) skin-on salmon fillets
Kosher salt and freshly ground black pepper, to taste	1 teaspoon ground ginger	
	½ teaspoon smoked paprika	

1. Select Air Fry, set temperature to 375°F (191°C) and set time to 20 minutes. Press Start to begin preheating. 2. In a bowl, toss the potatoes with 1 tablespoon of the oil until evenly coated. Season with salt and pepper. Transfer the potatoes to the baking pan. Once preheated, place the pan on the air fry position. 3. Meanwhile, in a bowl, combine the remaining 1 tablespoon oil, the turmeric, cumin, ginger, paprika, and cayenne. Add the salmon fillets and turn in the spice mixture until fully coated all over. 4. After the potatoes have cooked for 20 minutes, place the salmon fillets, skin-side up, on top of the potatoes, and continue cooking until the potatoes are tender, the salmon is cooked, and the salmon skin is slightly crisp. 5. Transfer the salmon fillets to two plates and serve with the potatoes while both are warm.

Salmon with Cauliflower

Prep time: 10 minutes | Cook time: 25 minutes | Serves 4

1 pound (454 g) salmon fillet, diced	1 tablespoon dried cilantro	1 teaspoon ground turmeric
1 cup cauliflower, shredded	1 tablespoon coconut oil, melted	¼ cup coconut cream

1. Select Roast, Air Fry Fan, set temperature to 350°F (177°C) and set time to 25 minutes. Press Start to begin preheating. 2. Mix salmon with cauliflower, dried cilantro, ground turmeric, coconut cream, and coconut oil in baking pan. 3. Once preheated, place the pan on the roast position. Stir the meal every 5 minutes to avoid the burning.

Tuna Nuggets in Hoisin Sauce

Prep time: 15 minutes | Cook time: 5 to 7 minutes | Serves 4

½ cup hoisin sauce	2 teaspoons dried lemongrass	8 ounces (227 g) fresh tuna, cut into 1-inch cubes
2 tablespoons rice wine vinegar	¼ teaspoon red pepper flakes	Cooking spray
2 teaspoons sesame oil	½ small onion, quartered and thinly sliced	3 cups cooked jasmine rice
1 teaspoon garlic powder		

1. Select Roast, Air Fry Fan, set temperature to 390°F (199°C) and set time to 3 minutes. Press Start to begin preheating. 2. Mix the hoisin sauce, vinegar, sesame oil, and seasonings together. Stir in the onions and tuna nuggets. 3. Spray a baking pan with nonstick spray and pour in tuna mixture. 4. Once preheated, place the pan on the roast position. Stir gently. 5. Cook 2 minutes and stir again, checking for doneness. Tuna should be barely cooked through, just beginning to flake and still very moist. If necessary, continue cooking and stirring in 1-minute intervals until done. 6. Serve warm over hot jasmine rice.

Savory Shrimp

Prep time: 5 minutes | Cook time: 8 to 10 minutes | Serves 4

1 pound (454 g) fresh large shrimp, peeled and deveined
1 tablespoon avocado oil
2 teaspoons minced garlic, divided
½ teaspoon red pepper flakes
Sea salt and freshly ground black pepper, to taste
2 tablespoons unsalted butter, melted
2 tablespoons chopped fresh parsley

1. Select Air Fry, set temperature to 350°F (177°C) and set time to 6 minutes. Press Start to begin preheating. 2. Place the shrimp in a large bowl and toss with the avocado oil, 1 teaspoon of minced garlic, and red pepper flakes. Season with salt and pepper. 3. Arrange the shrimp in a single layer in the crisper tray, working in batches if necessary. Once preheated, place the tray on the air fry position. Flip the shrimp and cook for 2 to 4 minutes more, until the internal temperature of the shrimp reaches 120°F (49°C). (The time it takes to cook will depend on the size of the shrimp.) 4. While the shrimp are cooking, melt the butter in a small saucepan over medium heat and stir in the remaining 1 teaspoon of garlic. 5. Transfer the cooked shrimp to a large bowl, add the garlic butter, and toss well. Top with the parsley and serve warm.

Cucumber and Salmon Salad

Prep time: 10 minutes | Cook time: 8 to 10 minutes | Serves 2

1 pound (454 g) salmon fillet
1½ tablespoons olive oil, divided
1 tablespoon sherry vinegar
1 tablespoon capers, rinsed and drained
1 seedless cucumber, thinly sliced
¼ Vidalia onion, thinly sliced
2 tablespoons chopped fresh parsley
Salt and freshly ground black pepper, to taste

1. Select Roast, Air Fry Fan, set temperature to 400°F (204°C) and set time to 8 to 10 minutes. Press Start to begin preheating. 2. Lightly coat the salmon with ½ tablespoon of the olive oil. Place skin-side down on the pizza rack. It will be done until the fish is opaque and flakes easily with a fork. Transfer the salmon to a plate and let cool to room temperature. Remove the skin and carefully flake the fish into bite-size chunks. 3. In a small bowl, whisk the remaining 1 tablespoon olive oil and the vinegar until thoroughly combined. Add the flaked fish, capers, cucumber, onion, and parsley. Season to taste with salt and freshly ground black pepper. Toss gently to coat. Serve immediately or cover and refrigerate for up to 4 hours.

Cripsy Shrimp with Cilantro

Prep time: 40 minutes | Cook time: 10 minutes | Serves 4

1 pound (454 g) raw large shrimp, peeled and deveined with tails on or off
½ cup chopped fresh cilantro
Juice of 1 lime
½ cup all-purpose flour
1 egg
¾ cup bread crumbs
Salt and freshly ground black pepper, to taste
Cooking oil spray
1 cup cocktail sauce

1. Place the shrimp in a resealable plastic bag and add the cilantro and lime juice. Seal the bag. Shake it to combine. Marinate the shrimp in the refrigerator for 30 minutes. 2. Place the flour in a small bowl. 3. In another small bowl, beat the egg. 4. Place the bread crumbs in a third small bowl, season with salt and pepper, and stir to combine. 5. Select Air Fry, set temperature to 400°F (204°C) and set time to 8 minutes. Press Start to begin preheating. 6. Remove the shrimp from the plastic bag. Dip each in the flour, the egg, and the bread crumbs to coat. Gently press the

crumbs onto the shrimp. 7. Spray the crisper tray with cooking oil. Place the shrimp in the tray. It is okay to stack them. Spray the shrimp with the cooking oil. 8. Once preheated, place the tray on the air fry position. 9. After 4 minutes, remove the tray and flip the shrimp one at a time. Reinsert the tray to resume cooking. 10. When the cooking is complete, the shrimp should be crisp. Let cool for 5 minutes. Serve with cocktail sauce.

Salmon Burgers with Creamy Broccoli Slaw

Prep time: 15 minutes | Cook time: 10 minutes | Serves 4

For the salmon burgers	crumbs	For the broccoli slaw	½ teaspoon salt
1 pound salmon fillets, bones and skin removed	1 teaspoon salt	3 cups chopped or shredded broccoli	2 tablespoons apple cider vinegar
1 egg	½ teaspoon cayenne pepper	½ cup shredded carrots	1 cup nonfat plain Greek yogurt
¼ cup fresh dill, chopped	2 garlic cloves, minced	¼ cup sunflower seeds	
1 cup whole wheat bread	4 whole wheat buns	2 garlic cloves, minced	

To make the salmon burgers 1. Select Bake, Air Fry Fan, set temperature to 360°F (182°C) and set time to 5 minutes. Press Start to begin preheating. 2. In a food processor, pulse the salmon fillets until they are finely chopped. 3. In a large bowl, combine the chopped salmon, egg, dill, bread crumbs, salt, cayenne, and garlic until it comes together. 4. Form the salmon into 4 patties. Place them on pizza rack, making sure that they don't touch each other. 5. Once preheated, place the rack on the bake position. Flip the salmon patties and bake for 5 minutes more. To make the broccoli slaw 6. In a large bowl, combine all of the ingredients for the broccoli slaw. Mix well. 7. Serve the salmon burgers on toasted whole wheat buns, and top with a generous portion of broccoli slaw.

Tuna Steak

Prep time: 10 minutes | Cook time: 12 minutes | Serves 4

| 1 pound (454 g) tuna steaks, boneless and cubed | 1 tablespoon mustard | 1 tablespoon apple cider vinegar |
| | 1 tablespoon avocado oil | |

1. Select Roast, Air Fry Fan, set temperature to 360°F (182°C) and set time to 12 minutes. Press Start to begin preheating. 2. Mix avocado oil with mustard and apple cider vinegar. Then brush tuna steaks with mustard mixture and put on the pizza rack. 3. Once preheated, place the rack on the roast position. After 6 minutes, turn the steaks. 4. Serve warm.

Air Fryer Fish Fry

Prep time: 5 minutes | Cook time: 15 minutes | Serves 4

2 cups low-fat buttermilk	4 (4-ounce) flounder fillets	¼ teaspoon cayenne pepper
½ teaspoon garlic powder	½ cup plain yellow cornmeal	Freshly ground black pepper
½ teaspoon onion powder	½ cup chickpea flour	

1. In a large bowl, combine the buttermilk, garlic powder, and onion powder. 2. Add the flounder, turning until well coated, and set aside to marinate for 20 minutes. 3. Select Air Fry, set temperature to 380°F (193°C) and set time to 12 minutes. Press Start to begin preheating. 4. In a shallow bowl, stir the cornmeal, chickpea flour, cayenne, and pepper together. 5. Dredge the fillets in the meal mixture, turning until well coated. Place in the baking pan. 5. Once preheated, place the pan on the air fry position.

Shrimp Pasta with Basil and Mushrooms

Prep time: 10 minutes | Cook time: 10 minutes | Serves 6

- 1 pound small shrimp, peeled and deveined
- ¼ cup plus 1 tablespoon olive oil, divided
- ¼ teaspoon garlic powder
- ¼ teaspoon cayenne
- 1 pound whole grain pasta
- 5 garlic cloves, minced
- 8 ounces baby bella mushrooms, sliced
- ½ cup Parmesan, plus more for serving (optional)
- 1 teaspoon salt
- ½ teaspoon black pepper
- ½ cup fresh basil

1. Select Roast, Air Fry Fan, set temperature to 380°F (193°C) and set time to 5 minutes. Press Start to begin preheating. 2. In a small bowl, combine the shrimp, 1 tablespoon olive oil, garlic powder, and cayenne. Toss to coat the shrimp. 3. Place the shrimp into the baking pan. Once preheated, place the pan on the roast position. Remove the shrimp and set aside. 4. Cook the pasta according to package directions. Once done cooking, reserve ½ cup pasta water, then drain. 5. Meanwhile, in a large skillet, heat ¼ cup of olive oil over medium heat. Add the garlic and mushrooms and cook down for 5 minutes. 6. Pour the pasta, reserved pasta water, Parmesan, salt, pepper, and basil into the skillet with the vegetable-and-oil mixture, and stir to coat the pasta. 7. Toss in the shrimp and remove from heat, then let the mixture sit for 5 minutes before serving with additional Parmesan, if desired.

Citrus-Soy Salmon with Bok Choy

Prep time: 30 minutes | Cook time: 12 minutes | Serves 2

Fish:
- ½ cup fresh orange juice
- ¼ cup soy sauce
- 3 tablespoons rice vinegar
- 2 garlic cloves, minced
- 1 tablespoon minced fresh ginger
- 1 tablespoon vegetable oil
- 2 teaspoons finely grated orange zest
- ½ teaspoon kosher salt
- 2 (5- to 6-ounce / 142- to 170-g) salmon fillets

Vegetables:
- 2 heads baby bok choy, halved lengthwise
- 2 ounces (57 g) shiitake mushrooms, stemmed
- 1 tablespoon toasted sesame oil
- Kosher salt, to taste
- ½ teaspoon sesame seeds, toasted

Make the Fish: 1. In a small bowl, whisk together the orange juice, soy sauce, vinegar, garlic, ginger, vegetable oil, orange zest, and salt. Set aside half the marinade. Place the salmon in a gallon-size resealable bag. Pour the remaining marinade over the salmon. Seal and massage to coat. Let stand at room temperature for 30 minutes. 2. Select Air Fry, set temperature to 400°F (204°C) and set time to 12 minutes. Press Start to begin preheating. 3. Place the salmon in the crisper tray. (Discard marinade.) Once preheated, place the tray on the air fry position. **Make the Vegetables:** 4. Brush the bok choy and mushroom caps all over with the sesame oil and season lightly with salt. 5. After the salmon has cooked for 6 minutes, add the vegetables around the salmon in the tray. Cook for the remaining 6 minutes. 6. To serve, drizzle the salmon with some of the reserved marinade and sprinkle the vegetables with the sesame seeds.

Crawfish Creole Casserole

Prep time: 20 minutes | Cook time: 25 minutes | Serves 4

- 1½ cups crawfish meat
- ½ cup chopped celery
- ½ cup chopped onion
- ½ cup chopped green bell pepper
- 2 large eggs, beaten
- 1 cup half-and-half
- 1 tablespoon butter, melted
- 1 tablespoon cornstarch
- 1 teaspoon Creole seasoning
- ¾ teaspoon salt
- ½ teaspoon freshly ground black pepper
- 1 cup shredded Cheddar cheese
- Cooking spray

1. In a medium bowl, stir together the crawfish, celery, onion, and green pepper. 2. In another medium bowl, whisk the eggs, half-and-half, butter, cornstarch, Creole seasoning, salt, and pepper until blended. Stir the egg mixture into the crawfish mixture. Add the cheese and stir to combine. 3. Select Bake, Air Fry Fan, set temperature to 300°F (149°C) and set time to 25 minutes. Press Start to begin preheating. Spritz a baking pan with oil. 4. Once preheated, transfer the crawfish mixture to the prepared pan and place it on the bake position. 5. Stir every 10 minutes, until a knife inserted into the center comes out clean. 6. Serve immediately.

Garlicky Cod Fillets

Prep time: 10 minutes | Cook time: 10 to 12 minutes | Serves 4

1 teaspoon olive oil	pepper, or more to taste	parsley, coarsely chopped	1 teaspoon dried basil
4 cod fillets	1 teaspoon cayenne	½ cup nondairy milk	½ teaspoon dried oregano
¼ teaspoon fine sea salt	pepper	1 Italian pepper, chopped	
¼ teaspoon ground black	½ cup fresh Italian	4 garlic cloves, minced	

1. Lightly coat the sides and bottom of a baking dish with the olive oil. Set aside. 2. In a large bowl, sprinkle the fillets with salt, black pepper, and cayenne pepper. 3. In a food processor, pulse the remaining ingredients until smoothly puréed. 4. Add the purée to the bowl of fillets and toss to coat, then transfer to the prepared baking pan. 5. Select Bake, Air Fry Fan, set temperature to 380°F (193°C) and set time to 10 to 12 minutes. Press Start to begin preheating. 6. Once preheated, put the baking pan on bake position. It will be done until the fish flakes when pressed lightly with a fork. 7. Remove from the basket and serve warm.

Lemon Mahi-Mahi

Prep time: 5 minutes | Cook time: 14 minutes | Serves 2

Oil, for spraying	1 tablespoon lemon juice	¼ teaspoon freshly ground black pepper	fresh dill
2 (6-ounce / 170-g) mahi-mahi fillets	1 tablespoon olive oil	1 tablespoon chopped	2 lemon slices
	¼ teaspoon salt		

1. Select Roast, Air Fry Fan, set temperature to 400°F (204°C) and set time to 12 to 14 minutes. Press Start to begin preheating. Line the pizza rack with parchment and spray lightly with oil. 2. Place the mahi-mahi in the prepared rack. 3. In a small bowl, whisk together the lemon juice and olive oil. Brush the mixture evenly over the mahi-mahi. 4. Sprinkle the mahi-mahi with the salt and black pepper and top with the dill. 5. Once preheated, place the rack on the roast position. It will be done until they flake easily. 6. Transfer to plates, top each with a lemon slice, and serve.

Lemon Pepper Shrimp

Prep time: 15 minutes | Cook time: 8 minutes | Serves 2

Oil, for spraying	3 tablespoons lemon juice	¼ teaspoon paprika
12 ounces (340 g) medium raw shrimp, peeled and deveined	1 tablespoon olive oil	¼ teaspoon granulated garlic
	1 teaspoon lemon pepper	

1. Select Air Fry, set temperature to 400°F (204°C) and set time to 6 to 8 minutes. Press Start to begin preheating. Line the pizza rack with parchment and spray lightly with oil. 2. In a medium bowl, toss together the shrimp, lemon juice, olive oil, lemon pepper, paprika, and garlic until evenly coated. 3. Once preheated, place the shrimp in the prepared rack on air fry position. 4. It will be done until pink and firm. Serve immediately.

Shrimp and Cherry Tomato Kebabs

Prep time: 15 minutes | Cook time: 5 minutes | Serves 4

1½ pounds (680 g) jumbo shrimp, cleaned, shelled and deveined	Sea salt and ground black pepper, to taste	½ teaspoon mustard seeds
1 pound (454 g) cherry tomatoes	1 teaspoon dried parsley flakes	½ teaspoon marjoram
2 tablespoons butter, melted	½ teaspoon dried basil	**Special Equipment:**
1 tablespoons Sriracha sauce	½ teaspoon dried oregano	4 to 6 wooden skewers, soaked in water for 30 minutes

1. Select Roast, Air Fry Fan, set temperature to 400°F (204°C) and set time to 5 minutes. Press Start to begin preheating. 2. Put all the ingredients in a large bowl and toss to coat well. 3. Make the kebabs: Thread, alternating jumbo shrimp and cherry tomatoes, onto the wooden skewers that fit into the air fryer. 4. Arrange the kebabs on pizza rack. You may need to cook in batches. 5. Once preheated, place the pan on the roast position. It will be done until the shrimp are pink and the cherry tomatoes are softened. Repeat with the remaining kebabs. Let the shrimp and cherry tomato kebabs cool for 5 minutes and serve hot.

Fried Shrimp

Prep time: 15 minutes | Cook time: 5 minutes | Serves 4

½ cup self-rising flour	½ teaspoon freshly ground black pepper	1 cup finely crushed panko bread crumbs	(about 1-pound / 907-g), peeled and deveined
1 teaspoon paprika	1 large egg, beaten	20 frozen large shrimp	Cooking spray
1 teaspoon salt			

1. In a shallow bowl, whisk the flour, paprika, salt, and pepper until blended. Add the beaten egg to a second shallow bowl and the bread crumbs to a third. 2. One at a time, dip the shrimp into the flour, the egg, and the bread crumbs, coating thoroughly. 3. Select Air Fry, set temperature to 400°F (204°C) and set time to 2 minutes. Press Start to begin preheating. Line the crisper tray with parchment paper. 4. Place the shrimp on the parchment and spritz with oil. 5. Once preheated, place the tray on the air fry position. Shake the tray, spritz the shrimp with oil, and air fry for 3 minutes more until lightly browned and crispy. Serve hot.

Blackened Red Snapper

Prep time: 13 minutes | Cook time: 8 to 10 minutes | Serves 4

1½ teaspoons black pepper	⅛ teaspoon cayenne pepper	fillet portions, skin on
¼ teaspoon thyme	1 teaspoon olive oil	4 thin slices lemon
¼ teaspoon garlic powder	4 (4-ounce / 113-g) red snapper	Cooking spray

1. Select Roast, Air Fry Fan, set temperature to 390°F (199°C) and set time to 8 to 10 minutes. Press Start to begin preheating. 2. Mix the spices and oil together to make a paste. Rub into both sides of the fish. 3. Spray the baking pan with nonstick cooking spray and lay snapper steaks in pan, skin-side down. 4. Place a lemon slice on each piece of fish. 5. Once preheated, place the pan on the roast position. The fish will not flake when done, but it should be white through the center.

Teriyaki Salmon

Prep time: 30 minutes | Cook time: 12 minutes | Serves 4

4 (6-ounce / 170-g) salmon fillets	½ cup soy sauce	brown sugar	1 teaspoon minced garlic
	¼ cup packed light	2 teaspoons rice vinegar	¼ teaspoon ground

ginger	½ teaspoon salt	ground black pepper
2 teaspoons olive oil	¼ teaspoon freshly	Oil, for spraying

1. Place the salmon in a small pan, skin-side up. 2. In a small bowl, whisk together the soy sauce, brown sugar, rice vinegar, garlic, ginger, olive oil, salt, and black pepper. 3. Pour the mixture over the salmon and marinate for about 30 minutes. 4. Select Roast, Air Fry Fan, set temperature to 400°F (204°C) and set time to 6 minutes. Press Start to begin preheating. Line the pizza rack with parchment and spray lightly with oil. Place the salmon on the prepared rack, skin-side down. You may need to work in batches. 5. Once preheated, place the pan on the roast position. Brush the salmon with more marinade, and cook for another 6 minutes, or until the internal temperature reaches 145°F (63°C). Serve immediately.

Catfish Bites

Prep time: 15 minutes | Cook time: 20 minutes | Serves 4

Oil, for spraying	1 cup buttermilk	2 teaspoons Creole seasoning
1 pound (454 g) catfish fillets, cut into 2-inch pieces	½ cup cornmeal	½ cup yellow mustard
	¼ cup all-purpose flour	

1. Line the pizza rack with parchment and spray lightly with oil. 2. Place the catfish pieces and buttermilk in a zip-top plastic bag, seal, and refrigerate for about 10 minutes. 3. Select Air Fry, set temperature to 400°F (204°C) and set time to 10 minutes. Press Start to begin preheating. 4. In a shallow bowl, mix together the cornmeal, flour, and Creole seasoning. 5. Remove the catfish from the bag and pat dry with a paper towel. 6. Spread the mustard on all sides of the catfish, then dip them in the cornmeal mixture until evenly coated. 7. Place the catfish on the prepared rack. You may need to work in batches. Spray lightly with oil. 8. Once preheated, place the rack on the air fry position. Flip carefully, spray with oil, and cook for another 10 minutes. Serve immediately.

Baked Grouper with Tomatoes and Garlic

Prep time: 5 minutes | Cook time: 12 minutes | Serves 4

4 grouper fillets	1 tomato, sliced	¼ cup fresh dill, roughly chopped	¼ cup olive oil
½ teaspoon salt	¼ cup sliced Kalamata olives		
3 garlic cloves, minced		Juice of 1 lemon	

1. Select Bake, Air Fry Fan, set temperature to 380°F (193°C) and set time to 10 to 12 minutes. Press Start to begin preheating. 2. Season the grouper fillets on all sides with salt, then place into the baking pan and top with the minced garlic, tomato slices, olives, and fresh dill. Drizzle the lemon juice and olive oil over the top of the grouper. 3. Once preheated, place the pan on the bake position. It will be done until the internal temperature reaches 145°F (63°C).

Parmesan Fish Fillets

Prep time: 8 minutes | Cook time: 17 minutes | Serves 4

⅓ cup grated Parmesan cheese	⅓ teaspoon mixed peppercorns	halved
½ teaspoon fennel seed	2 eggs, beaten	2 tablespoons dry white wine
½ teaspoon tarragon	4 (4-ounce / 113-g) fish fillets,	1 teaspoon seasoned salt

1. Select Bake, Air Fry Fan, set temperature to 345°F (174°C) and set time to 17 minutes. Press Start to begin preheating. 2. Place the grated Parmesan cheese, fennel seed, tarragon, and mixed peppercorns in a food processor

and pulse for about 20 seconds until well combined. Transfer the cheese mixture to a shallow dish. 3. Place the beaten eggs in another shallow dish. 4. Drizzle the dry white wine over the top of fish fillets. Dredge each fillet in the beaten eggs on both sides, shaking off any excess, then roll them in the cheese mixture until fully coated. Season with the salt. 5. Arrange the fillets on pizza rack. Once preheated, place the rack on the bake position. It will be done until the fish is cooked through and no longer translucent. Flip the fillets once halfway through the cooking time. 6. Cool for 5 minutes before serving.

Mouthwatering Cod over Creamy Leek Noodles

Prep time: 10 minutes | Cook time: 24 minutes | Serves 4

- 1 small leek, sliced into long thin noodles (about 2 cups)
- ½ cup heavy cream
- 2 cloves garlic, minced
- 1 teaspoon fine sea salt, divided
- 4 (4-ounce / 113-g) cod fillets (about 1 inch thick)
- ½ teaspoon ground black pepper

Coating:
- ¼ cup grated Parmesan cheese
- 2 tablespoons mayonnaise
- 2 tablespoons unsalted butter, softened
- 1 tablespoon chopped fresh thyme, or ½ teaspoon dried thyme leaves, plus more for garnish

1. Select Roast, Air Fry Fan, set temperature to 350°F (177°C) and set time to 10 minutes. Press Start to begin preheating. 2. Place the leek noodles in baking pan. 3. In a small bowl, stir together the cream, garlic, and ½ teaspoon of the salt. Pour the mixture over the leeks. Once preheated, place the pan on the roast position. The leeks will be very tender when done. 4. Pat the fish dry and season with the remaining ½ teaspoon of salt and the pepper. When the leeks are ready, open the air fryer oven and place the fish fillets on top of the leeks. Cook for 8 to 10 minutes, until the fish flakes easily with a fork (the thicker the fillets, the longer this will take). 5. While the fish cooks, make the coating: In a small bowl, combine the Parmesan, mayo, butter, and thyme. 6. When the fish is ready, remove it from the oven and increase the heat to 425°F (218°C) (or as high as your air fryer oven can go). Spread the fillets with a ½-inch-thick to ¾-inch-thick layer of the coating. 7. Place the fish back in the air fryer oven and cook for 3 to 4 minutes, until the coating browns. 8. Garnish with fresh or dried thyme, if desired. Store leftovers in an airtight container in the refrigerator for up to 3 days. Reheat in a casserole dish in a preheated 350°F (177°C) air fryer oven for 6 minutes, or until heated through.

Oregano Tilapia Fingers

Prep time: 15 minutes | Cook time: 9 minutes | Serves 4

- 1 pound (454 g) tilapia fillet
- ½ cup coconut flour
- 2 eggs, beaten
- ½ teaspoon ground paprika
- 1 teaspoon dried oregano
- 1 teaspoon avocado oil

1. Select Air Fry, set temperature to 370°F (188°C) and set time to 9 minutes. Press Start to begin preheating. 2. Cut the tilapia fillets into fingers and sprinkle with ground paprika and dried oregano. 3. Then dip the tilapia fingers in eggs and coat in the coconut flour. 4. Sprinkle fish fingers with avocado oil and transfer to baking pan. Once preheated, place the pan on the air fry position.

Stuffed Shrimp

Prep time: 20 minutes | Cook time: 12 minutes per batch | Serves 4

- 16 tail-on shrimp, peeled and deveined (last tail section intact)
- ¾ cup crushed panko bread crumbs
- Oil for misting or cooking spray

Stuffing:
- 2 (6-ounce / 170-g) cans lump crab meat
- 2 tablespoons chopped shallots

2 tablespoons chopped green onions

2 tablespoons chopped celery

2 tablespoons chopped green bell pepper

½ cup crushed saltine crackers

1 teaspoon Old Bay Seasoning

1 teaspoon garlic powder

¼ teaspoon ground thyme

2 teaspoons dried parsley flakes

2 teaspoons fresh lemon juice

2 teaspoons Worcestershire sauce

1 egg, beaten

1. Rinse shrimp. Remove tail section (shell) from 4 shrimp, discard, and chop the meat finely. 2. To prepare the remaining 12 shrimp, cut a deep slit down the back side so that the meat lies open flat. Do not cut all the way through. 3. Select Air Fry, set temperature to 360°F (182°C) and set time to 10 minutes. Press Start to begin preheating. 4. Place chopped shrimp in a large bowl with all of the stuffing ingredients and stir to combine. 5. Divide stuffing into 12 portions, about 2 tablespoons each. 6. Place one stuffing portion onto the back of each shrimp and form into a ball or oblong shape. Press firmly so that stuffing sticks together and adheres to shrimp. 7. Gently roll each stuffed shrimp in panko crumbs and mist with oil or cooking spray. Transfer to pizza rack. 8. Once preheated, place the rack on the air fry position. Mist with oil or spray and cook 2 minutes longer or until stuffing cooks through inside and is crispy outside. 9. Repeat step 8 to cook remaining shrimp.

BBQ Shrimp with Creole Butter Sauce

Prep time: 10 minutes | Cook time: 12 to 15 minutes | Serves 4

6 tablespoons unsalted butter

⅓ cup Worcestershire sauce

3 cloves garlic, minced

Juice of 1 lemon

1 teaspoon paprika

1 teaspoon Creole seasoning

1½ pounds (680 g) large uncooked shrimp, peeled and deveined

2 tablespoons fresh parsley

1. Select Air Fry, set temperature to 370°F (188°C) and set time to 12 to 15 minutes. Press Start to begin preheating. 2. In a large microwave-safe bowl, combine the butter, Worcestershire, and garlic. Microwave on high for 1 to 2 minutes until the butter is melted. Stir in the lemon juice, paprika, and Creole seasoning. Add the shrimp and toss until thoroughly coated. 3. Transfer the mixture to baking pan. Once preheated, place the pan on the air fry position. Pausing halfway through the cooking time to turn the shrimp. The shrimp will be cooked through when done. Top with the parsley just before serving.

Cayenne Flounder Cutlets

Prep time: 15 minutes | Cook time: 10 minutes | Serves 2

1 egg

1 cup Pecorino Romano cheese, grated

Sea salt and white pepper, to taste

½ teaspoon cayenne pepper

1 teaspoon dried parsley flakes

2 flounder fillets

1. Select Roast, Air Fry Fan, set temperature to 390°F (199°C) and set time to 5 minutes. Press Start to begin preheating. 2. To make a breading station, whisk the egg until frothy. 3. In another bowl, mix Pecorino Romano cheese, and spices. 4. Dip the fish in the egg mixture and turn to coat evenly; then, dredge in the cracker crumb mixture, turning a couple of times to coat evenly. Transfer to the pizza rack. 5. Once preheated, place the pan on the roast position. Turn them over and cook another 5 minutes. Enjoy!

Tortilla Shrimp Tacos

Prep time: 10 minutes | Cook time: 6 minutes | Serves 4

Spicy Mayo:
- 3 tablespoons mayonnaise
- 1 tablespoon Louisiana-style hot pepper sauce

Cilantro-Lime Slaw:
- 2 cups shredded green cabbage
- ½ small red onion, thinly sliced
- 1 small jalapeño, thinly sliced
- 2 tablespoons chopped fresh cilantro
- Juice of 1 lime
- ¼ teaspoon kosher salt

Shrimp:
- 1 large egg, beaten
- 1 cup crushed tortilla chips
- 24 jumbo shrimp (about 1 pound / 454 g), peeled and deveined
- ⅛ teaspoon kosher salt
- Cooking spray
- 8 corn tortillas, for serving

1. For the spicy mayo: In a small bowl, mix the mayonnaise and hot pepper sauce. 2. For the cilantro-lime slaw: In a large bowl, toss together the cabbage, onion, jalapeño, cilantro, lime juice, and salt to combine. Cover and refrigerate to chill. 3. For the shrimp: Place the egg in a shallow bowl and the crushed tortilla chips in another. Season the shrimp with the salt. Dip the shrimp in the egg, then in the crumbs, pressing gently to adhere. Place on a work surface and spray both sides with oil. 4. Select Air Fry, set temperature to 360°F (182°C) and set time to 6 minutes. Press Start to begin preheating. 5. Working in batches, arrange a single layer of the shrimp in the crisper tray. Once preheated, place the tray on the air fry position. Flip halfway, until golden and cooked through in the center. 6. To serve, place 2 tortillas on each plate and top each with 3 shrimp. Top each taco with ¼ cup slaw, then drizzle with spicy mayo.

Bang Bang Shrimp

Prep time: 15 minutes | Cook time: 14 minutes | Serves 4

Sauce:
- ½ cup mayonnaise
- ¼ cup sweet chili sauce
- 2 to 4 tablespoons Sriracha
- 1 teaspoon minced fresh ginger

Shrimp:
- 1 pound (454 g) jumbo raw shrimp (21 to 25 count), peeled and deveined
- 2 tablespoons cornstarch or rice flour
- ½ teaspoon kosher salt
- Vegetable oil spray

1. For the sauce: In a large bowl, combine the mayonnaise, chili sauce, Sriracha, and ginger. Stir until well combined. Remove half of the sauce to serve as a dipping sauce. 2. For the shrimp: Select Air Fry, set temperature to 350°F (177°C) and set time to 10 minutes. Press Start to begin preheating. Place the shrimp in a medium bowl. Sprinkle the cornstarch and salt over the shrimp and toss until well coated. 3. Place the shrimp in the crisper tray in a single layer. Spray generously with vegetable oil spray. Once preheated, place the tray on the air fry position. Turn and spray with additional oil spray halfway through the cooking time. 4. Remove the shrimp and toss in the bowl with half of the sauce. Place the shrimp back in the air fryer oven. Set the temperature to 350°F (177°C) for an additional 4 to 5 minutes, or until the sauce has formed a glaze. 5. Serve the hot shrimp with the reserved sauce for dipping.

Shrimp Kebabs

Prep time: 15 minutes | Cook time: 6 minutes | Serves 4

- Oil, for spraying
- 1 pound (454 g) medium raw shrimp, peeled and deveined
- 4 tablespoons unsalted butter, melted
- 1 tablespoon Old Bay seasoning
- 1 tablespoon packed light brown sugar
- 1 teaspoon granulated garlic
- 1 teaspoon onion powder
- ½ teaspoon freshly ground black pepper

1. Select Roast, Air Fry Fan, set temperature to 400°F (204°C) and set time to 5 to 6 minutes. Press Start to begin preheating. Line the pizza rack with parchment and spray lightly with oil. 2. Thread the shrimp onto the skewers and place them in the prepared rack. 3. In a small bowl, mix together the butter, Old Bay, brown sugar, garlic, onion powder, and black pepper. Brush the sauce on the shrimp. 4. Once preheated, place the tray on the roast position. It will be done until pink and firm. Serve immediately.

Golden Shrimp

Prep time: 20 minutes | Cook time: 7 minutes | Serves 4

2 egg whites
½ cup coconut flour
1 cup Parmigiano-Reggiano, grated
½ teaspoon celery seeds
½ teaspoon porcini powder
½ teaspoon onion powder
1 teaspoon garlic powder
½ teaspoon dried rosemary
½ teaspoon sea salt
½ teaspoon ground black pepper
1½ pounds (680 g) shrimp, deveined

1. Select Air Fry, set temperature to 390°F (199°C) and set time to 5 to 7 minutes. Press Start to begin preheating. 2. Whisk the egg with coconut flour and Parmigiano-Reggiano. Add in seasonings and mix to combine well. 3. Dip your shrimp in the batter. Roll until they are covered on all sides. Transfer to crisper tray. 4. Once preheated, place the tray on the air fry position. It will be done until golden brown. Serve with lemon wedges if desired.

Friday Night Fish Fry

Prep time: 10 minutes | Cook time: 10 minutes | Serves 4

1 large egg
½ cup powdered Parmesan cheese (about 1½ ounces / 43 g)
1 teaspoon smoked paprika
¼ teaspoon celery salt
¼ teaspoon ground black pepper
4 (4-ounce / 113-g) cod fillets
Chopped fresh oregano or parsley, for garnish (optional)
Lemon slices, for serving (optional)

1. Spray the pizza rack with avocado oil. Select Roast, Air Fry Fan, set temperature to 400°F (204°C) and set time to 10 minutes. Press Start to begin preheating. 2. Crack the egg in a shallow bowl and beat it lightly with a fork. Combine the Parmesan cheese, paprika, celery salt, and pepper in a separate shallow bowl. 3. One at a time, dip the fillets into the egg, then dredge them in the Parmesan mixture. Using your hands, press the Parmesan onto the fillets to form a nice crust. As you finish, place the fish on pizza rack. 4. Once preheated, place the rack on the roast position. It will be done until it is cooked through and flakes easily with a fork. Garnish with fresh oregano or parsley and serve with lemon slices, if desired. 5. Store leftovers in an airtight container in the refrigerator for up to 3 days. Reheat in a preheated 400°F (204°C) air fryer oven for 5 minutes, or until warmed through.

Quick Shrimp Skewers

Prep time: 10 minutes | Cook time: 5 minutes | Serves 5

4 pounds (1.8 kg) shrimp, peeled
1 tablespoon dried rosemary
1 tablespoon avocado oil
1 teaspoon apple cider vinegar

1. Select Roast, Air Fry Fan, set temperature to 400°F (204°C) and set time to 5 minutes. Press Start to begin preheating. 2. Mix the shrimps with dried rosemary, avocado oil, and apple cider vinegar. Then sting the shrimps into skewers and put in the pizza rack. 3. Once preheated, place the rack on the roast position.

Salmon Spring Rolls

Prep time: 20 minutes | Cook time: 8 to 10 minutes | Serves 4

- ½ pound (227 g) salmon fillet
- 1 teaspoon toasted sesame oil
- 1 onion, sliced
- 8 rice paper wrappers
- 1 yellow bell pepper, thinly sliced
- 1 carrot, shredded
- ⅓ cup chopped fresh flat-leaf parsley
- ¼ cup chopped fresh basil

1. Select Bake, Air Fry Fan, set temperature to 370°F (188°C) and set time to 8 to 10 minutes. Press Start to begin preheating. Put the salmon in the baking pan and drizzle with the sesame oil. Add the onion. Once preheated, place the pan on the bake position. It will be done until the salmon just flakes when tested with a fork and the onion is tender. 2. Meanwhile, fill a small shallow bowl with warm water. One at a time, dip the rice paper wrappers into the water and place on a work surface. 3. Top each wrapper with one-eighth each of the salmon and onion mixture, yellow bell pepper, carrot, parsley, and basil. Roll up the wrapper, folding in the sides, to enclose the ingredients. 4. If you like, bake in the air fryer oven at 380°F (193°C) for 7 to 9 minutes, until the rolls are crunchy. Cut the rolls in half to serve.

Crustless Shrimp Quiche

Prep time: 15 minutes | Cook time: 20 minutes | Serves 2

- Vegetable oil
- 4 large eggs
- ½ cup half-and-half
- 4 ounces (113 g) raw shrimp, chopped (about 1 cup)
- 1 cup shredded Parmesan or Swiss cheese
- ¼ cup chopped scallions
- 1 teaspoon sweet smoked paprika
- 1 teaspoon herbes de Provence
- 1 teaspoon black pepper
- ½ to 1 teaspoon kosher salt

1. Select Bake, Air Fry Fan, set temperature to 300°F (149°C) and set time to 20 minutes. Press Start to begin preheating. Generously grease a baking pan with vegetable oil. (Be sure to grease the pan well, the proteins in eggs stick something fierce. Alternatively, line the bottom of the pan with parchment paper cut to fit and spray the parchment and sides of the pan generously with vegetable oil spray.) 2. In a large bowl, beat together the eggs and half-and-half. Add the shrimp, ¾ cup of the cheese, the scallions, paprika, herbes de Provence, pepper, and salt. Stir with a fork to thoroughly combine. Pour the egg mixture into the prepared pan. 3. Once preheated, place the pan on the bake position. After 17 minutes, sprinkle the remaining ¼ cup cheese on top and cook for the remaining 3 minutes, or until the cheese has melted, the eggs are set, and a toothpick inserted into the center comes out clean. 4. Serve the quiche warm or at room temperature.

Tilapia Sandwiches with Tartar Sauce

Prep time: 8 minutes | Cook time: 17 minutes | Serves 4

- ¾ cup mayonnaise
- 2 tablespoons dried minced onion
- 1 dill pickle spear, finely chopped
- 2 teaspoons pickle juice
- ¼ teaspoon salt
- ⅛ teaspoon freshly ground black pepper
- ⅓ cup all-purpose flour
- 1 egg, lightly beaten
- 1¾ cups panko bread crumbs
- 2 teaspoons lemon pepper
- 4 (6-ounce / 170-g) tilapia fillets
- Olive oil spray
- 4 hoagie rolls
- 4 butter lettuce leaves

1. To make the tartar sauce, in a small bowl, whisk the mayonnaise, dried onion, pickle, pickle juice, salt, and pepper until blended. Refrigerate while you make the fish. 2. Scoop the flour onto a plate; set aside. 3. Put the beaten egg in a medium shallow bowl. 4. On another plate, stir together the panko and lemon pepper. 5. Select Air Fry, set

temperature to 400°F (204°C) and set time to 17 minutes. Press Start to begin preheating. 6. Dredge the tilapia fillets in the flour, in the egg, and press into the panko mixture to coat. 7. Once preheated, spray crisper tray with olive oil and place a parchment paper liner into the tray. Place the prepared fillets on the liner in a single layer. Lightly spray the fillets with olive oil. Place the tray on the air fry position. 8. After 8 minutes, remove the tray, carefully flip the fillets, and spray them with more olive oil. Place the tray back to resume cooking. 9. When the cooking is complete, the fillets should be golden and crispy and a food thermometer should register 145°F (63°C). Place each cooked fillet in a hoagie roll, top with a little bit of tartar sauce and lettuce, and serve.

Crab Cakes with Mango Mayo

Prep time: 25 minutes | Cook time: 15 minutes | Serves 4

Crab Cakes:
½ cup chopped red onion
½ cup fresh cilantro leaves
1 small serrano chile or jalapeño, seeded and quartered
½ pound (227 g) lump crab meat
1 large egg
1 tablespoon mayonnaise
1 tablespoon whole-grain mustard
2 teaspoons minced fresh ginger
½ teaspoon ground cumin
½ teaspoon ground coriander
¼ teaspoon kosher salt
2 tablespoons fresh lemon juice
1½ cups panko bread crumbs
Vegetable oil spray

Mango Mayo:
½ cup diced fresh mango
½ cup mayonnaise
½ teaspoon grated lime zest
2 teaspoons fresh lime juice
Pinch of cayenne pepper

1. For the crab cakes: Select Bake, Air Fry Fan, set temperature to 375°F (191°C) and set time to 15 minutes. Press Start to begin preheating. 2. Combine the onion, cilantro, and serrano in a food processor. Pulse until minced. 3. In a large bowl, combine the minced vegetable mixture with the crab meat, egg, mayonnaise, mustard, ginger, cumin, coriander, and salt. Add the lemon juice and mix gently until thoroughly combined. Add 1 cup of the bread crumbs. Mix gently again until well blended. 4. Form into four evenly sized patties. Put the remaining ½ cup bread crumbs in a shallow bowl and press both sides of each patty into the bread crumbs. 5. Arrange the patties on pizza rack. Spray with vegetable oil spray. Once preheated, place the rack on the bake position. Turn and spray other side of the patties with vegetable oil spray halfway through the cooking time. It will be done until the crab cakes are golden brown and crisp. 6. Meanwhile, for the mayonnaise: In a blender, combine the mango, mayonnaise, lime zest, lime juice, and cayenne. Blend until smooth. 7. Serve the crab cakes warm, with the mango mayo.

Sea Bass with Potato Scales

Prep time: 10 minutes | Cook time: 10 minutes | Serves 2

2 (6- to 8-ounce / 170- to 227-g) fillets of sea bass
Salt and freshly ground black pepper, to taste
¼ cup mayonnaise
2 teaspoons finely chopped lemon zest
1 teaspoon chopped fresh thyme
2 Fingerling potatoes, very thinly sliced into rounds
Olive oil
½ clove garlic, crushed into a paste
1 tablespoon capers, drained and rinsed
1 tablespoon olive oil
1 teaspoon lemon juice, to taste

1. Select Roast, Air Fry Fan, set temperature to 400°F (204°C) and set time to 8 to 10 minutes. Press Start to begin preheating. 2. Season the fish well with salt and freshly ground black pepper. Mix the mayonnaise, lemon zest and thyme together in a small bowl. Spread a thin layer of the mayonnaise mixture on both fillets. Start layering rows of potato slices onto the fish fillets to simulate the fish scales. The second row should overlap the first row slightly. Dabbing a little more mayonnaise along the upper edge of the row of potatoes where the next row overlaps will help

the potato slices stick. Press the potatoes onto the fish to secure them well and season again with salt. Brush or spray the potato layer with olive oil. 3. Transfer the fish to the pizza rack. Once preheated, place the rack on the roast position. 4. While the fish is cooking, add the garlic, capers, olive oil and lemon juice to the remaining mayonnaise mixture to make the caper aïoli. 5. Serve the fish warm with a dollop of the aïoli on top or on the side.

Tuna-Stuffed Quinoa Patties

Prep time: 10 minutes | Cook time: 15 minutes | Serves 4

12 ounces (340 g) quinoa	3 eggs	Kosher salt and pepper, to taste
4 slices white bread with crusts removed	10 ounces (283 g) tuna packed in olive oil, drained	1¼ cups panko bread crumbs
		Vegetable oil, for spraying
½ cup milk	2 to 3 lemons	Lemon wedges, for serving

1. Rinse the quinoa in a fine-mesh sieve until the water runs clear. Bring 4 cups of salted water to a boil. Add the quinoa, cover, and reduce heat to low. Simmer the quinoa covered until most of the water is absorbed and the quinoa is tender, 15 to 20 minutes. Drain and allow to cool to room temperature. Meanwhile, soak the bread in the milk. 2. Mix the drained quinoa with the soaked bread and 2 of the eggs in a large bowl and mix thoroughly. In a medium bowl, combine the tuna, the remaining egg, and the juice and zest of 1 of the lemons. Season well with salt and pepper. Spread the panko on a plate. 3. Scoop up approximately ½ cup of the quinoa mixture and flatten into a patty. Place a heaping tablespoon of the tuna mixture in the center of the patty and close the quinoa around the tuna. Flatten the patty slightly to create an oval-shaped croquette. Dredge both sides of the croquette in the panko. Repeat with the remaining quinoa and tuna. 4. Spray the crisper tray with oil to prevent sticking, and select Air Fry, set temperature to 400°F (204°C) and set time to 8 minutes. Press Start to begin preheating. Arrange 4 or 5 of the croquettes in the tray, taking care to avoid overcrowding. Spray the tops of the croquettes with oil. Once preheated, place the pan on the air fry position. It will be done until the top side is browned and crispy. Carefully turn the croquettes over and spray the second side with oil. Air fry until the second side is browned and crispy, another 7 minutes. Repeat with the remaining croquettes. 5. Serve the croquetas warm with plenty of lemon wedges for spritzing.

Trout Amandine with Lemon Butter Sauce

Prep time: 20 minutes | Cook time: 8 minutes | Serves 4

Trout Amandine:	4 (4-ounce / 113-g) trout fillets, or salmon fillets	lemon juice
⅔ cup toasted almonds		½ teaspoon Worcestershire sauce
⅓ cup grated Parmesan cheese	Cooking spray	½ teaspoon salt
1 teaspoon salt	**Lemon Butter Sauce:**	½ teaspoon freshly ground black pepper
½ teaspoon freshly ground black pepper	8 tablespoons (1 stick) butter, melted	
		¼ teaspoon hot sauce
2 tablespoons butter, melted	2 tablespoons freshly squeezed	

1. In a blender or food processor, pulse the almonds for 5 to 10 seconds until finely processed. Transfer to a shallow bowl and whisk in the Parmesan cheese, salt, and pepper. Place the melted butter in another shallow bowl. 2. One at a time, dip the fish in the melted butter, then the almond mixture, coating thoroughly. 3. Select Bake, Air Fry Fan, set temperature to 300°F (149°C) and set time to 4 minutes. Press Start to begin preheating. Line the pizza rack with parchment paper. 4. Place the coated fish on the parchment and spritz with oil. 5. Once preheated, place the rack on the bake position. Flip the fish, spritz it with oil, and bake for 4 minutes more until the fish flakes easily with a fork. 6.

In a small bowl, whisk the butter, lemon juice, Worcestershire sauce, salt, pepper, and hot sauce until blended. 7. Serve with the fish.

Baked Tilapia with Garlic Aioli

Prep time: 5 minutes | Cook time: 15 minutes | Serves 4

Tilapia:
- 4 tilapia fillets
- 1 tablespoon extra-virgin olive oil
- 1 teaspoon garlic powder
- 1 teaspoon paprika
- 1 teaspoon dried basil
- A pinch of lemon-pepper seasoning

Garlic Aioli:
- 2 garlic cloves, minced
- 1 tablespoon mayonnaise
- Juice of ½ lemon
- 1 teaspoon extra-virgin olive oil
- Salt and pepper, to taste

1. Select Bake, Air Fry Fan, set temperature to 400°F (204°C) and set time to 15 minutes. Press Start to begin preheating. 2. On a clean work surface, brush both sides of each fillet with the olive oil. Sprinkle with the garlic powder, paprika, basil, and lemon-pepper seasoning. 3. Place the fillets in the baking pan. Once preheated, place the pan on the bake position. Flip the fillets halfway through. It will be done until the fish flakes easily and is no longer translucent in the center. 4. Meanwhile, make the garlic aioli: Whisk together the garlic, mayo, lemon juice, olive oil, salt, and pepper in a small bowl until smooth. 5. Remove the fish from the basket and serve with the garlic aioli on the side.

Crab Legs

Prep time: 5 minutes | Cook time: 15 minutes | Serves 4

- ¼ cup salted butter, melted and divided
- 3 pounds (1.4 kg) crab legs
- ¼ teaspoon garlic powder
- Juice of ½ medium lemon

1. Select Air Fry, set temperature to 400°F (204°C) and set time to 15 minutes. Press Start to begin preheating. 2. In a large bowl, drizzle 2 tablespoons butter over crab legs. Place crab legs into the crisper tray. 3. Once preheated, place the tray on the air fry position. 4. Shake the tray to toss the crab legs halfway through the cooking time. 5. In a small bowl, mix remaining butter, garlic powder, and lemon juice. 6. To serve, crack open crab legs and remove meat. Dip in lemon butter.

Tex-Mex Salmon Bowl

Prep time: 15 minutes | Cook time: 9 to 14 minutes | Serves 4

- 12 ounces (340 g) salmon fillets, cut into 1½-inch cubes
- 1 red onion, chopped
- 1 jalapeño pepper, minced
- 1 red bell pepper, chopped
- ¼ cup low-sodium salsa
- 2 teaspoons peanut oil or safflower oil
- 2 tablespoons low-sodium tomato juice
- 1 teaspoon chili powder

1. Select Bake, Air Fry Fan, set temperature to 370°F (188°C) and set time to 9 to 14 minutes. Press Start to begin preheating. 2. Mix together the salmon cubes, red onion, jalapeño, red bell pepper, salsa, peanut oil, tomato juice, chili powder in a medium metal bowl and stir until well incorporated. 3. Once preheated, place the bowl on the bake position. Stir once. It will be done until the salmon is cooked through and the veggies are fork-tender. 4. Serve warm.

Chapter 6 Snacks and Appetizers

Lemony Endive in Curried Yogurt

Prep time: 5 minutes | Cook time: 10 minutes | Serves 6

6 heads endive
½ cup plain and fat-free yogurt
3 tablespoons lemon juice
1 teaspoon garlic powder
½ teaspoon curry powder
Salt and ground black pepper, to taste

1. Wash the endives, and slice them in half lengthwise. 2. In a bowl, mix together the yogurt, lemon juice, garlic powder, curry powder, salt and pepper. 3. Brush the endive halves with the marinade, coating them completely. Allow to sit for at least 30 minutes or up to 24 hours. 4. Select Bake, Air Fry Fan, set temperature to 320°F (160°C) and set time to 10 minutes. Press Start to begin preheating. 5. Put the endives in the baking pan on bake position. 6. Serve hot.

Greek Yogurt Deviled Eggs

Prep time: 15 minutes | Cook time: 15 minutes | Serves 4

4 eggs
¼ cup nonfat plain Greek yogurt
1 teaspoon chopped fresh dill
⅛ teaspoon salt
⅛ teaspoon paprika
⅛ teaspoon garlic powder
Chopped fresh parsley, for garnish

1. Select Broil, set temperature to 260°F (127°C) and set time to 15 minutes. Press Start to begin preheating. 2. Place the eggs in a single layer in the pizza rack. Once preheated, place the rack on the broil position. 3. Quickly remove the eggs from the oven and place them into a cold water bath. Let the eggs cool in the water for 10 minutes before removing and peeling them. 4. After peeling the eggs, cut them in half. 5. Spoon the yolk into a small bowl. Add the yogurt, dill, salt, paprika, and garlic powder and mix until smooth. 6. Spoon or pipe the yolk mixture into the halved egg whites. Serve with a sprinkle of fresh parsley on top.

Homemade Sweet Potato Chips

Prep time: 5 minutes | Cook time: 15 minutes | Serves 2

1 large sweet potato, sliced thin
⅛ teaspoon salt
2 tablespoons olive oil

1. Select Air Fry, set temperature to 380°F (193°C) and set time to 10 minutes. Press Start to begin preheating. 2. In a small bowl, toss the sweet potatoes, salt, and olive oil together until the potatoes are well coated. 3. Once preheated, put the sweet potato slices into the crisper tray on air fry position and spread them out in a single layer. 4. Stir, then air fry for 3 to 5 minutes more, or until the chips reach the preferred level of crispiness.

Five-Ingredient Falafel with Garlic-Yogurt Sauce

Prep time: 5 minutes | Cook time: 15 minutes | Serves 4

For the falafel
1 (15-ounce) can chickpeas, drained and rinsed
½ cup fresh parsley
2 garlic cloves, minced
½ tablespoon ground cumin
1 tablespoon whole wheat flour
Salt
For the garlic-yogurt sauce
1 cup nonfat plain Greek yogurt
1 garlic clove, minced
1 tablespoon chopped fresh dill
2 tablespoons lemon juice

To make the falafel 1. Select Bake, Air Fry Fan, set temperature to 360°F (182°C) and set time to 15 minutes. Press Start to begin preheating. 2. Put the chickpeas into a food processor. Pulse until mostly chopped, then add the parsley, garlic, and cumin and pulse for another 1 to 2 minutes, or until the ingredients are combined and turning into a dough. 3. Add the flour. Pulse a few more times until combined. The dough will have texture, but the chickpeas should be pulsed into small bits. 4. Using clean hands, roll the dough into 8 balls of equal size, then pat the balls down a bit so they are about ½-thick disks. 5. Spray the baking pan with olive oil cooking spray, then place the falafel patties in the pan in a single layer, making sure they don't touch each other. 6. Once preheated, place the pan on the bake position. To make the garlic-yogurt sauce 7. In a small bowl, combine the yogurt, garlic, dill, and lemon juice. 8. Once the falafel are done cooking and nicely browned on all sides, remove them from the air fryer oven and season with salt. 9. Serve hot with a side of dipping sauce.

Pork and Cabbage Egg Rolls

Prep time: 15 minutes | Cook time: 12 minutes | Makes 12 egg rolls

Cooking oil spray
2 garlic cloves, minced
12 ounces (340 g) ground pork
1 teaspoon sesame oil
¼ cup soy sauce
2 teaspoons grated peeled fresh ginger
2 cups shredded green cabbage
4 scallions, green parts (white parts optional), chopped
24 egg roll wrappers

1. Spray a skillet with the cooking oil and place it over medium-high heat. Add the garlic and cook for 1 minute until fragrant. 2. Add the ground pork to the skillet. Using a spoon, break the pork into smaller chunks. 3. In a small bowl, whisk the sesame oil, soy sauce, and ginger until combined. Add the sauce to the skillet. Stir to combine and continue cooking for about 5 minutes until the pork is browned and thoroughly cooked. 4. Stir in the cabbage and scallions. Transfer the pork mixture to a large bowl. 5. Lay the egg roll wrappers on a flat surface. Dip a basting brush in water and glaze each egg roll wrapper along the edges with the wet brush. This will soften the dough and make it easier to roll. 6. Stack 2 egg roll wrappers (it works best if you double-wrap the egg rolls). Scoop 1 to 2 tablespoons of the pork mixture into the center of each wrapper stack. 7. Roll one long side of the wrappers up over the filling. Press firmly on the area with the filling, tucking it in lightly to secure it in place. Fold in the left and right sides. Continue rolling to close. Use the basting brush to wet the seam and seal the egg roll. Repeat with the remaining ingredients. 8. Select Air Fry, set temperature to 400°F (204°C) and set time to 12 minutes. Press Start to begin preheating. 9. Spray the crisper tray with cooking oil. Place the egg rolls into the tray. It is okay to stack them. Spray them with cooking oil. 10. Once preheated, place the pan on the air fry position. 11. After 8 minutes, use tongs to flip the egg rolls. Reinsert the tray to resume cooking. 12. When the cooking is complete, serve the egg rolls hot.

Old Bay Chicken Wings

Prep time: 10 minutes | Cook time: 12 to 15 minutes | Serves 4

2 tablespoons Old Bay seasoning
2 teaspoons baking powder
2 teaspoons salt
2 pounds (907 g) chicken wings, patted dry
Cooking spray

1. Select Air Fry, set temperature to 400°F (204°C) and set time to 12 to 15 minutes. Press Start to begin preheating. Lightly spray the pizza rack basket with cooking spray. 2. Combine the Old Bay seasoning, baking powder, and salt in a large zip-top plastic bag. Add the chicken wings, seal, and shake until the wings are thoroughly coated in the seasoning mixture. 3. Lay the chicken wings in the rack in a single layer and lightly mist with cooking spray. You may need to work in batches to avoid overcrowding. 4. Once preheated, place the rack on the air fry position. Flip the

wings halfway through, or until the wings are lightly browned and the internal temperature reaches at least 165°F (74°C) on a meat thermometer. 5. Remove from the oven to a plate and repeat with the remaining chicken wings. 6. Serve hot.

Garlic-Roasted Tomatoes and Olives

Prep time: 5 minutes | Cook time: 20 minutes | Serves 6

2 cups cherry tomatoes	1 cup black olives	1 tablespoon fresh oregano, minced
4 garlic cloves, roughly chopped	1 cup green olives	2 tablespoons olive oil
½ red onion, roughly chopped	1 tablespoon fresh basil, minced	¼ to ½ teaspoon salt

1. Select Roast, Air Fry Fan, set temperature to 380°F (193°C) and set time to 10 minutes. Press Start to begin preheating. 2. In a large bowl, combine all of the ingredients and toss together so that the tomatoes and olives are coated well with the olive oil and herbs. 3. Once preheated, pour the mixture into the baking pan on the roast position. Stir the mixture well, then continue roasting for an additional 10 minutes. 4. Remove from the oven, transfer to a serving bowl, and enjoy.

Honey-Mustard Chicken Wings

Prep time: 10 minutes | Cook time: 24 minutes | Serves 2

2 pounds (907 g) chicken wings	2 tablespoons butter	Pinch ground cayenne pepper
Salt and freshly ground black pepper, to taste	¼ cup honey	2 teaspoons Worcestershire sauce
	¼ cup spicy brown mustard	

1. Prepare the chicken wings by cutting off the wing tips and discarding (or freezing for chicken stock). Divide the drumettes from the wingettes by cutting through the joint. Place the chicken wing pieces in a large bowl. 2. Select Roast, Air Fry Fan, set temperature to 400°F (204°C) and set time to 10 minutes. Press Start to begin preheating. 3. Season the wings with salt and freshly ground black pepper on pizza rack. Once preheated, place the rack on the roast position. You may need to work in two batches. Shake the rack half way through the cooking process. 4. While the wings are air frying, combine the remaining ingredients in a small saucepan over low heat. 5. When both batches are done, toss all the wings with the honey-mustard sauce and toss them all back into the oven for another 4 minutes to heat through and finish cooking. Remove the wings from the air fryer oven and serve.

Egg Roll Pizza Sticks

Prep time: 10 minutes | Cook time: 5 minutes | Serves 4

Olive oil	8 egg roll wrappers	Marinara sauce, for dipping
8 pieces reduced-fat string cheese	24 slices turkey pepperoni	(optional)

1. Select Bake, Air Fry Fan, set temperature to 375°F (191°C) and set time to 5 minutes. Press Start to begin preheating. Spray the crisper tray lightly with olive oil. Fill a small bowl with water. 2. Place each egg roll wrapper diagonally on a work surface. It should look like a diamond. 3. Place 3 slices of turkey pepperoni in a vertical line down the center of the wrapper. 4. Place 1 Mozzarella cheese stick on top of the turkey pepperoni. 5. Fold the top and bottom corners of the egg roll wrapper over the cheese stick. 6. Fold the left corner over the cheese stick and roll the cheese stick up to resemble a spring roll. Dip a finger in the water and seal the edge of the roll 7. Repeat with the rest of the pizza sticks. 8. Place them in the tray in a single layer, making sure to leave a little space between each one. Lightly spray the pizza sticks with oil. You may need to cook these in batches. 9. Once preheated, place the tray on the

bake position. It will be done until the pizza sticks are lightly browned and crispy. 10. These are best served hot while the cheese is melted. Accompany with a small bowl of marinara sauce, if desired.

Cream Cheese Wontons

Prep time: 15 minutes | Cook time: 6 minutes | Makes 20 wontons

Oil, for spraying

20 wonton wrappers

4 ounces (113 g) cream cheese

1. Select Air Fry, set temperature to 400°F (204°C) and set time to 6 minutes. Press Start to begin preheating. Line the crisper tray with parchment and spray lightly with oil. 2. Pour some water in a small bowl. 3. Lay out a wonton wrapper and place 1 teaspoon of cream cheese in the center. 4. Dip your finger in the water and moisten the edge of the wonton wrapper. Fold over the opposite corners to make a triangle and press the edges together. 5. Pinch the corners of the triangle together to form a classic wonton shape. Place the wonton in the prepared tray. Repeat with the remaining wrappers and cream cheese. You may need to work in batches. 6. Once preheated, place the tray on the air fry position. It will be done until golden brown around the edges.

Golden Onion Rings

Prep time: 15 minutes | Cook time: 14 minutes per batch | Serves 4

1 large white onion, peeled and cut into ½ to ¾-inch-thick slices (about 2 cups)

½ cup 2% milk

1 cup whole-wheat pastry flour, or all-purpose flour

2 tablespoons cornstarch

¾ teaspoon sea salt, divided

½ teaspoon freshly ground black pepper, divided

¾ teaspoon granulated garlic, divided

1½ cups whole-grain bread crumbs, or gluten-free bread crumbs

Cooking oil spray (coconut, sunflower, or safflower)

Ketchup, for serving (optional)

1. Carefully separate the onion slices into rings—a gentle touch is important here. 2. Place the milk in a shallow bowl and set aside. 3. Make the first breading: In a medium bowl, stir together the flour, cornstarch, ¼ teaspoon of salt, ¼ teaspoon of pepper, and ¼ teaspoon of granulated garlic. Set aside. 4. Make the second breading: In a separate medium bowl, stir together the bread crumbs with the remaining ½ teaspoon of salt, the remaining ½ teaspoon of garlic, and the remaining ½ teaspoon of pepper. Set aside. 5. Select Air Fry, set temperature to 390°F (199°C) and set time to 14 minutes. Press Start to begin preheating. 6. Spray the crisper tray with cooking oil. 7. To make the onion rings, dip one ring into the milk and into the first breading mixture. Dip the ring into the milk again and back into the first breading mixture, coating thoroughly. Dip the ring into the milk one last time and then into the second breading mixture, coating thoroughly. Gently lay the onion ring in the basket. Repeat with additional rings and, as you place them into the basket, do not overlap them too much. Once all the onion rings are in the tray, generously spray the tops with cooking oil. 8. Once preheated, place the tray on the air fry position. 9. After 4 minutes, open the unit and spray the rings generously with cooking oil. Close the unit to resume cooking. After 3 minutes, remove the tray and spray the onion rings again. Remove the rings, turn them over, and place them back into the tray. Generously spray them again with oil. Put the tray back to resume cooking. After 4 minutes, generously spray the rings with oil one last time. Resume cooking for the remaining 3 minutes, or until the onion rings are very crunchy and brown. 10. When the cooking is complete, serve the hot rings with ketchup, or other sauce of choice.

Spinach and Crab Meat Cups

Prep time: 10 minutes | Cook time: 10 minutes | Makes 30 cups

1 (6-ounce / 170-g) can crab meat,

drained to yield ⅓ cup meat

¼ cup frozen spinach, thawed,

drained, and chopped	3 tablespoons plain yogurt	30 mini frozen phyllo shells,
1 clove garlic, minced	¼ teaspoon lemon juice	thawed
½ cup grated Parmesan cheese	½ teaspoon Worcestershire sauce	Cooking spray

1. Select Bake, Air Fry Fan, set temperature to 390°F (199°C) and set time to 5 minutes. Press Start to begin preheating. 2. Remove any bits of shell that might remain in the crab meat. 3. Mix the crab meat, spinach, garlic, and cheese together. 4. Stir in the yogurt, lemon juice, and Worcestershire sauce and mix well. 5. Spoon a teaspoon of filling into each phyllo shell. 6. Spray the baking pan with cooking spray and arrange half the shells in the pan. Once preheated, place the pan on the bake position. Repeat with the remaining shells. 7. Serve immediately.

Garlic Edamame

Prep time: 5 minutes | Cook time: 10 minutes | Serves 4

Olive oil	½ teaspoon salt	pepper
1 (16-ounce / 454-g) bag frozen	½ teaspoon garlic salt	½ teaspoon red pepper flakes
edamame in pods	¼ teaspoon freshly ground black	(optional)

1. Select Roast, Air Fry Fan, set temperature to 375°F (191°C) and set time to 5 minutes. Press Start to begin preheating. Spray the baking pan lightly with olive oil. 2. In a medium bowl, add the frozen edamame and lightly spray with olive oil. Toss to coat. 3. In a small bowl, mix together the salt, garlic salt, black pepper, and red pepper flakes (if using). Add the mixture to the edamame and toss until evenly coated. 4. Place half the edamame in the pan. Do not overfill the pan. 5. Once preheated, place the pan on the roast position. Shake the pan and cook until the edamame is starting to brown and get crispy, 3 to 5 more minutes. 6. Repeat with the remaining edamame and serve immediately.

Artichoke and Olive Pita Flatbread

Prep time: 5 minutes | Cook time: 10 minutes | Serves 4

2 whole wheat pitas	½ cup canned artichoke hearts,	¼ cup crumbled feta
2 tablespoons olive oil, divided	sliced	Chopped fresh parsley, for garnish
2 garlic cloves, minced	¼ cup Kalamata olives	(optional)
¼ teaspoon salt	¼ cup shredded Parmesan	

1. Select Bake, Air Fry Fan, set temperature to 380°F (193°C) and set time to 10 minutes. Press Start to begin preheating. 2. Brush each pita with 1 tablespoon olive oil, then sprinkle the minced garlic and salt over the top. 3. Distribute the artichoke hearts, olives, and cheeses evenly between the two pitas, and place both into the baking pan. 4. Once preheated, place the pan on the bake position. Remove the pitas and cut them into 4 pieces each before serving. Sprinkle parsley over the top, if desired.

Cheesy Steak Fries

Prep time: 5 minutes | Cook time: 20 minutes | Serves 5

1 (28-ounce / 794-g) bag frozen	Salt and pepper, to taste	2 scallions, green parts only,
steak fries	½ cup beef gravy	chopped
Cooking spray	1 cup shredded Mozzarella cheese	

1. Select Air Fry, set temperature to 400°F (204°C) and set time to 10 minutes. Press Start to begin preheating. 2.

Place the frozen steak fries in the crisper tray. Once preheated, place the tray on the air fry position. Shake the tray and spritz the fries with cooking spray. Sprinkle with salt and pepper. Air fry for an additional 8 minutes. 3. Pour the beef gravy into a medium, microwave-safe bowl. Microwave for 30 seconds, or until the gravy is warm. 4. Sprinkle the fries with the cheese. Air fry for an additional 2 minutes, until the cheese is melted. 5. Transfer the fries to a serving dish. Drizzle the fries with gravy and sprinkle the scallions on top for a green garnish. Serve.

String Bean Fries

Prep time: 15 minutes | Cook time: 5 to 6 minutes | Serves 4

- ½ pound (227 g) fresh string beans
- 2 eggs
- 4 teaspoons water
- ½ cup white flour
- ½ cup bread crumbs
- ¼ teaspoon salt
- ¼ teaspoon ground black pepper
- ¼ teaspoon dry mustard (optional)
- Oil for misting or cooking spray

1. Select Air Fry, set temperature to 360°F (182°C) and set time to 3 minutes. Press Start to begin preheating. 2. Trim stem ends from string beans, wash, and pat dry. 3. In a shallow dish, beat eggs and water together until well blended. 4. Place flour in a second shallow dish. 5. In a third shallow dish, stir together the bread crumbs, salt, pepper, and dry mustard if using. 6. Dip each string bean in egg mixture, flour, egg mixture again, then bread crumbs. 7. When you finish coating all the string beans, place them in crisper tray. 8. Once preheated, place the tray on the air fry position. 9. Stop and mist string beans with oil or cooking spray. 10. Cook for 2 to 3 more minutes or until string beans are crispy and nicely browned.

Mexican Potato Skins

Prep time: 10 minutes | Cook time: 55 minutes | Serves 6

- Olive oil
- 6 medium russet potatoes, scrubbed
- Salt and freshly ground black pepper, to taste
- 1 cup fat-free refried black beans
- 1 tablespoon taco seasoning
- ½ cup salsa
- ¾ cup reduced-fat shredded Cheddar cheese

1. Select Bake, Air Fry Fan, set temperature to 400°F (204°C) and set time to 30 to 40 minutes. Press Start to begin preheating. Spray the baking pan lightly with olive oil. 2. Spray the potatoes lightly with oil and season with salt and pepper. Pierce each potato a few times with a fork. 3. Place the potatoes in the pan. Once preheated, place the pan on the bake position. 4. While the potatoes are cooking, in a small bowl, mix together the beans and taco seasoning. Set aside until the potatoes are cool enough to handle. 5. Cut each potato in half lengthwise. Scoop out most of the insides, leaving about ¼ inch in the skins so the potato skins hold their shape. 6. Season the insides of the potato skins with salt and black pepper. Lightly spray the insides of the potato skins with oil. You may need to cook them in batches. 7. Place them into the baking pan, skin-side down, and bake until crisp and golden, 8 to 10 minutes. 8. Transfer the skins to a work surface and spoon ½ tablespoon of seasoned refried black beans into each one. Top each with 2 teaspoons salsa and 1 tablespoon shredded Cheddar cheese. 9. Place filled potato skins in the pan in a single layer. Lightly spray with oil. 10. Bake until the cheese is melted and bubbly, 2 to 3 minutes.

Cheese Wafers

Prep time: 30 minutes | Cook time: 5 to 6 minutes per batch | Makes 4 dozen

- 4 ounces (113 g) sharp Cheddar cheese, grated
- ¼ cup butter
- ½ cup flour
- ¼ teaspoon salt
- ½ cup crisp rice cereal
- Oil for misting or cooking spray

1. Cream the butter and grated cheese together. You can do it by hand, but using a stand mixer is faster and easier. 2.

Sift flour and salt together. Add it to the cheese mixture and mix until well blended. 3. Stir in cereal. 4. Place dough on wax paper and shape into a long roll about 1 inch in diameter. Wrap well with the wax paper and chill for at least 4 hours. 5. When ready to cook, Select Bake, Air Fry Fan, set temperature to 360°F (182°C) and set time to 5 to 6 minutes. Press Start to begin preheating. 6. Cut cheese roll into ¼-inch slices. 7. Spray the baking pan with oil or cooking spray and place slices in a single layer, close but not touching. 8. Once preheated, place the pan on the bake position. It will be done until golden brown. When done, place them on paper towels to cool. 9. Repeat previous step to cook remaining cheese bites.

Asian Five-Spice Wings

Prep time: 30 minutes | Cook time: 13 to 15 minutes | Serves 4

- 2 pounds (907 g) chicken wings
- ½ cup Asian-style salad dressing
- 2 tablespoons Chinese five-spice powder

1. Cut off wing tips and discard or freeze for stock. Cut remaining wing pieces in two at the joint. 2. Place wing pieces in a large sealable plastic bag. Pour in the Asian dressing, seal bag, and massage the marinade into the wings until well coated. Refrigerate for at least an hour. 3. Select Air Fry, set temperature to 360°F (182°C) and set time to 13 to 15 minutes. Press Start to begin preheating. Remove wings from bag, drain off excess marinade, and place wings in pizza rack. 4. Once preheated, place the rack on the air fry position. It will be done until juices run clear. About halfway through cooking time, shake the rack or stir wings for more even cooking. 5. Transfer cooked wings to plate in a single layer. Sprinkle half of the Chinese five-spice powder on the wings, turn, and sprinkle other side with remaining seasoning.

Asiago Shishito Peppers

Prep time: 5 minutes | Cook time: 10 minutes | Serves 4

- Oil, for spraying
- 6 ounces (170 g) shishito peppers
- 1 tablespoon olive oil
- ½ teaspoon salt
- ½ teaspoon lemon pepper
- ⅓ cup grated Asiago cheese, divided

1. Select Roast, Air Fry Fan, set temperature to 350°F (177°C) and set time to 10 minutes. Press Start to begin preheating. Line the baking pan with parchment and spray lightly with oil. 2. Rinse the shishitos and pat dry with paper towels. 3. In a large bowl, mix together the shishitos, olive oil, salt, and lemon pepper. Place the shishitos in the prepared pan. 4. Once preheated, place the pan on the roast position. It will be done until blistered but not burned. 5. Sprinkle with half of the cheese and cook for 1 more minute. 6. Transfer to a serving plate. Immediately sprinkle with the remaining cheese and serve.

Spiced Nuts

Prep time: 5 minutes | Cook time: 25 minutes | Makes 3 cups

- 1 egg white, lightly beaten
- ¼ cup sugar
- 1 teaspoon salt
- ½ teaspoon ground cinnamon
- ¼ teaspoon ground cloves
- ¼ teaspoon ground allspice
- Pinch ground cayenne pepper
- 1 cup pecan halves
- 1 cup cashews
- 1 cup almonds

1. Combine the egg white with the sugar and spices in a bowl. 2. Select Bake, Air Fry Fan, set temperature to 300°F (149°C) and set time to 25 minutes. Press Start to begin preheating. 3. Spray or brush the crisper tray with vegetable

oil. Toss the nuts together in the spiced egg white and transfer the nuts to the tray. 4. Once preheated, place the tray on the bake position. Stir the nuts in the tray a few times during the cooking process. Taste the nuts (carefully because they will be very hot) to see if they are crunchy and nicely toasted. Cook for a few more minutes if necessary. 5. Serve warm or cool to room temperature and store in an airtight container for up to two weeks.

Ranch Oyster Snack Crackers

Prep time: 3 minutes | Cook time: 12 minutes | Serves 6

Oil, for spraying	seasoning	½ teaspoon granulated garlic	1 (9-ounce / 255-g) bag oyster crackers
¼ cup olive oil	1 teaspoon chili powder		
2 teaspoons dry ranch	½ teaspoon dried dill	½ teaspoon salt	

1. Select Air Fry, set temperature to 325°F (163°C) and set time to 10 to 12 minutes. Press Start to begin preheating. Line the crisper tray with parchment and spray lightly with oil. 2. In a large bowl, mix together the olive oil, ranch seasoning, chili powder, dill, garlic, and salt. Add the crackers and toss until evenly coated. 3. Place the mixture in the prepared tray. 4. Once preheated, place the tray on the air fry position. Shake or stirring every 3 to 4 minutes, or until crisp and golden brown.

Shishito Peppers with Herb Dressing

Prep time: 10 minutes | Cook time: 6 minutes | Serves 2 to 4

6 ounces (170 g) shishito peppers	1 tablespoon finely chopped fresh tarragon
1 tablespoon vegetable oil	1 tablespoon finely chopped fresh chives
Kosher salt and freshly ground black pepper, to taste	Finely grated zest of ½ lemon
½ cup mayonnaise	1 tablespoon fresh lemon juice
2 tablespoons finely chopped fresh basil leaves	Flaky sea salt, for serving
2 tablespoons finely chopped fresh flat-leaf parsley	

1. Select Roast, Air Fry Fan, set temperature to 400°F (204°C) and set time to 6 minutes. Press Start to begin preheating. 2. In a bowl, toss together the shishitos and oil to evenly coat and season with kosher salt and black pepper. Transfer to the baking pan. Once preheated, place the pan on the roast position. Shake the basket halfway through. It will be done until the shishitos are blistered and lightly charred. 3. Meanwhile, in a small bowl, whisk together the mayonnaise, basil, parsley, tarragon, chives, lemon zest, and lemon juice. 4. Pile the peppers on a plate, sprinkle with flaky sea salt, and serve hot with the dressing.

Grilled Ham and Cheese on Raisin Bread

Prep time: 5 minutes | Cook time: 10 minutes | Serves 1

2 slices raisin bread	3 slices thinly sliced honey ham (about 3 ounces / 85 g)
2 tablespoons butter, softened	4 slices Muenster cheese (about 3 ounces / 85 g)
2 teaspoons honey mustard	2 toothpicks

1. Select Pizza, Air Fry Fan, set temperature to 370°F (188°C) and set time to 5 minutes. Press Start to begin preheating. 2. Spread the softened butter on one side of both slices of raisin bread and place the bread, buttered side down on the counter. Spread the honey mustard on the other side of each slice of bread. Layer 2 slices of cheese, the ham and the remaining 2 slices of cheese on one slice of bread and top with the other slice of bread. Remember to leave the buttered side of the bread on the outside. 3. Transfer the sandwich to the pizza rack and secure the sandwich

with toothpicks. 4. Once preheated, place the rack on the pizza position. Flip the sandwich over, remove the toothpicks and cook for another 5 minutes. Cut the sandwich in half and enjoy!

Carrot Chips

Prep time: 15 minutes | Cook time: 8 to 10 minutes | Serves 4

1 tablespoon olive oil, plus more for greasing the basket

1 teaspoon seasoned salt

4 to 5 medium carrots, trimmed and thinly sliced

1. Select Air Fry, set temperature to 390°F (199°C) and set time to 8 to 10 minutes. Press Start to begin preheating. Grease the crisper tray with the olive oil. 2. Toss the carrot slices with 1 tablespoon of olive oil and salt in a medium bowl until thoroughly coated. 3. Arrange the carrot slices in the greased tray. You may need to work in batches to avoid overcrowding. 4. Once preheated, place the tray on the air fry position. It will be done until the carrot slices are crisp-tender. Shake the tray once during cooking. 5. Transfer the carrot slices to a bowl and repeat with the remaining carrots. 6. Allow to cool for 5 minutes and serve.

Sausage Balls with Cheese

Prep time: 10 minutes | Cook time: 10 to 11 minutes | Serves 8

12 ounces (340 g) mild ground sausage

3 ounces (85 g) cream cheese, at room temperature

1½ cups baking mix

1 to 2 tablespoons olive oil

1 cup shredded mild Cheddar cheese

1. Select Bake, Air Fry Fan, set temperature to 325°F (163°C) and set time to 10 to 11 minutes. Press Start to begin preheating. Line the baking pan with parchment paper. 2. Mix together the ground sausage, baking mix, Cheddar cheese, and cream cheese in a large bowl and stir to incorporate. 3. Divide the sausage mixture into 16 equal portions and roll them into 1-inch balls with your hands. 4. Arrange the sausage balls on the parchment, leaving space between each ball. You may need to work in batches to avoid overcrowding. 5. Brush the sausage balls with the olive oil. Once preheated, place the pan on the bake position. Shake the pan halfway through, or until the balls are firm and lightly browned on both sides. 6. Remove from the oven to a plate and repeat with the remaining balls. 7. Serve warm.

Rosemary-Garlic Shoestring Fries

Prep time: 5 minutes | Cook time: 18 minutes | Serves 2

1 large russet potato (about 12 ounces / 340 g), scrubbed clean, and julienned

1 tablespoon vegetable oil

Leaves from 1 sprig fresh rosemary

Kosher salt and freshly ground

black pepper, to taste

1 garlic clove, thinly sliced

Flaky sea salt, for serving

1. Select Air Fry, set temperature to 400°F (204°C) and set time to 18 minutes. Press Start to begin preheating. 2. Place the julienned potatoes in a large colander and rinse under cold running water until the water runs clear. Spread the potatoes out on a double-thick layer of paper towels and pat dry. 3. In a large bowl, combine the potatoes, oil, and rosemary. Season with kosher salt and pepper and toss to coat evenly. Place the potatoes in the crisper tray. Once preheated, place the tray on the air fry position. Shake the tray every 5 minutes and adding the garlic in the last 5 minutes of cooking, or until the fries are golden brown and crisp. 4. Transfer the fries to a plate and sprinkle with flaky sea salt while they're hot. Serve immediately.

Dark Chocolate and Cranberry Granola Bars

Prep time: 5 minutes | Cook time: 15 minutes | Serves 6

2 cups certified gluten-free quick oats

2 tablespoons sugar-free dark chocolate chunks

2 tablespoons unsweetened dried cranberries

3 tablespoons unsweetened shredded coconut

½ cup raw honey

1 teaspoon ground cinnamon

⅛ teaspoon salt

2 tablespoons olive oil

1. Select Bake, Air Fry Fan, set temperature to 360°F (182°C) and set time to 15 minutes. Press Start to begin preheating. Line a baking pan with parchment paper that comes up the side so you can lift it out after cooking. 2. In a large bowl, mix together all of the ingredients until well combined. 3. Press the oat mixture into the pan in an even layer. 4. Once preheated, place the pan on the bake position. 5. Remove the pan, and lift the granola cake out of the pan using the edges of the parchment paper. 6. Allow to cool for 5 minutes before slicing into 6 equal bars. 7. Serve immediately, or wrap in plastic wrap and store at room temperature for up to 1 week.

Onion Pakoras

Prep time: 30 minutes | Cook time: 10 minutes per batch | Serves 2

2 medium yellow or white onions, sliced (2 cups)

½ cup chopped fresh cilantro

2 tablespoons vegetable oil

1 tablespoon chickpea flour

1 tablespoon rice flour, or 2 tablespoons chickpea flour

1 teaspoon ground turmeric

1 teaspoon cumin seeds

1 teaspoon kosher salt

½ teaspoon cayenne pepper

Vegetable oil spray

1. In a large bowl, combine the onions, cilantro, oil, chickpea flour, rice flour, turmeric, cumin seeds, salt, and cayenne. Stir to combine. Cover and let stand for 30 minutes or up to overnight. (This allows the onions to release moisture, creating a batter.) Mix well before using. 2. Select Roast, Air Fry Fan, set temperature to 350°F (177°C) and set time to 8 minutes. Press Start to begin preheating. Spray the baking pan generously with vegetable oil spray. Drop half of the batter in 6 heaping tablespoons into the pan. Once preheated, place the pan on the roast position and cook. Carefully turn the pakoras over and spray with oil spray. Set the air fryer oven for 2 minutes, or until the batter is cooked through and crisp. 3. Repeat with remaining batter to make 6 more pakoras, checking at 6 minutes for doneness. Serve hot.

Kale Chips with Sesame

Prep time: 15 minutes | Cook time: 8 minutes | Serves 5

8 cups deribbed kale leaves, torn into 2-inch pieces

1½ tablespoons olive oil

¾ teaspoon chili powder

¼ teaspoon garlic powder

½ teaspoon paprika

2 teaspoons sesame seeds

1. Select Air Fry, set temperature to 350°F (177°C) and set time to 8 minutes. Press Start to begin preheating. 2. In a large bowl, toss the kale with the olive oil, chili powder, garlic powder, paprika, and sesame seeds until well coated. Put the kale in the crisper tray. 3. Once preheated, place the tray on the air fry position. Flip the kale twice during cooking, or until the kale is crispy. 4. Serve warm.

Garlic-Parmesan Croutons

Prep time: 3 minutes | Cook time: 12 minutes | Serves 4

Oil, for spraying

4 cups cubed French bread

1 tablespoon grated Parmesan cheese

3 tablespoons olive oil

1 tablespoon granulated garlic

½ teaspoon unsalted salt

1. Select Air Fry, set temperature to 350°F (177°C) and set time to 10 to 12 minutes. Press Start to begin preheating. Line the crisper tray with parchment and spray lightly with oil. 2. In a large bowl, mix together the bread, Parmesan cheese, olive oil, garlic, and salt, tossing with your hands to evenly distribute the seasonings. Transfer the coated bread cubes to the prepared tray. 3. Once preheated, place the pan on the air fry position. Stir once after 5 minutes, or until crisp and golden brown.

Air Fried Pot Stickers

Prep time: 10 minutes | Cook time: 18 to 20 minutes | Makes 30 pot stickers

½ cup finely chopped cabbage

¼ cup finely chopped red bell pepper

2 green onions, finely chopped

1 egg, beaten

2 tablespoons cocktail sauce

2 teaspoons low-sodium soy sauce

30 wonton wrappers

1 tablespoon water, for brushing the wrappers

1. Select Air Fry, set temperature to 360°F (182°C) and set time to 9 to 10 minutes. Press Start to begin preheating. 2. In a small bowl, combine the cabbage, pepper, green onions, egg, cocktail sauce, and soy sauce, and mix well. 3. Put about 1 teaspoon of the mixture in the center of each wonton wrapper. Fold the wrapper in half, covering the filling; dampen the edges with water, and seal. You can crimp the edges of the wrapper with your fingers so they look like the pot stickers you get in restaurants. Brush them with water. 4. Place the pot stickers in the crisper tray. Once preheated, place the tray on the air fry position. It will be done until the pot stickers are hot and the bottoms are lightly browned. 5. Serve hot.

Greek Street Tacos

Prep time: 10 minutes | Cook time: 3 minutes | Makes 8 small tacos

8 small flour tortillas (4-inch diameter)

8 tablespoons hummus

4 tablespoons crumbled feta cheese

4 tablespoons chopped kalamata or other olives (optional)

Olive oil for misting

1. Select Air Fry, set temperature to 390°F (199°C) and set time to 3 minutes. Press Start to begin preheating. 2. Place 1 tablespoon of hummus or tapenade in the center of each tortilla. Top with 1 teaspoon of feta crumbles and 1 teaspoon of chopped olives, if using. 3. Using your finger or a small spoon, moisten the edges of the tortilla all around with water. 4. Fold tortilla over to make a half-moon shape. Press center gently. Then press the edges firmly to seal in the filling. 5. Mist both sides with olive oil. 6. Place in crisper tray very close but try not to overlap. 7. Once preheated, place the tray on the air fry position. It will be done until lightly browned and crispy.

Roasted Mushrooms with Garlic

Prep time: 3 minutes | Cook time: 22 to 27 minutes | Serves 4

16 garlic cloves, peeled

2 teaspoons olive oil, divided

16 button mushrooms

½ teaspoon dried marjoram

⅛ teaspoon freshly ground black pepper

1 tablespoon white wine or low-sodium vegetable broth

1. Select Roast, Air Fry Fan, set temperature to 350°F (177°C) and set time to 12 minutes. Press Start to begin preheating. 2. In a baking pan, mix the garlic with 1 teaspoon of olive oil. Once preheated, place the pan on the roast position. 3. Add the mushrooms, marjoram, and pepper. Stir to coat. Drizzle with the remaining 1 teaspoon of olive oil and the white wine. 4. Return to the oven and roast for 10 to 15 minutes more, or until the mushrooms and garlic cloves are tender. Serve.

Crunchy Basil White Beans

Prep time: 2 minutes | Cook time: 19 minutes | Serves 2

1 (15 ounce) can cooked white beans
2 tablespoons olive oil
1 teaspoon fresh sage, chopped
¼ teaspoon garlic powder
¼ teaspoon salt, divided
1 teaspoon chopped fresh basil

1. Select Bake, Air Fry Fan, set temperature to 380°F (193°C) and set time to 10 minutes. Press Start to begin preheating. 2. In a medium bowl, mix together the beans, olive oil, sage, garlic, ⅛ teaspoon salt, and basil. 3. Pour the white beans into the baking pan and spread them out in a single layer. 4. Once preheated, place the pan on the bake position. Stir and continue cooking for an additional 5 to 9 minutes, or until they reach your preferred level of crispiness. 5. Toss with the remaining ⅛ teaspoon salt before serving.

Rumaki

Prep time: 30 minutes | Cook time: 10 to 12 minutes per batch | Makes about 24 rumaki

10 ounces (283 g) raw chicken livers
1 can sliced water chestnuts, drained
¼ cup low-sodium teriyaki sauce
12 slices turkey bacon

1. Cut livers into 1½-inch pieces, trimming out tough veins as you slice. 2. Place livers, water chestnuts, and teriyaki sauce in small container with lid. If needed, add another tablespoon of teriyaki sauce to make sure livers are covered. Refrigerate for 1 hour. 3. When ready to cook, cut bacon slices in half crosswise. Select Air Fry, set temperature to 390°F (199°C) and set time to 10 to 12 minutes. Press Start to begin preheating. 4. Wrap 1 piece of liver and 1 slice of water chestnut in each bacon strip. Secure with toothpick. 5. When you have wrapped half of the livers, place them in the baking pan in a single layer. 6. Once preheated, place the pan on the air fry position. It will be done until liver is done and bacon is crispy. 7. While first batch cooks, wrap the remaining livers.

Baked Ricotta

Prep time: 10 minutes | Cook time: 15 minutes | Makes 2 cups

1 (15-ounce / 425-g) container whole milk Ricotta cheese
3 tablespoons grated Parmesan cheese, divided
2 tablespoons extra-virgin olive oil
1 teaspoon chopped fresh thyme leaves
1 teaspoon grated lemon zest
1 clove garlic, crushed with press
¼ teaspoon salt
¼ teaspoon pepper
Toasted baguette slices or crackers, for serving

1. Select Bake, Air Fry Fan, set temperature to 380°F (193°C) and set time to 10 minutes. Press Start to begin preheating. 2. Whisk together the Ricotta, 2 tablespoons of the Parmesan, oil, thyme, lemon zest, garlic, salt, and pepper. Pour into a baking dish. Cover the dish tightly with foil. 3. Once preheated, place the dish on the bake

position. Remove the foil cover and sprinkle with the remaining 1 tablespoon of the Parmesan. Bake for 5 more minutes, or until bubbly at edges and the top is browned. 4. Serve warm with toasted baguette slices or crackers.

Bacon-Wrapped Pickle Spears

Prep time: 10 minutes | Cook time: 8 minutes | Serves 4

8 to 12 slices bacon

¼ cup (2 ounces / 57 g) cream

cheese, softened

¼ cup shredded Mozzarella cheese

8 dill pickle spears

½ cup ranch dressing

1. Select Air Fry, set temperature to 400°F (204°C) and set time to 8 minutes. Press Start to begin preheating. Lay the bacon slices on a flat surface. In a medium bowl, combine the cream cheese and Mozzarella. Stir until well blended. Spread the cheese mixture over the bacon slices. 2. Place a pickle spear on a bacon slice and roll the bacon around the pickle in a spiral, ensuring the pickle is fully covered. (You may need to use more than one slice of bacon per pickle to fully cover the spear.) Tuck in the ends to ensure the bacon stays put. Repeat to wrap all the pickles. 3. Place the wrapped pickles in the crisper tray in a single layer. Once preheated, place the tray on the air fry position. It will be done until the bacon is cooked through and crisp on the edges. 4. Serve the pickle spears with ranch dressing on the side.

Jalapeño Poppers

Prep time: 10 minutes | Cook time: 20 minutes | Serves 4

Oil, for spraying

8 ounces (227 g) cream cheese

¾ cup gluten-free bread crumbs, divided

2 tablespoons chopped

fresh parsley

½ teaspoon granulated garlic

½ teaspoon salt

10 jalapeño peppers, halved and seeded

1. Select Roast, Air Fry Fan, set temperature to 370°F (188°C) and set time to 20 minutes. Press Start to begin preheating. Line the pizza rack with parchment and spray lightly with oil. 2. In a medium bowl, mix together the cream cheese, half of the bread crumbs, the parsley, garlic, and salt. 3. Spoon the mixture into the jalapeño halves. Gently press the stuffed jalapeños in the remaining bread crumbs. 4. Place the stuffed jalapeños on the rack. 5. Once preheated, place the rack on the roast position. It will be done until the cheese is melted and the bread crumbs are crisp and golden brown.

Italian Rice Balls

Prep time: 20 minutes | Cook time: 10 minutes | Makes 8 rice balls

1½ cups cooked sticky rice

½ teaspoon Italian seasoning blend

¾ teaspoon salt, divided

8 black olives, pitted

1 ounce (28 g) Mozzarella cheese, cut into tiny pieces (small enough to stuff into olives)

2 eggs

⅓ cup Italian bread crumbs

¾ cup panko bread crumbs

Cooking spray

1. Stuff each black olive with a piece of Mozzarella cheese. Set aside. 2. In a bowl, combine the cooked sticky rice, Italian seasoning blend, and ½ teaspoon of salt and stir to mix well. Form the rice mixture into a log with your hands and divide it into 8 equal portions. Mold each portion around a black olive and roll into a ball. 3. Transfer to the freezer to chill for 10 to 15 minutes until firm. 4. Select Air Fry, set temperature to 390°F (199°C) and set time to 10 minutes. Press Start to begin preheating. 5. In a shallow dish, place the Italian bread crumbs. In a separate shallow dish, whisk the eggs. In a third shallow dish, combine the panko bread crumbs and remaining salt. 6. One by one, roll the rice balls in the Italian bread crumbs, then dip in the whisked eggs, finally coat them with the panko bread

crumbs. 7. Arrange the rice balls in the crisper tray and spritz both sides with cooking spray. 8. Once preheated, place the tray on the air fry position. It will be done until the rice balls are golden brown. Flip the balls halfway through the cooking time. 9. Serve warm.

Stuffed Fried Mushrooms

Prep time: 20 minutes | Cook time: 10 to 11 minutes | Serves 10

½ cup panko bread crumbs
½ teaspoon freshly ground black pepper
½ teaspoon onion powder
½ teaspoon cayenne pepper
1 (8-ounce / 227-g) package cream cheese, at room temperature
20 cremini or button mushrooms, stemmed
1 to 2 tablespoons oil

1. In a medium bowl, whisk the bread crumbs, black pepper, onion powder, and cayenne until blended. 2. Add the cream cheese and mix until well blended. Fill each mushroom top with 1 teaspoon of the cream cheese mixture 3. Select Roast, Air Fry Fan, set temperature to 360°F (182°C) and set time to 5 minutes. Press Start to begin preheating. Line the pizza rack with a piece of parchment paper. 4. Place the mushrooms on the parchment and spritz with oil. 5. Once preheated, place the rack on the roast position. Shake the rack and cook for 5 to 6 minutes more until the filling is firm and the mushrooms are soft.

Parmesan French Fries

Prep time: 10 minutes | Cook time: 25 minutes | Serves 2 to 3

2 to 3 large russet potatoes, peeled and cut into ½-inch sticks
2 teaspoons vegetable or canola oil
¾ cup grated Parmesan cheese
½ teaspoon salt
Freshly ground black pepper, to taste
1 teaspoon fresh chopped parsley

1. Bring a large saucepan of salted water to a boil on the stovetop while you peel and cut the potatoes. Blanch the potatoes in the boiling salted water for 4 minutes. 2. Select Air Fry, set temperature to 400°F (204°C) and set time to 25 minutes. Press Start to begin preheating. 3. Strain the potatoes and rinse them with cold water. Dry them well with a clean kitchen towel. 4. Toss the dried potato sticks gently with the oil and place them in the crisper tray. Once preheated, place the tray on the air fry position. Shake the tray a few times while the fries cook to help them brown evenly. 5. Combine the Parmesan cheese, salt and pepper. With 2 minutes left on the cooking time, sprinkle the fries with the Parmesan cheese mixture. Toss the fries to coat them evenly with the cheese mixture and continue to air fry for the final 2 minutes, until the cheese has melted and just starts to brown. Sprinkle the finished fries with chopped parsley, a little more grated Parmesan cheese if you like, and serve.

Garlicky and Cheesy French Fries

Prep time: 5 minutes | Cook time: 20 to 25 minutes | Serves 4

3 medium russet potatoes, rinsed, dried, and cut into thin wedges or classic fry shapes
2 tablespoons extra-virgin olive oil
1 tablespoon granulated garlic
⅓ cup grated Parmesan cheese
½ teaspoon salt
¼ teaspoon freshly ground black pepper
Cooking oil spray
2 tablespoons finely chopped fresh parsley (optional)

1. In a large bowl combine the potato wedges or fries and the olive oil. Toss to coat. 2. Sprinkle the potatoes with the granulated garlic, Parmesan cheese, salt, and pepper, and toss again. 3. Select Air Fry, set temperature to 400°F (204°C) and set time to 20 to 25 minutes. Press Start to begin preheating. 4. Spray the baking pan with cooking oil.

Place the potatoes into the pan. 5. Once preheated, place the pan on the air fry position. 6. After about 10 minutes, remove the pan and shake it so the fries at the bottom come up to the top. Reinsert the pan to resume cooking. 7. When the cooking is complete, top the fries with the parsley (if using) and serve hot.

Zucchini Fries with Roasted Garlic Aïoli

Prep time: 20 minutes | Cook time: 12 minutes | Serves 4

- 1 tablespoon vegetable oil
- ½ head green or savoy cabbage, finely shredded

Roasted Garlic Aïoli:
- 1 teaspoon roasted garlic
- ½ cup mayonnaise
- 2 tablespoons olive oil
- Juice of ½ lemon
- Salt and pepper, to taste

Zucchini Fries:
- ½ cup flour
- 2 eggs, beaten
- 1 cup seasoned bread crumbs
- Salt and pepper, to taste
- 1 large zucchini, cut into ½-inch sticks
- Olive oil

1. Make the aïoli: Combine the roasted garlic, mayonnaise, olive oil and lemon juice in a bowl and whisk well. Season the aïoli with salt and pepper to taste. 2. Prepare the zucchini fries. Create a dredging station with three shallow dishes. Place the flour in the first shallow dish and season well with salt and freshly ground black pepper. Put the beaten eggs in the second shallow dish. In the third shallow dish, combine the bread crumbs, salt and pepper. Dredge the zucchini sticks, coating with flour first, then dipping them into the eggs to coat, and finally tossing in bread crumbs. Shake the dish with the bread crumbs and pat the crumbs onto the zucchini sticks gently with your hands so they stick evenly. 3. Place the zucchini fries on a flat surface and let them sit at least 10 minutes before air frying to let them dry out a little. Select Air Fry, set temperature to 400°F (204°C) and set time to 12 minutes. Press Start to begin preheating. 4. Spray the zucchini sticks with olive oil, and place them into the crisper tray. You can air fry the zucchini in two layers, placing the second layer in the opposite direction to the first. Turn and rotate the fries halfway through the cooking time. Spray with additional oil when you turn them over. 5. Serve zucchini fries warm with the roasted garlic aïoli.

Crispy Chili Chickpeas

Prep time: 5 minutes | Cook time: 15 minutes | Serves 4

- 1 (15-ounce) can cooked chickpeas, drained and rinsed
- 1 tablespoon olive oil
- ¼ teaspoon salt
- ⅛ teaspoon chili powder
- ⅛ teaspoon garlic powder
- ⅛ teaspoon paprika

1. Select Air Fry, set temperature to 380°F (193°C) and set time to 15 minutes. Press Start to begin preheating. 2. In a medium bowl, toss all of the ingredients together until the chickpeas are well coated. 3. Pour the chickpeas into the crisper tray and spread them out in a single layer. 4. Once preheated, place the tray on the air fry position. Stir once halfway through the cook time.

Chapter 7 Desserts

Cinnamon and Pecan Pie

Prep time: 10 minutes | Cook time: 25 minutes | Serves 4

- 1 pie dough
- ½ teaspoons cinnamon
- ¾ teaspoon vanilla extract
- 2 eggs
- ¾ cup maple syrup
- ⅛ teaspoon nutmeg
- 3 tablespoons melted butter, divided
- 2 tablespoons sugar
- ½ cup chopped pecans

1. Select Air Fry, set temperature to 370°F (188°C) and set time to 10 minutes. Press Start to begin preheating. 2. In a small bowl, coat the pecans in 1 tablespoon of melted butter. 3. Transfer the pecans to the crisper tray. Once preheated, place the tray on the air fry position. 4. Put the pie dough in a greased baking pan and add the pecans on top. 5. In a bowl, mix the rest of the ingredients. Pour this over the pecans. 6. Put the pan in the oven. Select Pizza, set temperature to 370°F (188°C) and set time to 25 minutes. Press Start. 7. Serve immediately.

Orange-Anise-Ginger Skillet Cookie

Prep time: 20 minutes | Cook time: 15 minutes | Serves 2 to 4

Cookie:
Vegetable oil
1 cup plus 2 tablespoons all-purpose flour
1 tablespoon grated orange zest
1 teaspoon ground ginger
1 teaspoon aniseeds, crushed
¼ teaspoon kosher salt
4 tablespoons (½ stick) unsalted butter, at room temperature
½ cup granulated sugar, plus more for sprinkling
3 tablespoons dark molasses
1 large egg
Icing:
½ cup confectioners' sugar
2 to 3 teaspoons milk

1. For the cookie: Select Bake, Air Fry Fan, set temperature to 325°F (163°C) and set time to 15 minutes. Press Start to begin preheating. Generously grease a baking pan with vegetable oil. 2. In a medium bowl, whisk together the flour, orange zest, ginger, aniseeds, and salt. 3. In a medium bowl using a hand mixer, beat the butter and sugar on medium-high speed until well combined, about 2 minutes. Add the molasses and egg and beat until light in color, about 2 minutes. Add the flour mixture and mix on low until just combined. Use a rubber spatula to scrape the dough into the prepared pan, spreading it to the edges and smoothing the top. Sprinkle with sugar. 4. Once preheated, place the pan on the bake position. It will be done until sides are browned but the center is still quite soft. 5. Let cool in the pan on a wire rack for 15 minutes. Turn the cookie out of the pan onto the rack. 6. For the icing: Whisk together the sugar and 2 teaspoons of milk. Add 1 teaspoon milk if needed for the desired consistency. Spread, or drizzle onto the cookie.

Indian Toast and Milk

Prep time: 10 minutes | Cook time: 20 minutes | Serves 4

1 cup sweetened condensed milk
1 cup evaporated milk
1 cup half-and-half
1 teaspoon ground cardamom, plus additional for garnish
1 pinch saffron threads
4 slices white bread
2 to 3 tablespoons ghee or butter, softened
2 tablespoons crushed pistachios, for garnish (optional)

1. Select Bake, Air Fry Fan, set temperature to 350°F (177°C) and set time to 15 minutes. Press Start to begin preheating. 2. In a baking pan, combine the condensed milk, evaporated milk, half-and-half, cardamom, and saffron. Stir until well combined. 3. Once preheated, place the pan on the bake position. Stir halfway through the cooking time. Remove the sweetened milk and set aside. 3. Cut each slice of bread into two triangles. Brush each side with ghee. Transfer the bread to pizza rack and place on bake position. Set the temperature to 350°F (177°C) for 5 minutes or until golden brown and toasty. 4. Remove the bread from the oven. Arrange two triangles in each of four wide, shallow bowls. Pour the hot milk mixture on top of the bread and let soak for 30 minutes. 5. Garnish with pistachios if using, and sprinkle with additional cardamom.

Vanilla Pound Cake

Prep time: 10 minutes | Cook time: 25 minutes | Serves 6

- 1 cup blanched finely ground almond flour
- ¼ cup salted butter, melted
- ½ cup granular erythritol
- 1 teaspoon vanilla extract
- 1 teaspoon baking powder
- ½ cup full-fat sour cream
- 1 ounce (28 g) full-fat cream cheese, softened
- 2 large eggs

1. Select Bake, Air Fry Fan, set temperature to 300°F (149°C) and set time to 25 minutes. Press Start to begin preheating. 2. In a large bowl, mix almond flour, butter, and erythritol. 3. Add in vanilla, baking powder, sour cream, and cream cheese and mix until well combined. Add eggs and mix. 4. Pour batter into baking pan. 5. Once preheated, place the pan on the bake position. 6. When the cake is done, a toothpick inserted in center will come out clean. The center should not feel wet. Allow it to cool completely, or the cake will crumble when moved.

Pumpkin Cookie with Cream Cheese Frosting

Prep time: 10 minutes | Cook time: 7 minutes | Serves 6

- ½ cup blanched finely ground almond flour
- ½ cup powdered erythritol, divided
- 2 tablespoons butter, softened
- 1 large egg
- ½ teaspoon unflavored gelatin
- ½ teaspoon baking powder
- ½ teaspoon vanilla extract
- ½ teaspoon pumpkin pie spice
- 2 tablespoons pure pumpkin purée
- ½ teaspoon ground cinnamon, divided
- ¼ cup low-carb, sugar-free chocolate chips
- 3 ounces (85 g) full-fat cream cheese, softened

1. Select Bake, Air Fry Fan, set temperature to 300°F (149°C) and set time to 7 minutes. Press Start to begin preheating. 2. In a large bowl, mix almond flour and ¼ cup erythritol. Stir in butter, egg, and gelatin until combined. 3. Stir in baking powder, vanilla, pumpkin pie spice, pumpkin purée, and ¼ teaspoon cinnamon, then fold in chocolate chips. 4. Pour batter into a baking pan. Once preheated, place pan on the bake position. 5. When fully cooked, the top will be golden brown and a toothpick inserted in center will come out clean. Let cool at least 20 minutes. 6. To make the frosting: mix cream cheese, remaining ¼ teaspoon cinnamon, and remaining ¼ cup erythritol in a large bowl. Using an electric mixer, beat until it becomes fluffy. Spread onto the cooled cookie. Garnish with additional cinnamon if desired.

Pears with Honey-Lemon Ricotta

Prep time: 10 minutes | Cook time: 8 minutes | Serves 4

- 2 large Bartlett pears
- 3 tablespoons butter, melted
- 3 tablespoons brown sugar
- ½ teaspoon ground ginger
- ¼ teaspoon ground cardamom
- ½ cup whole-milk ricotta cheese
- 1 tablespoon honey, plus additional for drizzling
- 1 teaspoon pure almond extract
- 1 teaspoon pure lemon extract

1. Select Bake, Air Fry Fan, set temperature to 375°F (191°C) and set time to 8 to 10 minutes. Press Start to begin preheating. Peel each pear and cut in half lengthwise. Use a melon baller to scoop out the core. Place the pear halves in a medium bowl, add the melted butter, and toss. Add the brown sugar, ginger, and cardamom; toss to coat. 2. Place the pear halves, cut side down, on pizzas rack. Once preheated, place the rack on the bake position. It will be done until the pears are lightly browned and tender, but not mushy. 3. Meanwhile, in a medium bowl, combine the ricotta, honey, and almond and lemon extracts. Beat with an electric mixer on medium speed until the mixture is light and

fluffy, about 1 minute. 4. To serve, divide the ricotta mixture among four small shallow bowls. Place a pear half, cut side up, on top of the cheese. Drizzle with additional honey and serve.

Butter Flax Cookies

Prep time: 25 minutes | Cook time: 20 minutes | Serves 4

8 ounces (227 g) almond meal	1 teaspoon baking powder	1 large egg, room temperature.
2 tablespoons flaxseed meal	A pinch of grated nutmeg	1 stick butter, room temperature
1 ounce (28 g) monk fruit	A pinch of coarse salt	1 teaspoon vanilla extract

1. Select Bake, Air Fry Fan, set temperature to 350°F (177°C) and set time to 10 minutes. Press Start to begin preheating. 2. Mix the almond meal, flaxseed meal, monk fruit, baking powder, grated nutmeg, and salt in a bowl. 3. In a separate bowl, whisk the egg, butter, and vanilla extract. 4. Stir the egg mixture into dry mixture; mix to combine well or until it forms a nice, soft dough. 5. Roll your dough out and cut out with a cookie cutter of your choice. Transfer to the baking ban. Once preheated, place the pan on the bake position. Decrease the temperature to 330°F (166°C) and cook for 10 minutes longer. Bon appétit!

Applesauce and Chocolate Brownies

Prep time: 10 minutes | Cook time: 15 minutes | Serves 8

¼ cup unsweetened cocoa powder	½ teaspoons baking powder	½ cup granulated sugar	¼ cup miniature semisweet chocolate chips
¼ cup all-purpose flour	3 tablespoons unsalted butter, melted	1 large egg	
¼ teaspoon kosher salt		3 tablespoons unsweetened applesauce	Coarse sea salt, to taste

1. Select Bake, Air Fry Fan, set temperature to 300°F (149°C) and set time to 15 minutes. Press Start to begin preheating. 2. In a large bowl, whisk together the cocoa powder, all-purpose flour, kosher salt, and baking powder. 3. In a separate large bowl, combine the butter, granulated sugar, egg, and applesauce, then use a spatula to fold in the cocoa powder mixture and the chocolate chips until well combined. 4. Spray a baking pan with nonstick cooking spray, then pour the mixture into the pan. Once preheated, place the pan on the bake position. It will be done until a toothpick comes out clean when inserted in the middle. 5. Remove the brownies from the air fryer oven, sprinkle some coarse sea salt on top, and allow to cool in the pan for 20 minutes before cutting and serving.

Jelly Doughnuts

Prep time: 5 minutes | Cook time: 5 minutes | Serves 8

1 (16.3-ounce / 462-g) package large refrigerator biscuits	Cooking spray	jam
	1¼ cups good-quality raspberry	Confectioners' sugar, for dusting

1. Select Bake, Air Fry Fan, set temperature to 350°F (177°C) and set time to 5 minutes. Press Start to begin preheating. 2. Separate biscuits into 8 rounds. Spray both sides of rounds lightly with oil. 3. Spray the baking pan with oil and place 3 to 4 rounds in the pan. Once preheated, place the pan on the bake position. It will be done until golden brown. Allow doughnuts to cool. Repeat with the remaining rounds. 4. Fill a pastry bag, fitted with small plain tip, with raspberry jam; use tip to poke a small hole in the side of each doughnut, then fill the centers with the jam. Dust doughnuts with confectioners' sugar. Serve immediately.

Sweet Potato Donut Holes

Prep time: 10 minutes | Cook time: 4 to 5 minutes per batch | Makes 18 donut holes

- 1 cup flour
- 1/3 cup sugar
- 1/4 teaspoon baking soda
- 1 teaspoon baking powder
- 1/8 teaspoon salt
- 1/2 cup cooked mashed purple sweet potatoes
- 1 egg, beaten
- 2 tablespoons butter, melted
- 1 teaspoon pure vanilla extract
- Oil for misting or cooking spray

1. Select Bake, Air Fry Fan, set temperature to 390°F (199°C) and set time to 4 to 5 minutes. Press Start to begin preheating. 2. In a large bowl, stir together the flour, sugar, baking soda, baking powder, and salt. 3. In a separate bowl, combine the potatoes, egg, butter, and vanilla and mix well. 4. Add potato mixture to dry ingredients and stir into a soft dough. 5. Shape dough into 1½-inch balls. Mist lightly with oil or cooking spray. 6. Place 9 donut holes in baking pan, leaving a little space in between. Once preheated, place the pan on the bake position. It will be done until done in center and lightly browned outside. 7. Repeat step 6 to cook remaining donut holes.

Crustless Peanut Butter Cheesecake

Prep time: 10 minutes | Cook time: 10 minutes | Serves 2

- 4 ounces (113 g) cream cheese, softened
- 2 tablespoons confectioners' erythritol
- 1 tablespoon all-natural, no-sugar-added peanut butter
- 1/2 teaspoon vanilla extract
- 1 large egg, whisked

1. Select Bake, Air Fry Fan, set temperature to 300°F (149°C) and set time to 10 minutes. Press Start to begin preheating. 2. In a medium bowl, mix cream cheese and erythritol until smooth. Add peanut butter and vanilla, mixing until smooth. Add egg and stir just until combined. 3. Spoon mixture into an ungreased baking pan. Once preheated, place the pan on the bake position. Edges will be firm, but center will be mostly set with only a small amount of jiggle when done. 4. Let pan cool at room temperature 30 minutes, cover with plastic wrap, then place into refrigerator at least 2 hours. Serve chilled.

Coconut Muffins

Prep time: 5 minutes | Cook time: 25 minutes | Serves 5

- 1/2 cup coconut flour
- 2 tablespoons cocoa powder
- 3 tablespoons erythritol
- 1 teaspoon baking powder
- 2 tablespoons coconut oil
- 2 eggs, beaten
- 1/2 cup coconut shred

1. Select Bake, Air Fry Fan, set temperature to 350°F (177°C) and set time to 25 minutes. Press Start to begin preheating. 2. In the mixing bowl, mix all ingredients. 3. Then pour the mixture into the molds of the muffin and place on the bake position once preheated. 4. Serve and enjoy.

Apple Dutch Baby

Prep time: 30 minutes | Cook time: 16 minutes | Serves 2 to 3

Batter:
- 2 large eggs
- 1/4 cup all-purpose flour
- 1/4 teaspoon baking powder
- 1½ teaspoons granulated sugar
- Pinch kosher salt
- 1/2 cup whole milk
- 1 tablespoon butter, melted
- 1/2 teaspoon pure vanilla extract
- 1/4 teaspoon ground nutmeg

Apples:
- 2 tablespoon butter
- 4 tablespoons granulated sugar
- 1/4 teaspoon ground cinnamon
- 1/4 teaspoon ground nutmeg

1 small tart apple (such as Granny Smith), peeled, cored, and sliced

Vanilla ice cream (optional), for serving

Make the Batter: 1. In a medium bowl, combine the eggs, flour, baking powder, sugar, and salt. Whisk lightly. While whisking continuously, slowly pour in the milk. Whisk in the melted butter, vanilla, and nutmeg. Let the batter stand for 30 minutes. (You can also cover and refrigerate overnight.) **Make the Apples:** 2. Select Air Fry, set temperature to 400°F (204°C) and set time to 2 minutes. Press Start to begin preheating. Place the butter in the baking pan. Once preheated, place the pan on the air fry position. 3. In a small bowl, combine 2 tablespoons of the sugar with the cinnamon and nutmeg and stir until well combined. 4. When the pan is hot and the butter is melted, brush some butter up the sides of the pan. Sprinkle the spiced sugar mixture over the butter. Arrange the apple slices in the pan in a single layer and sprinkle the remaining 2 tablespoons sugar over the apples. Set the temperature to 400°F (204°C) for 2 minutes, or until the mixture bubbles. 5. Gently pour the batter over the apples. Set the temperature to 350°F (177°C) for 12 minutes, or until the pancake is golden brown around the edges, the center is cooked through, and a toothpick emerges clean. 6. Serve immediately with ice cream, if desired.

Carrot Cake with Cream Cheese Icing

Prep time: 10 minutes | Cook time: 55 minutes | Serves 6 to 8

- 1¼ cups all-purpose flour
- 1 teaspoon baking powder
- ½ teaspoon baking soda
- 1 teaspoon ground cinnamon
- ¼ teaspoon ground nutmeg
- ¼ teaspoon salt
- 2 cups grated carrot (about 3 to 4 medium carrots or 2 large)
- ¾ cup granulated sugar
- ¼ cup brown sugar
- 2 eggs
- ¾ cup canola or vegetable oil
- **Icing:**
- 8 ounces (227 g) cream cheese, softened at room temperature
- 8 tablespoons butter (1 stick), softened at room temperature
- 1 cup powdered sugar
- 1 teaspoon pure vanilla extract

1. Grease a cake pan that fits your air fryer oven. 2. Combine the flour, baking powder, baking soda, cinnamon, nutmeg and salt in a bowl. Add the grated carrots and toss well. In a separate bowl, beat the sugars and eggs together until light and frothy. Drizzle in the oil, beating constantly. Fold the egg mixture into the dry ingredients until everything is just combined and you no longer see any traces of flour. Pour the batter into the cake pan and wrap the pan completely in greased aluminum foil. 3. Select Bake, Air Fry Fan, set temperature to 350°F (177°C) and set time to 40 minutes. Press Start to begin preheating. 4. Once preheated, place the pan on the bake position and cook. Remove the aluminum foil cover and bake for an additional 15 minutes or until a skewer inserted into the center of the cake comes out clean and the top is nicely browned. 5. While the cake is cooking, beat the cream cheese, butter, powdered sugar and vanilla extract together using a hand mixer, stand mixer or food processor (or a lot of elbow grease!). 6. Remove the cake pan from the air fryer oven and let the cake cool in the cake pan for 10 minutes or so. Then remove the cake from the pan and let it continue to cool completely. Frost the cake with the cream cheese icing and serve.

Nutty Pear Crumble

Prep time: 10 minutes | Cook time: 30 minutes | Serves 2 to 4

- 2 ripe d'Anjou pears (1 pound / 454 g), peeled, cored, and roughly chopped
- ¼ cup packed light brown sugar
- 2 tablespoons cornstarch
- 1 teaspoon kosher salt
- ¼ cup granulated sugar
- 3 tablespoons unsalted butter, at room temperature

1/3 cup all-purpose flour

2½ tablespoons Dutch-process cocoa powder

¼ cup chopped blanched hazelnuts

Vanilla ice cream or whipped cream, for serving (optional)

1. Select Bake, Air Fry Fan, set temperature to 320°F (160°C) and set time to 30 minutes. Press Start to begin preheating. 2. In a baking pan, combine the pears, brown sugar, cornstarch, and ½ teaspoon salt and toss until the pears are evenly coated in the sugar. 3. In a bowl, combine the remaining ½ teaspoon salt with the granulated sugar, butter, flour, and cocoa powder and pinch and press the butter into the other ingredients with your fingers until a sandy, shaggy crumble dough forms. Stir in the hazelnuts. Sprinkle the crumble topping evenly over the pears. 4. Once preheated, place the pan on the bake position. It will be done until the crumble is crisp and the pears are bubbling in the center. 5. Carefully remove the pan from the air fryer oven and serve the hot crumble in bowls, topped with ice cream or whipped cream, if you like.

Double Chocolate Brownies

Prep time: 5 minutes | Cook time: 15 to 20 minutes | Serves 8

1 cup almond flour

½ cup unsweetened cocoa powder

½ teaspoon baking powder

⅓ cup Swerve

¼ teaspoon salt

½ cup unsalted butter, melted and cooled

3 eggs

1 teaspoon vanilla extract

2 tablespoons mini semisweet chocolate chips

1. Select Bake, Air Fry Fan, set temperature to 350°F (177°C) and set time to 15 to 20 minutes. Select Start/Stop to begin preheating. Line the baking pan with parchment paper and brush with oil. 2. In a large bowl, combine the almond flour, cocoa powder, baking powder, Swerve, and salt. Add the butter, eggs, and vanilla. Stir until thoroughly combined. (The batter will be thick.) Spread the batter into the prepared pan and scatter the chocolate chips on top. 3. Once preheated, place the pan on the bake position. It will be done until the edges are set. (The center should still appear slightly undercooked.) Let cool completely before slicing. To store, cover and refrigerate the brownies for up to 3 days.

Apple Wedges with Apricots

Prep time: 5 minutes | Cook time: 15 to 18 minutes | Serves 4

4 large apples, peeled and sliced into 8 wedges

2 tablespoons olive oil

½ cup dried apricots, chopped

1 to 2 tablespoons sugar

½ teaspoon ground cinnamon

1. Select Air Fry, set temperature to 350°F (180°C) and set time to 12 to 15 minutes. Press Start to begin preheating. 2. Toss the apple wedges with the olive oil in a mixing bowl until well coated. 3. Place the apple wedges in the crisper tray. 4. Sprinkle with the dried apricots. Once preheated, place the tray on the air fry position. 5. Meanwhile, thoroughly combine the sugar and cinnamon in a small bowl. 6. Remove the apple wedges from the oven to a plate. Serve sprinkled with the sugar mixture.

Coconut Mixed Berry Crisp

Prep time: 5 minutes | Cook time: 20 minutes | Serves 6

1 tablespoon butter, melted

12 ounces (340 g) mixed berries

⅓ cup granulated Swerve

1 teaspoon pure vanilla extract

½ teaspoon ground cinnamon

¼ teaspoon ground cloves

¼ teaspoon grated nutmeg

½ cup coconut chips, for garnish

1. Select Air Fry, set temperature to 330°F (166°C) and set time to 20 minutes. Press Start to begin preheating. Coat a baking pan with melted butter. 2. Put the remaining ingredients except the coconut chips in the prepared baking pan. 3. Once preheated, place the pan on the air fry position. 4. Serve garnished with the coconut chips.

Maple Bacon Moonshine Bread Pudding

Prep time: 20 minutes | Cook time: 15 minutes | Serves 6

1 cup whole milk

1 (4.6-ounce / 130-g) package cook-and-serve vanilla pudding and pie filling

¼ cup granulated sugar

2 large eggs, beaten

1 tablespoon butter, melted

1 teaspoon ground cinnamon

1 teaspoon vanilla extract

4 cups loosely packed cubed French bread

¼ cup packed light brown sugar

½ cup chopped toasted pecans

¾ cup maple bacon moonshine, plus 3 tablespoons

1 to 2 tablespoons oil

1. In a large bowl, whisk the milk, pudding mix, granulated sugar, eggs, melted butter, cinnamon, and vanilla until blended. Add the bread cubes and let soak for 10 minutes. 2. In a small bowl, stir together the brown sugar, pecans, and ¾ cup moonshine. Stir the pecan mixture into the bread mixture. 3. Select Bake, Air Fry Fan, set temperature to 355°F (179°C) and set time to 10 minutes. Press Start to begin preheating. Spritz a baking pan with oil. 4. Transfer the bread mixture to the prepared pan. 5. Once preheated, place the pan on the bake position. The bottom of the pudding will still be mushy. Stir. Bake for 5 minutes more and stir again. The pudding will be soft, but not runny, and a knife inserted into the middle will have soft crumbs attached. 6. Drizzle the remaining 3 tablespoons of maple bacon moonshine over the pudding.

Fried Cheesecake Bites

Prep time: 30 minutes | Cook time: 2 minutes | Makes 16 bites

8 ounces (227 g) cream cheese, softened

½ cup plus 2 tablespoons Swerve, divided

4 tablespoons heavy cream, divided

½ teaspoon vanilla extract

½ cup almond flour

1. In a stand mixer fitted with a paddle attachment, beat the cream cheese, ½ cup of the Swerve, 2 tablespoons of the heavy cream, and the vanilla until smooth. Using a small ice-cream scoop, divide the mixture into 16 balls and arrange them on a rimmed baking sheet lined with parchment paper. Freeze for 45 minutes until firm. 2. Line the crisper tray with parchment paper and select Air Fry, set temperature to 350°F (177°C) and set time to 2 minutes. Press Start to begin preheating. 3. In a small shallow bowl, combine the almond flour with the remaining 2 tablespoons Swerve. 4. In another small shallow bowl, place the remaining 2 tablespoons cream. 5. One at a time, dip the frozen cheesecake balls into the cream and then roll in the almond flour mixture, pressing lightly to form an even coating. Arrange the balls in a single layer in the crisper tray, leaving room between them. Once preheated, place the tray on the air fry position. The coating will be lightly browned when done.

Pecan Butter Cookies

Prep time: 5 minutes | Cook time: 24 minutes | Makes 12 cookies

1 cup chopped pecans

½ cup salted butter, melted

½ cup coconut flour

¾ cup erythritol, divided

1 teaspoon vanilla extract

1. Select Bake, Air Fry Fan, set temperature to 325°F (163°C) and set time to 8 minutes. Press Start to begin

preheating. 2. In a food processor, blend together pecans, butter, flour, ½ cup erythritol, and vanilla 1 minute until a dough forms. 3. Form dough into twelve individual cookie balls, about 1 tablespoon each. 4. Cut a piece of parchment to fit the baking pan. Place cookies on parchment. You may need to work in batches. Once preheated, place the pan on the bake position. Repeat cooking with remaining batches. 5. When the timer goes off, allow cookies to cool 5 minutes on a large serving plate until cool enough to handle. While still warm, dust cookies with remaining erythritol. Allow to cool completely, about 15 minutes, before serving.

Gingerbread

Prep time: 5 minutes | Cook time: 20 minutes | Makes 1 loaf

Cooking spray	ginger	½ teaspoon baking soda	½ cup buttermilk
1 cup flour	¼ teaspoon cinnamon	⅛ teaspoon salt	2 tablespoons oil
2 tablespoons sugar	1 teaspoon baking powder	1 egg	1 teaspoon pure vanilla extract
¾ teaspoon ground		¼ cup molasses	

1. Select Bake, Air Fry Fan, set temperature to 330°F (166°C) and set time to 20 minutes. Press Start to begin preheating. 2. Spray a baking dish lightly with cooking spray. 3. In a medium bowl, mix together all the dry ingredients. 4. In a separate bowl, beat the egg. Add molasses, buttermilk, oil, and vanilla and stir until well mixed. 5. Pour liquid mixture into dry ingredients and stir until well blended. 6. Pour batter into baking dish. Once preheated, place the dish on the bake position. It will be done until toothpick inserted in center of loaf comes out clean.

Funnel Cake

Prep time: 10 minutes | Cook time: 5 minutes | Serves 4

Oil, for spraying	dusting	½ teaspoon ground cinnamon
1 cup self-rising flour, plus more for	1 cup fat-free vanilla Greek yogurt	¼ cup confectioners' sugar

1. Select Air Fry, set temperature to 375°F (191°C) and set time to 5 minutes. Press Start to begin preheating. Line the crisper tray with parchment and spray lightly with oil. 2. In a large bowl, mix together the flour, yogurt, and cinnamon until the mixture forms a ball. 3. Place the dough on a lightly floured work surface and knead for about 2 minutes. 4. Cut the dough into 4 equal pieces, then cut each of those into 6 pieces. You should have 24 total pieces. 5. Roll the pieces into 8- to 10-inch-long ropes. Loosely mound the ropes into 4 piles of 6 ropes. 6. Place the dough piles in the prepared tray and spray liberally with oil. You may need to work in batches. 7. Once preheated, place the tray on the air fry position. It will be done until lightly browned. 8. Dust with the confectioners' sugar before serving.

Grilled Pineapple Dessert

Prep time: 5 minutes | Cook time: 12 minutes | Serves 4

Oil for misting or cooking spray	1 tablespoon honey	toasted
4 ½-inch-thick slices fresh pineapple, core removed	¼ teaspoon brandy	Vanilla frozen yogurt or coconut sorbet
	2 tablespoons slivered almonds,	

1. Select Air Fry, set temperature to 390°F (199°C) and set time to 6 minutes. Press Start to begin preheating. Spray both sides of pineapple slices with oil or cooking spray. Place into crisper tray. 2. Once preheated, place the tray on the air fry position. Turn slices over and cook for an additional 6 minutes. 3. Mix together the honey and brandy. 4. Remove cooked pineapple slices from the oven, sprinkle with toasted almonds, and drizzle with honey mixture. 5. Serve with a scoop of frozen yogurt or sorbet on the side.

Homemade Mint Pie

Prep time: 15 minutes | Cook time: 25 minutes | Serves 2

1 tablespoon instant coffee	2 tablespoons erythritol	1 teaspoon spearmint, dried
2 tablespoons almond butter, softened	1 teaspoon dried mint	4 teaspoons coconut flour
	3 eggs, beaten	Cooking spray

1. Select Pizza, Air Fry Fan, set temperature to 365°F (185°C) and set time to 25 minutes. Press Start to begin preheating. Spray the baking pan with cooking spray. 2. Then mix all ingredients in the mixer bowl. 3. When you get a smooth mixture, transfer it in the pan. Flatten it gently. Once preheated, place the pan on the pizza position. 4. Serve.

Fried Oreos

Prep time: 7 minutes | Cook time: 6 minutes per batch | Makes 12 cookies

Oil for misting or nonstick spray	1 teaspoon vanilla extract	sandwich cookies
1 cup complete pancake and waffle mix	½ cup water, plus 2 tablespoons	1 tablespoon confectioners' sugar
	12 Oreos or other chocolate	

1. Spray baking pan with oil or nonstick spray. 2. Select Air Fry, set temperature to 390°F (199°C) and set time to 6 minutes. Press Start to begin preheating. 3. In a medium bowl, mix together the pancake mix, vanilla, and water. 4. Dip 4 cookies in batter and place in baking pan. Once preheated, place the pan on the air fry position. It will be done until browned. 5. Repeat steps 4 for the remaining cookies. 6. Sift sugar over warm cookies.

Molten Chocolate Almond Cakes

Prep time: 5 minutes | Cook time: 13 minutes | Serves 3

Butter and flour for the ramekins	¼ cup sugar	(or 4 chunks of chocolate)
4 ounces (113 g) bittersweet chocolate, chopped	½ teaspoon pure vanilla extract, or almond extract	Cocoa powder or powdered sugar, for dusting
½ cup (1 stick) unsalted butter	1 tablespoon all-purpose flour	Toasted almonds, coarsely chopped
2 eggs	3 tablespoons ground almonds	
2 egg yolks	8 to 12 semisweet chocolate discs	

1. Butter and flour three (6-ounce / 170-g) ramekins. (Butter the ramekins and then coat the butter with flour by shaking it around in the ramekin and dumping out any excess.) 2. Melt the chocolate and butter together, either in the microwave or in a double boiler. In a separate bowl, beat the eggs, egg yolks and sugar together until light and smooth. Add the vanilla extract. Whisk the chocolate mixture into the egg mixture. Stir in the flour and ground almonds. 3. Select Bake, Air Fry Fan, set temperature to 330°F (166°C) and set time to 13 minutes. Press Start to begin preheating. 4. Transfer the batter carefully to the buttered ramekins, filling halfway. Place two or three chocolate discs in the center of the batter and then fill the ramekins to ½-inch below the top with the remaining batter. Once preheated, place the ramekins on the bake position. The sides of the cake should be set, but the centers should be slightly soft. Remove the ramekins from the air fryer oven and let the cakes sit for 5 minutes. (If you'd like the cake a little less molten, bake for 14 minutes and let the cakes sit for 4 minutes.) 5. Run a butter knife around the edge of the ramekins and invert the cakes onto a plate. Lift the ramekin off the plate slowly and carefully so that the cake doesn't break. Dust with cocoa powder or powdered sugar and serve with a scoop of ice cream and some coarsely chopped toasted almonds.

Cinnamon Cupcakes with Cream Cheese Frosting

Prep time: 10 minutes | Cook time: 20 to 25 minutes | Serves 6

½ cup plus 2 tablespoons almond flour

2 tablespoons low-carb vanilla protein powder

⅛ teaspoon salt

1 teaspoon baking powder

¼ teaspoon ground cinnamon

¼ cup unsalted butter

¼ cup Swerve

2 eggs

½ teaspoon vanilla extract

2 tablespoons heavy cream

Cream Cheese Frosting:

4 ounces (113 g) cream cheese, softened

2 tablespoons unsalted butter, softened

½ teaspoon vanilla extract

2 tablespoons powdered Swerve

1 to 2 tablespoons heavy cream

1. Select Bake, Air Fry Fan, set temperature to 320°F (160°C) and set time to 20 to 25 minutes. Press Start to begin preheating. Lightly coat 6 silicone muffin cups with oil and set aside. 2. In a medium bowl, combine the almond flour, protein powder, salt, baking powder, and cinnamon; set aside. 3. In a stand mixer fitted with a paddle attachment, beat the butter and Swerve until creamy. Add the eggs, vanilla, and heavy cream, and beat again until thoroughly combined. Add half the flour mixture at a time to the butter mixture, mixing after each addition, until you have a smooth, creamy batter. 4. Divide the batter evenly among the muffin cups, filling each one about three-fourths full. Once preheated, place the muffin cups on the bake position. It will be done until a toothpick inserted into the center of a cupcake comes out clean. Allow to cool completely. 5. To make the cream cheese frosting: In a stand mixer fitted with a paddle attachment, beat the cream cheese, butter, and vanilla until fluffy. Add the Swerve and mix again until thoroughly combined. With the mixer running, add the heavy cream a tablespoon at a time until the frosting is smooth and creamy. Frost the cupcakes as desired.

Chocolate Peppermint Cheesecake

Prep time: 5 minutes | Cook time: 18 minutes | Serves 6

Crust:

½ cup butter, melted

½ cup coconut flour

2 tablespoons stevia

Cooking spray

Topping:

4 ounces (113 g) unsweetened baker's chocolate

1 cup mascarpone cheese, at room temperature

1 teaspoon vanilla extract

2 drops peppermint extract

1. Select Bake, Air Fry Fan, set temperature to 350°F (177°C) and set time to 18 minutes. Press Start to begin preheating. Lightly coat a baking pan with cooking spray. 2. In a mixing bowl, whisk together the butter, flour, and stevia until well combined. Transfer the mixture to the prepared baking pan. 3. Once preheated, place the pan on the bake position. It will be done until a toothpick inserted in the center comes out clean. 4. Remove the crust from the oven to a wire rack to cool. 5. Once cooled completely, place it in the freezer for 20 minutes. 6. When ready, combine all the ingredients for the topping in a small bowl and stir to incorporate. 7. Spread this topping over the crust and let it sit for another 15 minutes in the freezer. 8. Serve chilled.

Simple Pineapple Sticks

Prep time: 5 minutes | Cook time: 10 minutes | Serves 4

½ fresh pineapple, cut into sticks

¼ cup desiccated coconut

1. Select Air Fry, set temperature to 400°F (204°C) and set time to 10 minutes. Press Start to begin preheating. 2. Coat the pineapple sticks in the desiccated coconut and put each one in the crisper tray. 3. Once preheated, place the

tray on the air fry position. 4. Serve immediately

Mini Peanut Butter Tarts

Prep time: 25 minutes | Cook time: 12 to 15 minutes | Serves 8

1 cup pecans
1 cup finely ground blanched almond flour
2 tablespoons unsalted butter, at room temperature
½ cup plus 2 tablespoons Swerve, divided
½ cup heavy (whipping) cream
2 tablespoons mascarpone cheese
4 ounces (113 g) cream cheese
½ cup sugar-free peanut butter
1 teaspoon pure vanilla extract
⅛ teaspoon sea salt
½ cup stevia-sweetened chocolate chips
1 tablespoon coconut oil
¼ cup chopped peanuts or pecans

1. Select Bake, Air Fry Fan, set temperature to 300°F (149°C) and set time to 12 to 15 minutes. Press Start to begin preheating. Place the pecans in the bowl of a food processor; process until they are finely ground. 2. Transfer the ground pecans to a medium bowl and stir in the almond flour. Add the butter and 2 tablespoons of Swerve, and stir until the mixture becomes wet and crumbly. 3. Divide the mixture among 8 silicone muffin cups, pressing the crust firmly with your fingers into the bottom and part way up the sides of each cup. 4. Once preheated, place the muffin cups on the bake position, working in batches if necessary. It will be done until the crusts begin to brown. Remove the cups from the air fryer oven and set them aside to cool. 5. In the bowl of a stand mixer, combine the heavy cream and mascarpone cheese. Beat until peaks form. Transfer to a large bowl. 6. In the same stand mixer bowl, combine the cream cheese, peanut butter, remaining ½ cup of Swerve, vanilla, and salt. Beat at medium-high speed until smooth. 7. Reduce the speed to low and add the heavy cream mixture back a spoonful at a time, beating after each addition. 8. Spoon the peanut butter mixture over the crusts, and freeze the tarts for 30 minutes. 9. Place the chocolate chips and coconut oil in the top of a double boiler over high heat. Stir until melted, then remove from the heat. 10. Drizzle the melted chocolate over the peanut butter tarts. Top with the chopped nuts and freeze the tarts for another 15 minutes, until set. 11. Store the peanut butter tarts in an airtight container in the refrigerator for up to 1 week or in the freezer for up to 1 month.

Pumpkin Spice Pecans

Prep time: 5 minutes | Cook time: 6 minutes | Serves 4

1 cup whole pecans
¼ cup granular erythritol
1 large egg white
½ teaspoon ground cinnamon
½ teaspoon pumpkin pie spice
½ teaspoon vanilla extract

1. Select Air Fry, set temperature to 300°F (149°C) and set time to 6 minutes. Press Start to begin preheating. 2. Toss all ingredients in a large bowl until pecans are coated. Place into the crisper tray. 3. Once preheated, place the tray on the air fry position. 4. Toss two to three times during cooking. 5. Allow to cool completely. Store in an airtight container up to 3 days.

Gluten-Free Spice Cookies

Prep time: 10 minutes | Cook time: 12 minutes | Serves 4

4 tablespoons (½ stick) unsalted butter, at room temperature
2 tablespoons agave nectar
1 large egg
2 tablespoons water
2½ cups almond flour
½ cup sugar
2 teaspoons ground ginger
1 teaspoon ground cinnamon
½ teaspoon freshly grated nutmeg
1 teaspoon baking soda
¼ teaspoon kosher salt

1. Select Bake, Air Fry Fan, set temperature to 325°F (163°C) and set time to 12 minutes. Press Start to begin preheating. Line the baking pan with parchment paper cut to fit. 2. In a large bowl using a hand mixer, beat together the butter, agave, egg, and water on medium speed until light and fluffy. 3. Add the almond flour, sugar, ginger, cinnamon, nutmeg, baking soda, and salt. Beat on low speed until well combined. 4. Roll the dough into 2-tablespoon balls and arrange them on the parchment paper in the pan. (They don't really spread too much, but try to leave a little room between them.) It will be done until the tops of cookies are lightly browned. 5. Allow to cool completely. Store in an airtight container for up to a week.

Almond Shortbread

Prep time: 10 minutes | Cook time: 12 minutes | Serves 8

½ cup (1 stick) unsalted butter

½ cup sugar

1 teaspoon pure almond extract

1 cup all-purpose flour

1. In bowl of a stand mixer fitted with the paddle attachment, beat the butter and sugar on medium speed until light and fluffy, 3 to 4 minutes. Add the almond extract and beat until combined, about 30 seconds. Turn the mixer to low. Add the flour a little at a time and beat for about 2 minutes more until well-incorporated. 2. Select Pizza, Air Fry Fan, set temperature to 375°F (191°C) and set time to 12 minutes. Press Start to begin preheating. Pat the dough into an even layer in a baking pan. Once preheated, place the pan on the pizza position. 3. Carefully remove the pan from air fryer oven. While the shortbread is still warm and soft, cut it into 8 wedges. 4. Let cool in the pan for 5 minutes. Remove the wedges from the pan and let cool completely before serving.

Tortilla Fried Pies

Prep time: 10 minutes | Cook time: 5 minutes per batch | Makes 12 pies

12 small flour tortillas (4-inch diameter)

½ cup fig preserves

¼ cup sliced almonds

2 tablespoons shredded, unsweetened coconut

Oil for misting or cooking spray

1. Select Pizza, Air Fry Fan, set temperature to 390°F (199°C) and set time to 5 minutes. Press Start to begin preheating. Wrap refrigerated tortillas in damp paper towels and heat in microwave 30 seconds to warm. 2. Working with one tortilla at a time, place 2 teaspoons fig preserves, 1 teaspoon sliced almonds, and ½ teaspoon coconut in the center of each. 3. Moisten outer edges of tortilla all around. 4. Fold one side of tortilla over filling to make a half-moon shape and press down lightly on center. Using the tines of a fork, press down firmly on edges of tortilla to seal in filling. 5. Mist both sides with oil or cooking spray. 6. Place hand pies in pizza rack close but not overlapping. It's fine to lean some against the sides and corners of the basket. You may need to cook in 2 batches. 7. Once preheated, place the rack on the pizza position. It will be done until lightly browned. Serve hot. 8. Refrigerate any leftover pies in a closed container. To serve later, toss them back in the oven and cook for 2 or 3 minutes to reheat.

Zucchini Nut Muffins

Prep time: 15 minutes | Cook time: 15 minutes | Serves 4

¼ cup vegetable oil, plus more for greasing

¾ cup all-purpose flour

¾ teaspoon ground cinnamon

¼ teaspoon kosher salt

¼ teaspoon baking soda

¼ teaspoon baking powder

2 large eggs

½ cup sugar

½ cup grated zucchini

¼ cup chopped walnuts

1. Select Bake, Air Fry Fan, set temperature to 325°F (163°C) and set time to 15 minutes. Press Start to begin preheating. Generously grease a baking pan with vegetable oil. 2. In a medium bowl, sift together the flour, cinnamon, salt, baking soda, and baking powder. 3. In a separate medium bowl, beat together the eggs, sugar, and vegetable oil. Add the dry ingredients to the wet ingredients. Add the zucchini and nuts and stir gently until well combined. Transfer the batter to the prepared baking pan. 4. Once preheated, place the pan on the bake position. It will be done until a cake tester or toothpick inserted into the center comes out clean. If it doesn't, cook for 3 to 5 minutes more and test again. 5. Let cool in the pan for 10 minutes. Carefully remove from the pan and let cool completely before serving.

Mini Cheesecake

Prep time: 10 minutes | Cook time: 15 minutes | Serves 2

½ cup walnuts
2 tablespoons salted butter
2 tablespoons granular erythritol
4 ounces (113 g) full-fat cream cheese, softened
1 large egg
½ teaspoon vanilla extract
⅛ cup powdered erythritol

1. Select Bake, Air Fry Fan, set temperature to 400°F (204°C) and set time to 5 minutes. Press Start to begin preheating. Place walnuts, butter, and granular erythritol in a food processor. Pulse until ingredients stick together and a dough forms. 2. Press dough into a baking pan. 3. Once preheated, place the pan on the bake position. 4. When done, remove the crust and let cool. 5. In a medium bowl, mix cream cheese with egg, vanilla extract, and powdered erythritol until smooth. 6. Spoon mixture on top of baked walnut crust and place into the air fryer oven. 7. Adjust the temperature to 300°F (149°C) and bake for 10 minutes. 8. Once done, chill for 2 hours before serving.

Lemon Bars

Prep time: 15 minutes | Cook time: 25 minutes | Serves 6

¾ cup whole-wheat pastry flour
2 tablespoons confectioners' sugar
¼ cup butter, melted
½ cup granulated sugar
1 tablespoon packed grated lemon zest
¼ cup freshly squeezed lemon juice
⅛ teaspoon sea salt
¼ cup unsweetened plain applesauce
2 teaspoons cornstarch
¾ teaspoon baking powder
Cooking oil spray (sunflower, safflower, or refined coconut)

1. In a small bowl, stir together the flour, confectioners' sugar, and melted butter just until well combined. Place in the refrigerator. 2. In a medium bowl, stir together the granulated sugar, lemon zest and juice, salt, applesauce, cornstarch, and baking powder. 3. Select Bake, Air Fry Fan, set temperature to 350°F (177°C) and set time to 25 minutes. Press Start to begin preheating. 4. Spray a baking pan lightly with cooking oil. Remove the crust mixture from the refrigerator and gently press it into the bottom of the prepared pan in an even layer. 5. Once preheated, place the pan on the bake position. 6. After 5 minutes, check the crust. It should be slightly firm to the touch. Remove the pan and spread the lemon filling over the crust. Reinsert the pan into the oven and resume baking for 18 to 20 minutes, or until the top is nicely browned. 7. When baking is complete, let cool for 30 minutes. Refrigerate to cool completely. Cut into pieces and serve.

Crumbly Coconut-Pecan Cookies

Prep time: 10 minutes | Cook time: 25 minutes | Serves 10

1½ cups coconut flour
1½ cups extra-fine almond flour
½ teaspoon baking powder
⅓ teaspoon baking soda
3 eggs plus an egg yolk, beaten
¾ cup coconut oil, at room temperature
1 cup unsalted pecan nuts, roughly chopped

¾ cup monk fruit	⅓ teaspoon ground cloves	½ teaspoon pure coconut extract
¼ teaspoon freshly grated nutmeg	½ teaspoon pure vanilla extract	⅛ teaspoon fine sea salt

1. Select Bake, Air Fry Fan, set temperature to 370°F (188°C) and set time to 25 minutes. Press Start to begin preheating. Line the baking pan with parchment paper. 2. Mix the coconut flour, almond flour, baking powder, and baking soda in a large mixing bowl. 3. In another mixing bowl, stir together the eggs and coconut oil. Add the wet mixture to the dry mixture. 4. Mix in the remaining ingredients and stir until a soft dough forms. 5. Drop about 2 tablespoons of dough on the parchment paper for each cookie and flatten each biscuit until it's 1 inch thick. 6. Once preheated, place the pan on the bake position. the cookies will be golden and firm to the touch. Remove from the oven to a plate. Let the cookies cool to room temperature and serve.

Lemon Raspberry Muffins

Prep time: 5 minutes | Cook time: 15 minutes | Serves 6

2 cups almond flour	⅓ teaspoon ground anise star	1 cup sour cream
¾ cup Swerve	½ teaspoon grated lemon zest	½ cup coconut oil
1¼ teaspoons baking powder	¼ teaspoon salt	½ cup raspberries
⅓ teaspoon ground allspice	2 eggs	

1. Select Bake, Air Fry Fan, set temperature to 345°F (174°C) and set time to 15 minutes. Press Start to begin preheating. 2. In a mixing bowl, mix the almond flour, Swerve, baking powder, allspice, anise, lemon zest, and salt. 3. In another mixing bowl, beat the eggs, sour cream, and coconut oil until well mixed. Add the egg mixture to the flour mixture and stir to combine. Mix in the raspberries. 4. Scrape the batter into the six muffin cups, filling each about three-quarters full. 5. Once preheated, place the muffin cups on the bake position. You may need to work in batches. It will be done until the tops are golden and a toothpick inserted in the middle comes out clean. 6. Allow the muffins to cool for 10 minutes before removing and serving.

Coconut-Custard Pie

Prep time: 10 minutes | Cook time: 20 to 23 minutes | Serves 4

1 cup milk	1 teaspoon vanilla	Cooking spray
¼ cup plus 2 tablespoons sugar	2 eggs	½ cup shredded, sweetened
¼ cup biscuit baking mix	2 tablespoons melted butter	coconut

1. Place all ingredients except coconut in a medium bowl. 2. Using a hand mixer, beat on high speed for 3 minutes. 3. Let sit for 5 minutes. 4. Select Pizza, Air Fry Fan, set temperature to 330°F (166°C) and set time to 20 to 23 minutes. Press Start to begin preheating. 5. Spray a baking pan with cooking spray. 6. Pour filling into pan and sprinkle coconut over top. Once preheated, place the pan on the pizza position. 7. Serve.

Cardamom Custard

Prep time: 10 minutes | Cook time: 25 minutes | Serves 2

1 cup whole milk	¼ teaspoon vanilla bean paste or	plus more for sprinkling
1 large egg	pure vanilla extract	
2 tablespoons plus 1 teaspoon sugar	¼ teaspoon ground cardamom,	

1. Select Bake, Air Fry Fan, set temperature to 350°F (177°C) and set time to 25 minutes. Press Start to begin

preheating. 2. In a medium bowl, beat together the milk, egg, sugar, vanilla, and cardamom. 3. Divide the mixture between two 8-ounce (227-g) ramekins. Sprinkle lightly with cardamom. Cover each ramekin tightly with aluminum foil. Once preheated, place the ramekins on the bake position. It will be done until a toothpick inserted in the center comes out clean. 4. Let the custards cool on a wire rack for 5 to 10 minutes. 5. Serve warm, or refrigerate until cold and serve chilled.

Shortcut Spiced Apple Butter

Prep time: 5 minutes | Cook time: 1 hour | Makes 1¼ cups

Cooking spray

2 cups store-bought unsweetened applesauce

⅔ cup packed light brown sugar

3 tablespoons fresh lemon juice

½ teaspoon kosher salt

¼ teaspoon ground cinnamon

⅛ teaspoon ground allspice

1. Select Bake, Air Fry Fan, set temperature to 340°F (171°C) and set time to 60 minutes. Press Start to begin preheating. Spray a cake pan that will fit your air fryer oven with cooking spray. 2. Whisk together all the ingredients in a bowl until smooth, then pour into the greased pan. Once preheated, place the pan on the bake position. The apple mixture will be caramelized, reduced to a thick purée, and fragrant when done. 2. Remove the pan from the oven, stir to combine the caramelized bits at the edge with the rest, then let cool completely to thicken. Scrape the apple butter into a jar and store in the refrigerator for up to 2 weeks.

Chapter 8 Staples, Sauces, Dips, and Dressings

Peanut Sauce

Prep time: 5 minutes | Cook time: 0 minutes | Serves 4

⅓ cup peanut butter

¼ cup hot water

2 tablespoons soy sauce

2 tablespoons rice vinegar

Juice of 1 lime

1 teaspoon minced fresh ginger

1 teaspoon minced garlic

1 teaspoon black pepper

1. In a blender container, combine the peanut butter, hot water, soy sauce, vinegar, lime juice, ginger, garlic, and pepper. Blend until smooth. 2. Use immediately or store in an airtight container in the refrigerator for a week or more.

Tzatziki

Prep time: 10 minutes | Cook time: 0 minutes | Serves 4

1 large cucumber, peeled and grated (about 2 cups)

1 cup plain Greek yogurt

2 to 3 garlic cloves, minced

1 tablespoon tahini (sesame paste)

1 tablespoon fresh lemon juice

½ teaspoon kosher salt, or to taste

Chopped fresh parsley or dill, for garnish (optional)

1. In a medium bowl, combine the cucumber, yogurt, garlic, tahini, lemon juice, and salt. Stir until well combined. Cover and chill until ready to serve. 2. Right before serving, sprinkle with chopped fresh parsley, if desired.

Peachy Barbecue Sauce

Prep time: 10 minutes | Cook time: 0 minutes | Makes 2¼ cups

1 cup peach preserves

1 cup ketchup

2 tablespoons apple cider vinegar

2 tablespoons light brown sugar

1 teaspoon chili powder

½ teaspoon freshly ground black

pepper
½ teaspoon dry mustard

1. In a medium bowl, stir together the peach preserves, ketchup, and vinegar until blended. 2. In a small bowl, whisk the brown sugar, chili powder, pepper, and dry mustard to combine. Add the brown sugar mixture to the peach preserves mixture. Mix well to combine. 3. Transfer the barbecue sauce to an airtight container. Refrigerate for up to 1 week until ready to use as a sauce or marinade.

Pecan Tartar Sauce

Prep time: 10 minutes | Cook time: 10 minutes | Makes 1¼ cups

4 tablespoons pecans, finely chopped
½ cup sour cream
½ cup mayonnaise
½ teaspoon grated lemon zest
1½ tablespoons freshly squeezed lemon juice
2½ tablespoons chopped fresh
parsley
1 teaspoon paprika
2 tablespoons chopped dill pickle

1. Select Bake, Air Fry Fan, set temperature to 325°F (163°C) and set time to 7 to 10 minutes. Press Start to begin preheating. Spread the pecans in a single layer on a parchment sheet lightly spritzed with oil. 2. Once preheated, place the pecans in baking pan on bake position. Stir every 2 minutes. Let cool. 3. In a medium bowl, mix the sour cream, mayonnaise, lemon zest, and lemon juice until blended. 4. Stir in the parsley paprika, dill pickle, and pecans. Cover and refrigerate to chill for at least 1 hour to blend the flavors. This sauce should be used within 2 weeks.

Alfredo Sauce

Prep time: 10 minutes | Cook time: 10 minutes | Serves 6

¼ cup butter
1 cup cream cheese
1½ cups heavy (whipping) cream
2 teaspoons minced garlic
¼ teaspoon salt
¼ teaspoon freshly ground black
pepper
1 cup grated Parmesan cheese

1. Make the sauce. In a medium saucepan over medium heat, stir together the butter, cream cheese, and cream. Cook, whisking until the sauce is smooth and the butter and cheese are melted. Add the garlic, salt, and pepper and whisk until well blended. Whisk in the Parmesan. 2. Simmer. Bring the sauce to a simmer and cook until it is slightly thickened, about 5 minutes. 3. Store. Cool the sauce completely and store in a sealed container in the refrigerator for up to 3 days.

Marinara Sauce

Prep time: 15 minutes | Cook time: 40 minutes | Makes 8 cups

1 small onion, diced
1 small red bell pepper, stemmed, seeded and chopped
2 tablespoons plus ¼ cup extra-virgin olive oil, divided
2 tablespoons butter
4 to 6 garlic cloves, minced
2 teaspoon salt, divided
½ teaspoon freshly ground black pepper
2 (32-ounce / 907-g) cans crushed tomatoes (with basil, if possible), with their juices
½ cup thinly sliced basil leaves,
divided
2 tablespoons chopped fresh rosemary
1 to 2 teaspoons crushed red pepper flakes (optional)

1. In a food processor, combine the onion and bell pepper and blend until very finely minced. 2. In a large skillet, heat 2 tablespoons olive oil and the butter over medium heat. Add the minced onion, and red pepper and sauté until just

starting to get tender, about 5 minutes. 3. Add the garlic, salt, and pepper and sauté until fragrant, another 1 to 2 minutes. 4. Reduce the heat to low and add the tomatoes and their juices, remaining ¼ cup olive oil, ¼ cup basil, rosemary, and red pepper flakes (if using). Stir to combine, then bring to a simmer and cover. Cook over low heat for 30 to 60 minutes to allow the flavors to blend. 5. Add remaining ¼ cup chopped fresh basil after removing from heat, stirring to combine. Serve.

Pepper Sauce

Prep time: 10 minutes | Cook time: 20 minutes | Makes 4 cups

- 2 red hot fresh chiles, seeded
- 2 dried chiles
- ½ small yellow onion, roughly chopped
- 2 garlic cloves, peeled
- 2 cups water
- 2 cups white vinegar

1. In a medium saucepan, combine the fresh and dried chiles, onion, garlic, and water. Bring to a simmer and cook for 20 minutes, or until tender. Transfer to a food processor or blender. 2. Add the vinegar and blend until smooth.

Tomatillo Salsa

Prep time: 5 minutes | Cook time: 15 minutes | Serves 4

- 12 tomatillos
- 2 fresh serrano chiles
- 1 tablespoon minced garlic
- 1 cup chopped fresh cilantro leaves
- 1 tablespoon vegetable oil
- 1 teaspoon kosher salt

1. Select Bake, Air Fry Fan, set temperature to 350°F (177°C) and set time to 15 minutes. Press Start to begin preheating. 2. Remove and discard the papery husks from the tomatillos and rinse them under warm running water to remove the sticky coating. 3. Once preheated, place the tomatillos and peppers in baking pan on bake position. 3. Transfer the tomatillos and peppers to a blender, add the garlic, cilantro, vegetable oil, and salt, and blend until almost smooth. (If not using immediately, omit the salt and add it just before serving.) 4. Serve or store in an airtight container in the refrigerator for up to 10 days.

Gochujang Dip

Prep time: 5 minutes | Cook time: 0 minutes | Serves 4

- 2 tablespoons gochujang (Korean red pepper paste)
- 1 tablespoon mayonnaise
- 1 tablespoon toasted sesame oil
- 1 tablespoon minced fresh ginger
- 1 tablespoon minced garlic
- 1 teaspoon agave nectar

1. In a small bowl, combine the gochujang, mayonnaise, sesame oil, ginger, garlic, and agave. Stir until well combined. 2. Use immediately or store in the refrigerator, covered, for up to 3 days.

Hot Honey Mustard Dip

Prep time: 5 minutes | Cook time: 0 minutes | Makes 1⅓ cups

- ¾ cup mayonnaise
- ⅓ cup spicy brown mustard
- ¼ cup honey
- ½ teaspoon cayenne pepper

1. In a medium bowl, stir together the mayonnaise, mustard, and honey until blended. 2. Stir in the cayenne. Cover and chill for 3 hours so the flavors blend. 3. Keep refrigerated in an airtight container for up to 3 weeks.

Cucumber Yogurt Dip

Prep time: 5 minutes | Cook time: 0 minutes | Serves 2 to 3

1 cup plain, unsweetened, full-fat Greek yogurt

½ cup cucumber, peeled, seeded, and diced

1 tablespoon freshly squeezed lemon juice

1 tablespoon chopped fresh mint

1 small garlic clove, minced

Salt and freshly ground black pepper, to taste

1. In a food processor, combine the yogurt, cucumber, lemon juice, mint, and garlic. Pulse several times to combine, leaving noticeable cucumber chunks. 2. Taste and season with salt and pepper.

Artichoke Dip

Prep time: 15 minutes | Cook time: 0 minutes | Serves 3

1 (14-ounce / 397-g) can artichoke hearts, drained

1 pound (454 g) goat cheese

2 tablespoons extra-virgin olive oil

2 teaspoons lemon juice

1 garlic clove, minced

1 tablespoon chopped parsley

1 tablespoon chopped chives

½ tablespoon chopped basil

½ teaspoon sea salt

½ teaspoon freshly ground black pepper

Dash of cayenne pepper (optional)

½ cup freshly grated Pecorino Romano

1. In a food processor, combine all the ingredients, except the Pecorino Romano, and process until well incorporated and creamy. 2. Top with the freshly grated Pecorino Romano. Store in an airtight container in the refrigerator for up to 3 days.

Italian Dressing

Prep time: 5 minutes | Cook time: 0 minutes | Serves 12

¼ cup red wine vinegar

½ cup extra-virgin olive oil

¼ teaspoon salt

¼ teaspoon freshly ground black pepper

1 teaspoon dried Italian seasoning

1 teaspoon Dijon mustard

1 garlic clove, minced

1. In a small jar, combine the vinegar, olive oil, salt, pepper, Italian seasoning, mustard, and garlic. Close with a tight-fitting lid and shake vigorously for 1 minute. 2. Refrigerate for up to 1 week.

Tahini Dressing

Prep time: 5 minutes | Cook time: 0 minutes | Serves 8 to 10

½ cup tahini

¼ cup freshly squeezed lemon juice (about 2 to 3 lemons)

¼ cup extra-virgin olive oil

1 garlic clove, finely minced or ½ teaspoon garlic powder

2 teaspoons salt

1. In a glass mason jar with a lid, combine the tahini, lemon juice, olive oil, garlic, and salt. Cover and shake well until combined and creamy. Store in the refrigerator for up to 2 weeks.

Apple Cider Dressing

Prep time: 5 minutes | Cook time: 0 minutes | Serves 2

2 tablespoons apple cider vinegar

⅓ lemon, juiced

⅓ lemon, zested

Salt and freshly ground black

pepper, to taste

1. In a jar, combine the vinegar, lemon juice, and zest. Season with salt and pepper, cover, and shake well.

Orange Dijon Dressing

Prep time: 5 minutes | Cook time: 0 minutes | Serves 2

- ¼ cup extra-virgin olive oil
- 2 tablespoons freshly squeezed orange juice
- 1 orange, zested
- 1 teaspoon garlic powder
- ¾ teaspoon za'atar seasoning
- ½ teaspoon salt
- ¼ teaspoon Dijon mustard
- Freshly ground black pepper, to taste

1. In a jar, combine the olive oil, orange juice and zest, garlic powder, za'atar, salt, and mustard. Season with pepper and shake vigorously until completely mixed.

Miso-Ginger Dressing

Prep time: 10 minutes | Cook time: 0 minutes | Serves 4

- 1 tablespoon unseasoned rice vinegar
- 1 tablespoon red or white miso
- 1 teaspoon grated fresh ginger
- 1 garlic clove, minced
- 3 tablespoons extra-virgin olive oil

1. In a small bowl, combine the vinegar and miso into a paste. Add the ginger and garlic, and mix well. While whisking, drizzle in the olive oil. 2. Store in the refrigerator in an airtight container for up to 1 week.

Blue Cheese Dressing

Prep time: 5 minutes | Cook time: 0 minutes | Serves 12

- ¾ cup sugar-free mayonnaise
- ¼ cup sour cream
- ½ cup heavy (whipping) cream
- 1 teaspoon minced garlic
- 1 tablespoon freshly squeezed lemon juice
- 1 tablespoon apple cider vinegar
- 1 teaspoon hot sauce
- ½ teaspoon sea salt
- 4 ounces (113 g) blue cheese, crumbled (about ¾ cup)

1. In a medium bowl, whisk together the mayonnaise, sour cream, and heavy cream. 2. Stir in the garlic, lemon juice, apple cider vinegar, hot sauce, and sea salt. 3. Add the blue cheese crumbles, and stir until well combined. 4. Transfer to an airtight container, and refrigerate for up to 1 week.

Green Basil Dressing

Prep time: 10 minutes | Cook time: 0 minutes | Makes 1 cup

- 1 avocado, peeled and pitted
- ¼ cup sour cream
- ¼ cup extra-virgin olive oil
- ¼ cup chopped fresh basil
- 1 tablespoon freshly squeezed lime juice
- 1 teaspoon minced garlic
- Sea salt and freshly ground black pepper, to taste

1. Place the avocado, sour cream, olive oil, basil, lime juice, and garlic in a food processor and pulse until smooth, scraping down the sides of the bowl once during processing. 2. Season the dressing with salt and pepper. 3. Keep the dressing in an airtight container in the refrigerator for 1 to 2 weeks.

Traditional Caesar Dressing

Prep time: 10 minutes | Cook time: 5 minutes | Makes 1½ cups

- 2 teaspoons minced garlic
- 4 large egg yolks
- ¼ cup wine vinegar
- ½ teaspoon dry mustard
- Dash Worcestershire sauce
- 1 cup extra-virgin olive oil
- ¼ cup freshly squeezed lemon juice
- Sea salt and freshly ground black pepper, to taste

1. To a small saucepan, add the garlic, egg yolks, vinegar, mustard, and Worcestershire sauce and place over low heat. 2. Whisking constantly, cook the mixture until it thickens and is a little bubbly, about 5 minutes. 3. Remove from saucepan from the heat and let it stand for about 10 minutes to cool. 4. Transfer the egg mixture to a large stainless steel bowl. Whisking constantly, add the olive oil in a thin stream. 5. Whisk in the lemon juice and season the dressing with salt and pepper. 6. Transfer the dressing to an airtight container and keep in the refrigerator for up to 3 days.

Avocado Dressing

Prep time: 5 minutes | Cook time: 0 minutes | Makes 12 tablespoons

1 large avocado, pitted and peeled
½ cup water
2 tablespoons tahini
2 tablespoons freshly squeezed
lemon juice
1 teaspoon dried basil
1 teaspoon white wine vinegar
1 garlic clove
¼ teaspoon pink Himalayan salt
¼ teaspoon freshly ground black pepper

1. Combine all the ingredients in a food processor and blend until smooth.

Dijon and Balsamic Vinaigrette

Prep time: 5 minutes | Cook time: 0 minutes | Makes 12 tablespoons

6 tablespoons water
4 tablespoons Dijon mustard
4 tablespoons balsamic vinegar
1 teaspoon maple syrup
½ teaspoon pink Himalayan salt
¼ teaspoon freshly ground black pepper

1. In a bowl, whisk together all the ingredients.

Hemp Dressing

Prep time: 5 minutes | Cook time: 0 minutes | Makes 12 tablespoons

½ cup white wine vinegar
¼ cup tahini
¼ cup water
1 tablespoon hemp seeds
½ tablespoon freshly squeezed
lemon juice
1 teaspoon garlic powder
1 teaspoon dried oregano
1 teaspoon dried basil
1 teaspoon red pepper flakes
½ teaspoon onion powder
½ teaspoon pink Himalayan salt
½ teaspoon freshly ground black pepper

1. In a bowl, combine all the ingredients and whisk until mixed well.

Lemony Tahini

Prep time: 5 minutes | Cook time: 0 minutes | Serves 4

¾ cup water
½ cup tahini
3 garlic cloves, minced
Juice of 3 lemons
½ teaspoon pink Himalayan salt

1. In a bowl, whisk together all the ingredients until mixed well.

Cashew Mayo

Prep time: 5 minutes | Cook time: 0 minutes | Makes 18 tablespoons

1 cup cashews, soaked in hot water for at least 1 hour
¼ cup plus 3 tablespoons milk
1 tablespoon apple cider vinegar
1 tablespoon freshly squeezed lemon juice
1 tablespoon Dijon mustard
1 tablespoon aquafaba
⅛ teaspoon pink Himalayan salt

1. In a food processor, combine all the ingredients and blend until creamy and smooth.

Mushroom Apple Gravy

Prep time: 5 minutes | Cook time: 10 minutes | Serves 4

2 cups vegetable broth
½ cup finely chopped mushrooms
2 tablespoons whole wheat flour
1 tablespoon unsweetened applesauce
1 teaspoon onion powder
½ teaspoon dried thyme
¼ teaspoon dried rosemary
⅛ teaspoon pink Himalayan salt
Freshly ground black pepper, to taste

1. In a nonstick saucepan over medium-high heat, combine all the ingredients and mix well. Bring to a boil, stirring frequently, reduce the heat to low, and simmer, stirring constantly, until it thickens.

Homemade Remoulade Sauce

Prep time: 5 minutes | Cook time: 0 minutes | Serves 4

¾ cup mayonnaise
1 garlic clove, minced
2 tablespoons mustard
1 teaspoon horseradish
1 teaspoon Cajun seasoning
1 teaspoon dill pickle juice
½ teaspoon paprika
¼ teaspoon hot pepper sauce

1. Whisk together all the ingredients in a small bowl until completely mixed. 2. It can be used as a delicious dip for veggies, a sandwich or burger spread, or you can serve it with chicken fingers for a dipping sauce.

Sweet Ginger Teriyaki Sauce

Prep time: 5 minutes | Cook time: 0 minutes | Serves 4

¼ cup pineapple juice
¼ cup low-sodium soy sauce
2 tablespoons packed brown sugar
1 tablespoon arrowroot powder or cornstarch
1 tablespoon grated fresh ginger
1 teaspoon garlic powder

1. Mix together all the ingredients in a small bowl and whisk to incorporate. 2. Serve immediately, or transfer to an airtight container and refrigerate until ready to use.

Vegan Lentil Dip

Prep time: 10 minutes | Cook time: 15 minutes | Makes 3 cups

2½ cups water, divided
1 cup dried green or brown lentils, rinsed
⅓ cup tahini
1 garlic clove
½ teaspoon salt, plus additional as needed

1. Mix 2 cups of water and lentils in a medium pot and bring to a boil over high heat. 2. Once it starts to boil, reduce the heat to low, and bring to a simmer for 15 minutes, or until the lentils are tender. If there is any water remaining in the pot, simply drain it off. 3. Transfer the cooked lentils to a food processor, along with the remaining ingredients. Pulse until a hummus-like consistency is achieved. 4. Taste and add additional salt as needed. 5. It's tasty used as a sandwich spread, and you can also serve it over whole-wheat pita bread or crackers.

Lemon Cashew Dip

Prep time: 10 minutes | Cook time: 0 minutes | Makes 1 cup

¾ cup cashews, soaked in water for at least 4 hours and drained
Juice and zest of 1 lemon
¼ cup water

2 tablespoons chopped fresh dill

¼ teaspoon salt, plus additional as needed

1. Blend the cashew, lemon juice and zest, and water in a blender until smooth and creamy. 2. Fold in the dill and salt and blend again. 3. Taste and add additional salt as needed. 4. Transfer to the refrigerator to chill for at least 1 hour to blend the flavors. 5. This dip perfectly goes with the crackers or tacos. It also can be used as a sauce for roasted vegetables or a sandwich spread.

Cauliflower Alfredo Sauce

Prep time: 2 minutes | Cook time: 0 minutes | Makes 4 cups

2 tablespoons olive oil
6 garlic cloves, minced
3 cups unsweetened almond milk
1 (1-pound / 454-g) head

cauliflower, cut into florets
1 teaspoon salt
¼ teaspoon freshly ground black pepper

Juice of 1 lemon
4 tablespoons nutritional yeast

1. In a medium saucepan, heat the olive oil over medium-high heat. Add the garlic and sauté for 1 minute or until fragrant. Add the almond milk, stir, and bring to a boil. 2. Gently add the cauliflower. Stir in the salt and pepper and return to a boil. Continue cooking over medium-high heat for 5 minutes or until the cauliflower is soft. Stir frequently and reduce heat if needed to prevent the liquid from boiling over. 3. Carefully transfer the cauliflower and cooking liquid to a food processor, using a slotted spoon to scoop out the larger pieces of cauliflower before pouring in the liquid. Add the lemon and nutritional yeast and blend for 1 to 2 minutes until smooth. 4. Serve immediately.

Red Buffalo Sauce

Prep time: 5 minutes | Cook time: 20 minutes | Makes 2 cups

¼ cup olive oil
4 garlic cloves, roughly chopped
1 (5-ounce / 142-g) small red onion, roughly chopped

6 red chiles, roughly chopped (about 2 ounces / 56 g in total)
1 cup water
½ cup apple cider vinegar

½ teaspoon salt
½ teaspoon freshly ground black pepper

1. In a large nonstick sauté pan, heat ¼ cup olive oil over medium-high heat. Once it's hot, add the garlic, onion, and chiles. Cook for 5 minutes, stirring occasionally, until onions are golden brown. 2. Add the water and bring to a boil. Cook for about 10 minutes or until the water has nearly evaporated. 3. Transfer the cooked onion and chile mixture to a food processor or blender and blend briefly to combine. Add the apple cider vinegar, salt, and pepper. Blend again for 30 seconds. 4. Using a mesh sieve, strain the sauce into a bowl. Use a spoon or spatula to scrape and press all the liquid from the pulp.

Chapter 9 Desserts

Cream Cheese Danish

Prep time: 20 minutes | Cook time: 15 minutes | Serves 6

¾ cup blanched finely ground almond flour
1 cup shredded Mozzarella cheese

5 ounces (142 g) full-fat cream cheese, divided
2 large egg yolks

¾ cup powdered erythritol, divided
2 teaspoons vanilla extract, divided

1. Select Bake, Air Fry Fan, set temperature to 330ºF (166ºC) and set time to 15 minutes. Press Start to begin preheating. In a large microwave-safe bowl, add almond flour, Mozzarella, and 1 ounce (28 g) cream cheese. Mix and then microwave for 1 minute. 2. Stir and add egg yolks to the bowl. Continue stirring until soft dough forms. Add ½ cup erythritol to dough and 1 teaspoon vanilla. 3. Cut a piece of parchment to fit your baking pan. Wet your hands with warm water and press out the dough into a ¼-inch-thick rectangle. 4. In a medium bowl, mix remaining cream cheese, erythritol, and vanilla. Place this cream cheese mixture on the right half of the dough rectangle. Fold over the left side of the dough and press to seal. Place into the baking pan. 5. Once preheated, place the pan on the bake position. 6. After 7 minutes, flip over the Danish. 7. When done, remove the Danish from parchment and allow to completely cool before cutting.

Strawberry Pastry Rolls

Prep time: 20 minutes | Cook time: 5 to 6 minutes per batch | Serves 4

3 ounces (85 g) low-fat cream cheese	¼ teaspoon pure vanilla extract	¼ to ½ cup dark chocolate chips (optional)
2 tablespoons plain yogurt	8 ounces (227 g) fresh strawberries	
2 teaspoons sugar	8 sheets phyllo dough	
	Butter-flavored cooking spray	

1. In a medium bowl, combine the cream cheese, yogurt, sugar, and vanilla. Beat with hand mixer at high speed until smooth, about 1 minute. 2. Wash strawberries and destem. Chop enough of them to measure ½ cup. Stir into cheese mixture. 3. Select Bake, Air Fry Fan, set temperature to 330ºF (166ºC) and set time to 5 to 6 minutes. Press Start to begin preheating. 4. Phyllo dough dries out quickly, so cover your stack of phyllo sheets with waxed paper and then place a damp dish towel on top of that. Remove only one sheet at a time as you work. 5. To create one pastry roll, lay out a single sheet of phyllo. Spray lightly with butter-flavored spray, top with a second sheet of phyllo, and spray the second sheet lightly. 6. Place a quarter of the filling (about 3 tablespoons) about ½ inch from the edge of one short side. Fold the end of the phyllo over the filling and keep rolling a turn or two. Fold in both the left and right sides so that the edges meet in the middle of your roll. Then roll up completely. Spray outside of pastry roll with butter spray. 7. When you have 4 rolls, place them in the baking pan, seam side down, leaving some space in between each. Once preheated, place the pan on the bake position. It will be done until they turn a delicate golden brown. 8. Repeat step 7 for remaining rolls. 9. Allow pastries to cool to room temperature. 10. When ready to serve, slice the remaining strawberries. If desired, melt the chocolate chips in microwave or double boiler. Place 1 pastry on each dessert plate, and top with sliced strawberries. Drizzle melted chocolate over strawberries and onto plate.

Strawberry Scone Shortcake

Prep time: 10 minutes | Cook time: 20 minutes | Serves 4 to 6

1⅓ cups all-purpose flour	8 tablespoons (1 stick) unsalted butter, cubed and chilled	2 tablespoons powdered sugar, plus more for dusting
3 tablespoons granulated sugar	1⅓ cups heavy cream, chilled	½ teaspoon vanilla extract
1½ teaspoons baking powder	Turbinado sugar, for sprinkling	1 cup quartered fresh strawberries
1 teaspoon kosher salt		

1. Select Bake, Air Fry Fan, set temperature to 350ºF (177ºC) and set time to 20 minutes. Press Start to begin preheating. 2. In a large bowl, whisk together the flour, granulated sugar, baking powder, and salt. Add the butter and use your fingers to break apart the butter pieces while working them into the flour mixture, until pea-size pieces form. Pour ⅔ cup of the cream over the flour mixture and, using a rubber spatula, mix the ingredients together until just

combined. 3. Transfer the dough to a work surface and form into a 7-inch-wide disk. Brush the top with water, then sprinkle with some turbinado sugar. Using a large metal spatula, transfer the dough to the baking pan. Once preheated, place the pan on the bake position. It will be done until golden brown and fluffy. Let cool in the air fryer oven for 5 minutes, then turn out, right-side up, to cool completely. 4. Meanwhile, in a bowl, beat the remaining ⅔ cup cream, the powdered sugar, and vanilla until stiff peaks form. Split the scone like a hamburger bun and spread the strawberries over the bottom. Top with the whipped cream and cover with the top of the scone. Dust with powdered sugar and cut into wedges to serve.

5-Ingredient Brownies

Prep time: 10 minutes | Cook time: 25 minutes | Serves 6

Vegetable oil	½ cup chocolate chips	½ cup sugar
½ cup (1 stick) unsalted butter	3 large eggs	1 teaspoon pure vanilla extract

1. Select Bake, Air Fry Fan, set temperature to 350°F (177°C) and set time to 25 minutes. Press Start to begin preheating. Generously grease a baking pan with vegetable oil. 2. In a microwave-safe bowl, combine the butter and chocolate chips. Microwave on high for 1 minute. Stir very well. (You want the heat from the butter and chocolate to melt the remaining clumps. If you microwave until everything melts, the chocolate will be overcooked. If necessary, microwave for an additional 10 seconds, but stir well before you try that.) 3. In a medium bowl, combine the eggs, sugar, and vanilla. Whisk until light and frothy. While whisking continuously, slowly pour in the melted chocolate in a thin stream and whisk until everything is incorporated. 4. Pour the batter into the prepared pan. Once preheated, place the pan on the bake position. It will be done until a toothpick inserted into the center comes out clean. 5. Allow to cool for 30 minutes before cutting into squares.

Vanilla and Cardamon Walnuts Tart

Prep time: 5 minutes | Cook time: 13 minutes | Serves 6

1 cup coconut milk	½ stick butter, at room temperature	¼ teaspoon ground cardamom
½ cup walnuts, ground		¼ teaspoon ground cloves
½ cup Swerve	2 eggs	Cooking spray
½ cup almond flour	1 teaspoon vanilla essence	

1. Select Bake, Air Fry Fan, set temperature to 360°F (182°C) and set time to 13 minutes. Press Start to begin preheating. Coat a baking pan with cooking spray. 2. Combine all the ingredients except the oil in a large bowl and stir until well blended. Spoon the batter mixture into the baking pan. 3. Once preheated, place the pan on the bak3 position. Check the tart for doneness: If a toothpick inserted into the center of the tart comes out clean, it's done. 4. Remove from the oven and let it cool. Serve immediately.

Ricotta Lemon Poppy Seed Cake

Prep time: 10 minutes | Cook time: 55 minutes | Serves 4

Unsalted butter, at room temperature	¼ cup heavy cream	1 teaspoon pure lemon extract
	¼ cup full-fat ricotta cheese	Grated zest and juice of 1 lemon, plus more zest for garnish
1 cup almond flour	¼ cup coconut oil, melted	
½ cup sugar	2 tablespoons poppy seeds	
3 large eggs	1 teaspoon baking powder	

1. Select Bake, Air Fry Fan, set temperature to 325°F (163°C) and set time to 45 minutes. Press Start to begin preheating. Generously butter a baking pan. Line the bottom of the pan with parchment paper cut to fit. 2. In a large bowl, combine the almond flour, sugar, eggs, cream, ricotta, coconut oil, poppy seeds, baking powder, lemon extract, lemon zest, and lemon juice. Beat with a hand mixer on medium speed until well blended and fluffy. 3. Pour the batter into the prepared pan. Cover the pan tightly with aluminum foil. Once preheated, place the pan on the bake position. Remove the foil and cook for 10 to 15 minutes more, until a knife (do not use a toothpick) inserted into the center of the cake comes out clean. 4. Let the cake cool in the pan for 10 minutes. Remove the cake from pan and let it cool for 15 minutes before slicing. 5. Top with additional lemon zest, slice and serve.

Cherry Pie

Prep time: 15 minutes | Cook time: 35 minutes | Serves 6

All-purpose flour, for dusting	1 egg
2 refrigerated piecrusts, at room temperature	1 tablespoon water
1 (12.5-ounce / 354-g) can cherry pie filling	1 tablespoon sugar

1. Dust a work surface with flour and place the piecrust on it. Roll out the piecrust. Invert a baking pan on top of the dough. Trim the dough around the pan, making your cut ½ inch wider than the pan itself. 2. Repeat with the second piecrust but make the cut the same size as or slightly smaller than the pan. 3. Put the larger crust in the bottom of the baking pan. Don't stretch the dough. Gently press it into the pan. 4. Spoon in enough cherry pie filling to fill the crust. Do not overfill. 5. Using a knife or pizza cutter, cut the second piecrust into 1-inch-wide strips. Weave the strips in a lattice pattern over the top of the cherry pie filling. 6. Select Pizza, Air Fry Fan, set temperature to 325°F (163°C) and set time to 35 minutes. Press Start to begin preheating. 7. In a small bowl, whisk the egg and water. Gently brush the egg wash over the top of the pie. Sprinkle with the sugar and cover the pie with aluminum foil. 8. Once preheated, place the pan on the pizza position. 9. After 30 minutes, remove the foil and resume cooking for 3 to 5 minutes more. The finished pie should have a flaky golden brown crust and bubbling pie filling. 10. When the cooking is complete, serve warm. Refrigerate leftovers for a few days.

Bourbon Bread Pudding

Prep time: 10 minutes | Cook time: 20 minutes | Serves 4

3 slices whole grain bread, cubed	2 tablespoons bourbon	½ teaspoons ground cinnamon
1 large egg	½ teaspoons vanilla extract	2 teaspoons sparkling sugar
1 cup whole milk	¼ cup maple syrup, divided	

1. Select Bake, Air Fry Fan, set temperature to 270°F (132°C) and set time to 20 minutes. Press Start to begin preheating. 2. Spray a baking pan with nonstick cooking spray, then place the bread cubes in the pan. 3. In a medium bowl, whisk together the egg, milk, bourbon, vanilla extract, 3 tablespoons of maple syrup, and cinnamon. Pour the egg mixture over the bread and press down with a spatula to coat all the bread, then sprinkle the sparkling sugar on top. 4. Once preheated, place the pan on the bake position. Remove the pudding from the oven and allow to cool in the pan for 10 minutes. Drizzle the remaining 1 tablespoon of maple syrup on top. Slice and serve warm.

Pumpkin-Spice Bread Pudding

Prep time: 15 minutes | Cook time: 35 minutes | Serves 6

Bread Pudding:	½ cup canned pumpkin	⅓ cup sugar
¾ cup heavy whipping cream	⅓ cup whole milk	1 large egg plus 1 yolk

½ teaspoon pumpkin pie spice	4 tablespoons (½ stick) unsalted butter, melted	1 tablespoon unsalted butter
⅛ teaspoon kosher salt		½ cup heavy whipping cream
4 cups 1-inch cubed day-old baguette or crusty country bread	**Sauce:**	½ teaspoon pure vanilla extract
	⅓ cup pure maple syrup	

1. For the bread pudding: Select Bake, Air Fry Fan, set temperature to 350°F (177°C) and set time to 35 minutes. Press Start to begin preheating. 2. In a medium bowl, combine the cream, pumpkin, milk, sugar, egg and yolk, pumpkin pie spice, and salt. Whisk until well combined. 3. In a large bowl, toss the bread cubes with the melted butter. Add the pumpkin mixture and gently toss until the ingredients are well combined. 4. Transfer the mixture to a baking pan. Once preheated, place the pan on the bake position. It will be done until custard is set in the middle. 5. Meanwhile, for the sauce: In a small saucepan, combine the syrup and butter. Heat over medium heat, stirring, until the butter melts. Stir in the cream and simmer, stirring often, until the sauce has thickened, about 15 minutes. Stir in the vanilla. Remove the pudding from the air fryer. 6. Let the pudding stand for 10 minutes before serving with the warm sauce.

Graham Cracker Cheesecake

Prep time: 10 minutes | Cook time: 20 minutes | Serves 8

1 cup graham cracker crumbs	cream cheese, at room temperature	1 teaspoon vanilla extract
3 tablespoons butter, at room temperature	⅓ cup sugar	¼ cup chocolate syrup
	2 eggs, beaten	
1½ (8-ounce / 227-g) packages	1 tablespoon all-purpose flour	

1. In a small bowl, stir together the graham cracker crumbs and butter. Press the crust into the bottom of a 6-by-2-inch round baking pan and freeze to set while you prepare the filling. 2. In a medium bowl, stir together the cream cheese and sugar until mixed well. 3. One at a time, beat in the eggs. Add the flour and vanilla and stir to combine. 4. Transfer ⅔ cup of filling to a small bowl and stir in the chocolate syrup until combined. 5. Select Bake, Air Fry Fan, set temperature to 325°F (163°C) and set time to 20 minutes. Press Start to begin preheating. 6. Pour the vanilla filling into the pan with the crust. Drop the chocolate filling over the vanilla filling by the spoonful. With a clean butter knife stir the fillings in a zigzag pattern to marbleize them. Do not let the knife touch the crust. 7. Once preheated, place the pan on the bake position. 8. When the cooking is done, the cheesecake should be just set. Cool on a wire rack for 1 hour. Refrigerate the cheesecake until firm before slicing.

Chocolate Bread Pudding

Prep time: 10 minutes | Cook time: 10 to 12 minutes | Serves 4

Nonstick flour-infused baking spray	¾ cup chocolate milk	3 tablespoons peanut butter
1 egg	2 tablespoons cocoa powder	1 teaspoon vanilla extract
1 egg yolk	3 tablespoons light brown sugar	5 slices firm white bread, cubed

1. Spray a baking pan with the baking spray. Set aside. 2. In a medium bowl, whisk the egg, egg yolk, chocolate milk, cocoa powder, brown sugar, peanut butter, and vanilla until thoroughly combined. Stir in the bread cubes and let soak for 10 minutes. Spoon this mixture into the prepared pan. 3. Select Bake, Air Fry Fan, set temperature to 325°F (163°C) and set time to 12 minutes. Press Start to begin preheating. 4. Once preheated, place the pan on the bake position. 5. Check the pudding after about 10 minutes. It is done when it is firm to the touch. If not, resume cooking.

6. When the cooking is complete, let the pudding cool for 5 minutes. Serve warm.

Eggless Farina Cake

Prep time: 30 minutes | Cook time: 25 minutes | Serves 6

Vegetable oil	1 cup milk	1 teaspoon ground cardamom
2 cups hot water	1 cup sugar	1 teaspoon baking powder
1 cup chopped dried fruit, such as apricots, golden raisins, figs, and/or dates	¼ cup ghee, butter, or coconut oil, melted	½ teaspoon baking soda
		Whipped cream, for serving
1 cup farina (or very fine semolina)	2 tablespoons plain Greek yogurt or sour cream	

1. Grease a baking pan with vegetable oil. 2. In a small bowl, combine the hot water and dried fruit; set aside for 20 minutes to plump the fruit. 3. Meanwhile, in a large bowl, whisk together the farina, milk, sugar, ghee, yogurt, and cardamom. Let stand for 20 minutes to allow the farina to soften and absorb some of the liquid. 4. Select Bake, Air Fry Fan, set temperature to 325°F (163°C) and set time to 25 minutes. Press Start to begin preheating. Drain the dried fruit and gently stir it into the batter. Add the baking powder and baking soda and stir until thoroughly combined. 5. Pour the batter into the prepared pan. Once preheated, place the pan on the bake position. It will be done until a toothpick inserted into the center of the cake comes out clean. 6. Let the cake cool in the pan on a wire rack for 10 minutes. Remove the cake from the pan and let cool on the rack for 20 minutes before slicing. 7. Slice and serve topped with whipped cream.

Mixed Berries with Pecan Streusel Topping

Prep time: 5 minutes | Cook time: 17 minutes | Serves 3

½ cup mixed berries	3 tablespoons almonds, slivered	2 tablespoons cold salted butter, cut into pieces
Cooking spray	3 tablespoons chopped pecans	
Topping:	2 tablespoons chopped walnuts	½ teaspoon ground cinnamon
1 egg, beaten	3 tablespoons granulated Swerve	

1. Select Bake, Air Fry Fan, set temperature to 340°F (171°C) and set time to 17 minutes. Press Start to begin preheating. Lightly spray a baking pan with cooking spray. 2. Make the topping: In a medium bowl, stir together the beaten egg, nuts, Swerve, butter, and cinnamon until well blended. 3. Put the mixed berries in the bottom of the baking pan and spread the topping over the top. 4. Once preheated, place the pan on the bake position. It will be done until the fruit is bubbly and topping is golden brown. 5. Allow to cool for 5 to 10 minutes before serving.

Peach Fried Pies

Prep time: 15 minutes | Cook time: 20 minutes | Makes 8 pies

1 (14.75-ounce / 418-g) can sliced peaches in heavy syrup	1 tablespoon cornstarch	2 refrigerated piecrusts
	1 large egg	
1 teaspoon ground cinnamon	All-purpose flour, for dusting	

1. Reserving 2 tablespoons of syrup, drain the peaches well. Chop the peaches into bite-size pieces, transfer to a medium bowl, and stir in the cinnamon. 2. In a small bowl, stir together the reserved peach juice and cornstarch until dissolved. Stir this slurry into the peaches. 3. In another small bowl, beat the egg. 4. Dust a cutting board or work surface with flour and spread the piecrusts on the prepared surface. Using a knife, cut each crust into 4 squares (8

squares total). 5. Place 2 tablespoons of peaches onto each dough square. Fold the dough in half and seal the edges. Using a pastry brush, spread the beaten egg on both sides of each hand pie. Using a knife, make 2 thin slits in the top of each pie. 6. Select Pizza, Air Fry Fan, set temperature to 350°F (177°C) and set time to 10 minutes. Press Start to begin preheating. 7. Line the pizza rack with parchment paper. Place 4 pies on the parchment. 8. Once preheated, place the rack on the pizza position. Flip the pies, brush with beaten egg, and cook for 5 minutes more. Repeat with the remaining pies.

Bananas Foster

Prep time: 5 minutes | Cook time: 7 minutes | Serves 2

1 tablespoon unsalted butter	lengthwise and then crosswise	2 tablespoons light rum
2 teaspoons dark brown sugar	2 tablespoons chopped pecans	Vanilla ice cream, for serving
1 banana, peeled and halved	⅛ teaspoon ground cinnamon	

1. Select Bake, Air Fry Fan, set temperature to 350°F (177°C) and set time to 2 minutes. Press Start to begin preheating. 2. In a baking pan, combine the butter and brown sugar. Once preheated, place the pan on the bake position. It will be done until the butter and sugar are melted. Swirl to combine. 3. Add the banana pieces and pecans, turning the bananas to coat. Set the temperature to 350°F (177°C) for 5 minutes, turning the banana pieces halfway through the cooking time. Sprinkle with the cinnamon. 4. Remove the pan from the oven and place on an unlit stovetop for safety. Add the rum to the pan, swirling to combine it with the butter mixture. Carefully light the sauce with a long-reach lighter. Spoon the flaming sauce over the banana pieces until the flames die out. 5. Serve the warm bananas and sauce over vanilla ice cream.

Lemon Poppy Seed Macaroons

Prep time: 10 minutes | Cook time: 14 minutes | Makes 1 dozen cookies

2 large egg whites, room temperature	plus more for garnish if desired	**Lemon Icing:**
⅓ cup Swerve confectioners'-style sweetener or equivalent amount of powdered sweetener	2 teaspoons poppy seeds	¼ cup Swerve confectioners'-style sweetener or equivalent amount of powdered sweetener
	1 teaspoon lemon extract	
	¼ teaspoon fine sea salt	
	2 cups unsweetened shredded coconut	1 tablespoon lemon juice
2 tablespoons grated lemon zest,		

1. Select Bake, Air Fry Fan, set temperature to 325°F (163°C) and set time to 12 to 14 minutes. Press Start to begin preheating. Line a pie pan or a casserole dish that will fit inside your air fryer oven with parchment paper. 2. Place the egg whites in a medium-sized bowl and use a hand mixer on high to beat the whites until stiff peaks form. Add the sweetener, lemon zest, poppy seeds, lemon extract, and salt. Mix on low until combined. Gently fold in the coconut with a rubber spatula. 3. Use a 1-inch cookie scoop to place the cookies on the parchment, spacing them about ¼ inch apart. Once preheated, place the pan on the bake position. It will be done until the cookies are golden and a toothpick inserted into the center comes out clean. 4. While the cookies bake, make the lemon icing: Place the sweetener in a small bowl. Add the lemon juice and stir well. If the icing is too thin, add a little more sweetener. If the icing is too thick, add a little more lemon juice. 5. Remove the cookies from the oven and allow to cool for about 10 minutes, then drizzle with the icing. Garnish with lemon zest, if desired. Store leftovers in an airtight container in the fridge for up to 5 days or in the freezer for up to a month.

Butter and Chocolate Chip Cookies

Prep time: 20 minutes | Cook time: 11 minutes | Serves 8

1 stick butter, at room temperature	1 fine almond flour	¼ teaspoon ground cinnamon
1¼ cups Swerve	⅔ cup coconut flour	¼ teaspoon ginger
¼ cup chunky peanut butter	⅓ cup cocoa powder, unsweetened	½ cup chocolate chips, unsweetened
1 teaspoon vanilla paste	1 ½ teaspoons baking powder	

1. Select Bake, Air Fry Fan, set temperature to 365°F (185°C) and set time to 11 minutes. Press Start to begin preheating. 2. In a mixing dish, beat the butter and Swerve until creamy and uniform. Stir in the peanut butter and vanilla. 3. In another mixing dish, thoroughly combine the flour, cocoa powder, baking powder, cinnamon, and ginger. 4. Add the flour mixture to the peanut butter mixture; mix to combine well. Afterwards, fold in the chocolate chips. Drop by large spoonfuls onto a parchment-lined baking pan. Once preheated, place the pan on the bake position. It will be done until golden brown on the top. Bon appétit!

Cream-Filled Sandwich Cookies

Prep time: 8 minutes | Cook time: 8 minutes | Makes 8 cookies

Oil, for spraying	crescent rolls	8 cream-filled sandwich cookies
1 (8-ounce / 227-g) can refrigerated	¼ cup milk	1 tablespoon confectioners' sugar

1. Select Bake, Air Fry Fan, set temperature to 350°F (177°C) and set time to 4 minutes. Press Start to begin preheating. Line the baking pan with parchment and spray lightly with oil. 2. Unroll the crescent dough and separate it into 8 triangles. Lay out the triangles on a work surface. 3. Pour the milk into a shallow bowl. Quickly dip each cookie in the milk, then place in the center of a dough triangle. 4. Wrap the dough around the cookie, cutting off any excess and pinching the ends to seal. You may be able to combine the excess into enough dough to cover additional cookies, if desired. 5. Place the wrapped cookies in the prepared pan, seam-side down, and spray lightly with oil. 6. Once preheated, place the pan on the bake position. Flip, spray with oil, and cook for another 3 to 4 minutes, or until puffed and golden brown. 7. Dust with the confectioners' sugar and serve.

Chocolate Lava Cakes

Prep time: 5 minutes | Cook time: 15 minutes | Serves 2

2 large eggs, whisked	almond flour	2 ounces (57 g) low-carb chocolate chips, melted
¼ cup blanched finely ground	½ teaspoon vanilla extract	

1. Select Bake, Air Fry Fan, set temperature to 320°F (160°C) and set time to 15 minutes. Press Start to begin preheating. 2. In a medium bowl, mix eggs with flour and vanilla. Fold in chocolate until fully combined. 3. Pour batter into two ramekins greased with cooking spray. Once preheated, place the ramekins on the bake position. Cakes will be set at the edges and firm in the center when done. Let cool 5 minutes before serving.

Grilled Peaches

Prep time: 5 minutes | Cook time: 10 minutes | Serves 4

Oil, for spraying	8 tablespoons (1 stick) unsalted butter, cubed	2 peaches, pitted and cut into quarters
¼ cup graham cracker crumbs	¼ teaspoon cinnamon	4 scoops vanilla ice cream
¼ cup packed light brown sugar		

1. Select Bake, Air Fry Fan, set temperature to 350°F (177°C) and set time to 5 minutes. Select Start/Stop to begin preheating. Line the baking pan with parchment and spray lightly with oil. 2. In a small bowl, mix together the graham cracker crumbs, brown sugar, butter, and cinnamon with a fork until crumbly. 3. Place the peach wedges in the prepared pan, skin-side up. You may need to work in batches. 4. Once preheated, place the pan on the bake position. Flip, and sprinkle with a spoonful of the graham cracker mixture. Cook for another 5 minutes, or until tender and caramelized. 5. Top with a scoop of vanilla ice cream and any remaining crumble mixture. Serve immediately.

Pecan Bars

Prep time: 5 minutes | Cook time: 40 minutes | Serves 12

2 cups coconut flour

5 tablespoons erythritol

4 tablespoons coconut oil, softened

½ cup heavy cream

1 egg, beaten

4 pecans, chopped

1. Select Bake, Air Fry Fan, set temperature to 350°F (177°C) and set time to 40 minutes. Press Start to begin preheating. 2. Mix coconut flour, erythritol, coconut oil, heavy cream, and egg. 3. Pour the batter in the baking pan and flatten well. Top the mixture with pecans. Once preheated, place the pan on the bake position. 4. Cut the cooked meal into the bars.

Cream Cheese Shortbread Cookies

Prep time: 30 minutes | Cook time: 20 minutes | Makes 12 cookies

¼ cup coconut oil, melted

2 ounces (57 g) cream cheese, softened

½ cup granular erythritol

1 large egg, whisked

2 cups blanched finely ground almond flour

1 teaspoon almond extract

1. Combine all ingredients in a large bowl to form a firm ball. 2. Place dough on a sheet of plastic wrap and roll into a 12-inch-long log shape. Roll log in plastic wrap and place in refrigerator 30 minutes to chill. 3. Remove log from plastic and slice into twelve equal cookies. Select Bake, Air Fry Fan, set temperature to 320°F (160°C) and set time to 10 minutes. Press Start to begin preheating. Cut one piece of parchment paper to fit your baking pan. Place cookies on parchment. Once preheated, place the pan on the bake position. Turn cookies halfway through cooking. They will be lightly golden when done. Repeat with remaining cookies. 4. Let cool 15 minutes before serving to avoid crumbling.

Baked Peaches with Yogurt and Blueberries

Prep time: 10 minutes | Cook time: 7 to 11 minutes | Serves 6

3 peaches, peeled, halved, and pitted

2 tablespoons packed brown sugar

1 cup plain Greek yogurt

¼ teaspoon ground cinnamon

1 teaspoon pure vanilla extract

1 cup fresh blueberries

1. Select Bake, Air Fry Fan, set temperature to 380°F (193°C) and set time to 7 to 11 minutes. Press Start to begin preheating. 2. Arrange the peaches on pizza rack, cut-side up. Top with a generous sprinkle of brown sugar. 3. Once preheated, place the rack on the bake position. The peaches will be lightly browned and caramelized when done. 4. Meanwhile, whisk together the yogurt, cinnamon, and vanilla in a small bowl until smooth. 5. Remove the peaches from the oven to a plate. Serve topped with the yogurt mixture and fresh blueberries.

Fried Golden Bananas

Prep time: 5 minutes | Cook time: 7 minutes | Serves 6

1 large egg	¼ cup plain bread crumbs	Cooking oil
¼ cup cornstarch	3 bananas, halved crosswise	Chocolate sauce, for drizzling

1. Select Air Fry, set temperature to 375°F (191°C) and set time to 4 minutes. Press Start to begin preheating. 2. Separate the biscuit dough into 8 biscuits and place them on a flat work surface. Use a small circle cookie cutter or a biscuit cutter to cut a hole in the center of each biscuit. You can also cut the holes using a knife. 3. Spray the crisper tray with cooking oil. 4. Put 4 donuts on the tray. Do not stack. Spray with cooking oil. Once preheated, place the tray on the air fry position. 5. Open the oven and flip the donuts. Air fry for an additional 4 minutes. 6. Remove the cooked donuts from the oven, then repeat steps 3, 4, and 5 for the remaining 4 donuts. 7. Drizzle chocolate sauce over the donuts and enjoy while warm.

Chocolate Chip-Pecan Biscotti

Prep time: 15 minutes | Cook time: 20 to 22 minutes | Serves 10

1¼ cups finely ground blanched almond flour	room temperature	chips, such as Lily's Sweets brand
¾ teaspoon baking powder	⅓ cup Swerve	Melted stevia-sweetened chocolate chips and chopped pecans, for topping (optional)
½ teaspoon xanthan gum	1 large egg, beaten	
¼ teaspoon sea salt	1 teaspoon pure vanilla extract	
3 tablespoons unsalted butter, at	⅓ cup chopped pecans	
	¼ cup stevia-sweetened chocolate	

1. In a large bowl, combine the almond flour, baking powder, xanthan gum, and salt. 2. Select Bake, Air Fry Fan, set temperature to 325°F (163°C) and set time to 12 minutes. Press Start to begin preheating. Line a cake pan that fits your air fryer oven with parchment paper. 3. In the bowl of a stand mixer, beat together the butter and Swerve. Add the beaten egg and vanilla, and beat for about 3 minutes. 4. Add the almond flour mixture to the butter-and-egg mixture; beat until just combined. 5. Stir in the pecans and chocolate chips. 6. Transfer the dough to the prepared pan, and press it into the bottom. 7. Once preheated, place the pan on the bake position. Remove from the air fryer oven and let cool for 15 minutes. Using a sharp knife, cut the cookie into thin strips, then return the strips to the cake pan with the bottom sides facing up. 8. Set the temperature to 300°F (149°C). Bake for 8 to 10 minutes. 9. Remove from the air fryer oven and let cool completely. If desired, dip one side of each biscotti piece into melted chocolate chips, and top with chopped pecans.

Peanut Butter-Honey-Banana Toast

Prep time: 10 minutes | Cook time: 9 minutes | Serves 4

2 tablespoons butter, softened	4 tablespoons peanut butter	4 tablespoons honey
4 slices white bread	2 bananas, peeled and thinly sliced	1 teaspoon ground cinnamon

1. Select Bake, Air Fry Fan, set temperature to 375°F (191°C) and set time to 5 minutes. Press Start to begin preheating. 2. Spread butter on one side of each slice of bread, then peanut butter on the other side. Arrange the banana slices on top of the peanut butter sides of each slice (about 9 slices per toast). Drizzle honey on top of the banana and sprinkle with cinnamon. 3. Cut each slice in half lengthwise so that it will better fit into the air fryer oven. Arrange two pieces of bread, butter sides down, on the pizza rack. Once preheated, place the rack on the bake position and cook. Then set the temperature to 400°F (204°C) for an additional 4 minutes, or until the bananas have started to brown. Repeat with remaining slices. Serve hot.

Cinnamon-Sugar Almonds

Prep time: 5 minutes | Cook time: 8 minutes | Serves 4

1 cup whole almonds

2 tablespoons salted butter, melted

1 tablespoon sugar

½ teaspoon ground cinnamon

1. Select Bake, Air Fry Fan, set temperature to 300°F (149°C) and set time to 8 minutes. Press Start to begin preheating. 2. In a medium bowl, combine the almonds, butter, sugar, and cinnamon. Mix well to ensure all the almonds are coated with the spiced butter. 3. Transfer the almonds to the baking pan and shake so they are in a single layer. 4. Once preheated, place the pan on the bake position. Stir the almonds halfway through the cooking time. 5. Let cool completely before serving.

Cream-Filled Sponge Cakes

Prep time: 10 minutes | Cook time: 10 minutes | Makes 4 cakes

Oil, for spraying

1 (8-ounce / 227-g) can refrigerated

crescent rolls

4 cream-filled sponge cakes

1 tablespoon confectioners' sugar

1. Select Bake, Air Fry Fan, set temperature to 200°F (93°C) and set time to 5 minutes. Press Start to begin preheating. Line the pizza rack with parchment and spray lightly with oil. 2. Unroll the dough into a single flat layer and cut it into 4 equal pieces. 3. Place 1 sponge cake in the center of each piece of dough. Wrap the dough around the cake, pinching the ends to seal. 4. Place the wrapped cakes in the prepared rack and spray lightly with oil. 5. Once preheated, place the rack on the bake position. Flip, spray with oil, and cook for another 5 minutes, or until golden brown. 6. Dust with the confectioners' sugar and serve.

Glazed Cherry Turnovers

Prep time: 10 minutes | Cook time: 14 minutes per batch | Serves 8

2 sheets frozen puff pastry, thawed

1 (21-ounce / 595-g) can premium cherry pie filling

2 teaspoons ground cinnamon

1 egg, beaten

1 cup sliced almonds

1 cup powdered sugar

2 tablespoons milk

1. Roll a sheet of puff pastry out into a square that is approximately 10-inches by 10-inches. Cut this large square into quarters. 2. Mix the cherry pie filling and cinnamon together in a bowl. Spoon ¼ cup of the cherry filling into the center of each puff pastry square. Brush the perimeter of the pastry square with the egg wash. Fold one corner of the puff pastry over the cherry pie filling towards the opposite corner, forming a triangle. Seal the two edges of the pastry together with the tip of a fork, making a design with the tines. Brush the top of the turnovers with the egg wash and sprinkle sliced almonds over each one. Repeat these steps with the second sheet of puff pastry. You should have eight turnovers at the end. 3. Select Air Fry, set temperature to 370°F (188°C) and set time to 14 minutes. Press Start to begin preheating. 4. Once preheated, place the turnovers in the crisper tray on the air fry position. You may need to work in batches. Carefully turn them over halfway through the cooking time. 5. While the turnovers are cooking, make the glaze by whisking the powdered sugar and milk together in a small bowl until smooth. Let the glaze sit for a minute so the sugar can absorb the milk. If the consistency is still too thick to drizzle, add a little more milk, a drop at a time, and stir until smooth. 6. Let the cooked cherry turnovers sit for at least 10 minutes. Then drizzle the glaze over each turnover in a zigzag motion. Serve warm or at room temperature.

Crispy Pineapple Rings

Prep time: 5 minutes | Cook time: 6 to 8 minutes | Serves 6

1 cup rice milk	½ teaspoon baking soda	Pinch of kosher salt
⅔ cup flour	½ teaspoon baking powder	1 medium pineapple, peeled and sliced
½ cup water	½ teaspoon vanilla essence	
¼ cup unsweetened flaked coconut	½ teaspoon ground cinnamon	
4 tablespoons sugar	¼ teaspoon ground anise star	

1. Select Air Fry, set temperature to 380°F (193°C) and set time to 6 to 8 minutes. Press Start to begin preheating. 2. In a large bowl, stir together all the ingredients except the pineapple. 3. Dip each pineapple slice into the batter until evenly coated. 4. Arrange the pineapple slices in the crisper tray. Once preheated, place the tray on the air fry position. It will be done until golden brown. 5. Remove from the oven to a plate and cool for 5 minutes before serving warm.

Lime Bars

Prep time: 10 minutes | Cook time: 33 minutes | Makes 12 bars

1½ cups blanched finely ground almond flour, divided	divided	2 large eggs, whisked
¾ cup confectioners' erythritol,	4 tablespoons salted butter, melted	
	½ cup fresh lime juice	

1. Select Bake, Air Fry Fan, set temperature to 300°F (149°C) and set time to 13 minutes. Press Start to begin preheating. 2. In a medium bowl, mix together 1 cup flour, ¼ cup erythritol, and butter. Press mixture into bottom of a cake pan. 3. Once preheated, place the pan on the bake position. Crust will be brown and set in the middle when done. 4. Allow to cool in pan 10 minutes. 5. In a medium bowl, combine remaining flour, remaining erythritol, lime juice, and eggs. Pour mixture over cooled crust and return to oven for 20 minutes at 300°F (149°C). Top will be browned and firm when done. 6. Let cool completely in pan, about 30 minutes, then chill covered in the refrigerator 1 hour. Serve chilled.

Strawberry Shortcake

Prep time: 10 minutes | Cook time: 25 minutes | Serves 6

2 tablespoons coconut oil	2 large eggs, whisked	powder	whipped cream
1 cup blanched finely ground almond flour	½ cup granular erythritol	1 teaspoon vanilla extract	6 medium fresh strawberries, hulled and sliced
	1 teaspoon baking	2 cups sugar-free	

1. Select Bake, Air Fry Fan, set temperature to 300°F (149°C) and set time to 25 minutes. Press Start to begin preheating. 2. In a large bowl, combine coconut oil, flour, eggs, erythritol, baking powder, and vanilla. Pour batter into a baking dish. 3. Once preheated, place the dish on the bake position. When done, shortcake should be golden and a toothpick inserted in the middle will come out clean. 4. Remove dish from fryer and let cool 1 hour. 5. Once cooled, top cake with whipped cream and strawberries to serve.

Apple Fries

Prep time: 10 minutes | Cook time: 7 minutes | Serves 8

Oil, for spraying	3 large eggs, beaten	¼ cup sugar
1 cup all-purpose flour	1 cup graham cracker crumbs	1 teaspoon ground cinnamon

3 large Gala apples, peeled, cored, and cut into wedges

1 cup caramel sauce, warmed

1. Select Air Fry, set temperature to 380°F (193°C) and set time to 5 minutes. Press Start to begin preheating. Line the crisper tray with parchment and spray lightly with oil. 2. Place the flour and beaten eggs in separate bowls and set aside. In another bowl, mix together the graham cracker crumbs, sugar, and cinnamon. 3. Working one at a time, coat the apple wedges in the flour, dip in the egg, and dredge in the graham cracker mix until evenly coated. 4. Place the apples in the prepared tray, taking care not to overlap, and spray lightly with oil. You may need to work in batches. 5. Once preheated, place the pan on the air fry position. Flip, spray with oil, and cook for another 2 minutes, or until crunchy and golden brown. 6. Drizzle the caramel sauce over the top and serve.

Lemon Curd Pavlova

Prep time: 10 minutes | Cook time: 1 hour | Serves 4

Shell:

3 large egg whites

¼ teaspoon cream of tartar

¾ cup Swerve confectioners'-style sweetener or equivalent amount of powdered sweetener

1 teaspoon grated lemon zest

1 teaspoon lemon extract

Lemon Curd:

1 cup Swerve confectioners'-style sweetener or equivalent amount of liquid or powdered sweetener

½ cup lemon juice

4 large eggs

½ cup coconut oil

For Garnish (Optional):

Blueberries

Swerve confectioners'-style sweetener or equivalent amount of powdered sweetener

1. Select Pizza, Air Fry Fan, set temperature to 275°F (135°C) and set time to 60 minutes. Press Start to begin preheating. Thoroughly grease a pie pan with butter or coconut oil. 2. Make the shell: In a small bowl, use a hand mixer to beat the egg whites and cream of tartar until soft peaks form. With the mixer on low, slowly sprinkle in the sweetener and mix until it's completely incorporated. 3. Add the lemon zest and lemon extract and continue to beat with the hand mixer until stiff peaks form. 4. Spoon the mixture into the greased pie pan, then smooth it across the bottom, up the sides, and onto the rim to form a shell. Once preheated, place the pan on the bake position. When done, turn off the air fryer oven and let the shell stand in the oven for 20 minutes. (The shell can be made up to 3 days ahead and stored in an airtight container in the refrigerator, if desired.) 5. While the shell bakes, make the lemon curd: In a medium-sized heavy-bottomed saucepan, whisk together the sweetener, lemon juice, and eggs. Add the coconut oil and place the pan on the stovetop over medium heat. Once the oil is melted, whisk constantly until the mixture thickens and thickly coats the back of a spoon, about 10 minutes. Do not allow the mixture to come to a boil. 6. Pour the lemon curd mixture through a fine-mesh strainer into a medium-sized bowl. Place the bowl inside a larger bowl filled with ice water and whisk occasionally until the curd is completely cool, about 15 minutes. 7. Place the lemon curd on top of the shell and garnish with blueberries and powdered sweetener, if desired. Store leftovers in the refrigerator for up to 4 days.

Dark Brownies

Prep time: 10 minutes | Cook time: 11 to 13 minutes | Serves 4

1 egg

½ cup granulated sugar

¼ teaspoon salt

½ teaspoon vanilla

¼ cup butter, melted

¼ cup flour, plus 2 tablespoons

¼ cup cocoa

Cooking spray

Optional:

Vanilla ice cream

Caramel sauce

Whipped cream

1. Select Bake, Air Fry Fan, set temperature to 330°F (166°C) and set time to 11 to 13 minutes. Press Start to begin preheating. 2. Beat together egg, sugar, salt, and vanilla until light. Add melted butter and mix well. 3. Stir in flour and cocoa. 4. Spray a baking pan lightly with cooking spray. 5. Spread batter in pan. Once preheated, place the pan on the bake position. Cool and cut into 4 large squares or 16 small brownie bites.

Baked Cheesecake

Prep time: 30 minutes | Cook time: 35 minutes | Serves 6

½ cup almond flour

1½ tablespoons unsalted butter, melted

2 tablespoons erythritol

1 (8-ounce / 227-g) package cream cheese, softened

¼ cup powdered erythritol

½ teaspoon vanilla paste

1 egg, at room temperature

Topping:

1½ cups sour cream

3 tablespoons powdered erythritol

1 teaspoon vanilla extract

1. Select Bake, Air Fry Fan, set temperature to 330°F (166°C) and set time to 35 minutes. Press Start to begin preheating. 2. Thoroughly combine the almond flour, butter, and 2 tablespoons of erythritol in a mixing bowl. Press the mixture into the bottom of lightly greased baking pan. 3. Then, mix the cream cheese, ¼ cup of powdered erythritol, vanilla, and egg using an electric mixer on low speed. Pour the batter into the pan, covering the crust. 4. Once preheated, place the pan on the bake position. It will be done until edges are puffed and the surface is firm. 5. Mix the sour cream, 3 tablespoons of powdered erythritol, and vanilla for the topping; spread over the crust and allow it to cool to room temperature. 6. Transfer to your refrigerator for 6 to 8 hours. Serve well chilled.

Pumpkin Pudding with Vanilla Wafers

Prep time: 10 minutes | Cook time: 12 to 17 minutes | Serves 4

1 cup canned no-salt-added pumpkin purée (not pumpkin pie filling)

¼ cup packed brown sugar

3 tablespoons all-purpose flour

1 egg, whisked

2 tablespoons milk

1 tablespoon unsalted butter, melted

1 teaspoon pure vanilla extract

4 low-fat vanilla wafers, crumbled

Nonstick cooking spray

1. Select Bake, Air Fry Fan, set temperature to 350°F (177°C) and set time to 12 to 17 minutes. Press Start to begin preheating. Coat a baking pan with nonstick cooking spray. Set aside. 2. Mix the pumpkin purée, brown sugar, flour, whisked egg, milk, melted butter, and vanilla in a medium bowl and whisk to combine. Transfer the mixture to the baking pan. 3. Once preheated, place the pan on the bake position. 4. Remove the pudding from the oven and allow it to cool. 5. Divide the pudding into four bowls and serve with the vanilla wafers sprinkled on top.

Coconut Flour Cake

Prep time: 10 minutes | Cook time: 25 minutes | Serves 6

2 tablespoons salted butter, melted

⅓ cup coconut flour

2 large eggs, whisked

½ cup granular erythritol

1 teaspoon baking powder

1 teaspoon vanilla extract

½ cup sour cream

1. Select Bake, Air Fry Fan, set temperature to 300°F (149°C) and set time to 25 minutes. Press Start to begin preheating. 2. Mix all ingredients in a large bowl. Pour batter into a baking dish that fits your air fryer oven. 3. Once preheated, place baking dish on the bake position. The cake will be dark golden on top, and a toothpick inserted in the center should come out clean when done. 3. Let cool in dish 15 minutes before slicing and serving.

Chocolate and Rum Cupcakes

Prep time: 5 minutes | Cook time: 15 minutes | Serves 6

¾ cup granulated erythritol	½ teaspoon baking soda	1 stick butter, at room temperature
1¼ cups almond flour	½ teaspoon ground cinnamon	3 eggs, whisked
1 teaspoon unsweetened baking powder	¼ teaspoon grated nutmeg	1 teaspoon pure rum extract
3 teaspoons cocoa powder	⅛ teaspoon salt	½ cup blueberries
	½ cup milk	Cooking spray

1. Select Bake, Air Fry Fan, set temperature to 345°F (174°C) and set time to 15 minutes. Press Start to begin preheating. Spray a 6-cup muffin tin with cooking spray. 2. In a mixing bowl, combine the erythritol, almond flour, baking powder, cocoa powder, baking soda, cinnamon, nutmeg, and salt and stir until well blended. 3. In another mixing bowl, mix together the milk, butter, egg, and rum extract until thoroughly combined. Slowly and carefully pour this mixture into the bowl of dry mixture. Stir in the blueberries. 4. Spoon the batter into the greased muffin cups, filling each about three-quarters full. 5. Once preheated, place the muffin tin on the bake position. It will be done until the center is springy and a toothpick inserted in the middle comes out clean. 6. Remove from the oven and allow to cool. Serve immediately.

Baked Apples and Walnuts

Prep time: 6 minutes | Cook time: 20 minutes | Serves 4

4 small Granny Smith apples	¼ cup light brown sugar	1 teaspoon ground cinnamon	nutmeg
⅓ cup chopped walnuts	2 tablespoons butter, melted	½ teaspoon ground	½ cup water, or apple juice

1. Cut off the top third of the apples. Spoon out the core and some of the flesh and discard. Place the apples in a baking pan. 2. Select Bake, Air Fry Fan, set temperature to 350°F (177°C) and set time to 20 minutes. Press Start to begin preheating. 3. In a small bowl, stir together the walnuts, brown sugar, melted butter, cinnamon, and nutmeg. Spoon this mixture into the centers of the hollowed-out apples. 4. Once preheated, place the baking pan on the bake position. 5. When the cooking is complete, the apples should be bubbly and fork-tender.

Vanilla Scones

Prep time: 20 minutes | Cook time: 10 minutes | Serves 6

4 ounces (113 g) coconut flour	2 teaspoons mascarpone	1 tablespoon erythritol
½ teaspoon baking powder	¼ cup heavy cream	Cooking spray
1 teaspoon apple cider vinegar	1 teaspoon vanilla extract	

1. Select Bake, Air Fry Fan, set temperature to 365°F (185°C) and set time to 10 minutes. Press Start to begin preheating. 2. In the mixing bowl, mix coconut flour with baking powder, apple cider vinegar, mascarpone, heavy cream, vanilla extract, and erythritol. 3. Knead the dough and cut into scones. 4. Then put them in the baking pan and sprinkle with cooking spray. 5. Once preheated, place the pan on the bake position.

Halle Berries-and-Cream Cobbler

Prep time: 10 minutes | Cook time: 25 minutes | Serves 4

12 ounces (340 g) cream cheese (1½ cups), softened	1 large egg	sweetener or equivalent amount of powdered sweetener
	¾ cup Swerve confectioners'-style	

½ teaspoon vanilla extract

¼ teaspoon fine sea salt

1 cup sliced fresh raspberries or strawberries

Biscuits:

3 large egg whites

¾ cup blanched almond flour

1 teaspoon baking powder

2½ tablespoons very cold unsalted butter, cut into pieces

¼ teaspoon fine sea salt

Frosting:

2 ounces (57 g) cream cheese (¼ cup), softened

1 tablespoon Swerve confectioners'-style sweetener or equivalent amount of powdered or liquid sweetener

1 tablespoon unsweetened, unflavored almond milk or heavy cream

Fresh raspberries or strawberries, for garnish

1. Select Pizza, Air Fry Fan, set temperature to 400°F (204°C) and set time to 5 minutes. Press Start to begin preheating. Grease a baking pan. 2. In a large mixing bowl, use a hand mixer to combine the cream cheese, egg, and sweetener until smooth. Stir in the vanilla and salt. Gently fold in the raspberries with a rubber spatula. Pour the mixture into the prepared pan and set aside. 3. Make the biscuits: Place the egg whites in a medium-sized mixing bowl or the bowl of a stand mixer. Using a hand mixer or stand mixer, whip the egg whites until very fluffy and stiff. 4. In a separate medium-sized bowl, combine the almond flour and baking powder. Cut in the butter and add the salt, stirring gently to keep the butter pieces intact. 5. Gently fold the almond flour mixture into the egg whites. Use a large spoon or ice cream scooper to scoop out the dough and form it into a 2-inch-wide biscuit, making sure the butter stays in separate clumps. Place the biscuit on top of the raspberry mixture in the pan. Repeat with remaining dough to make 4 biscuits. 6. Once preheated, place the pan on the pizza position and cook. Then lower the temperature to 325°F (163°C) and cook for another 17 to 20 minutes, until the biscuits are golden brown. 7. While the cobbler cooks, make the frosting: Place the cream cheese in a small bowl and stir to break it up. Add the sweetener and stir. Add the almond milk and stir until well combined. If you prefer a thinner frosting, add more almond milk. 8. Remove the cobbler from the air fryer oven and allow to cool slightly, then drizzle with the frosting. Garnish with fresh raspberries. 9. Store leftovers in an airtight container in the refrigerator for up to 3 days. Reheat the cobbler in a preheated 350°F (177°C) air fryer oven for 3 minutes, or until warmed through.

Chickpea Brownies

Prep time: 10 minutes | Cook time: 20 minutes | Serves 6

Vegetable oil

1 (15-ounce / 425-g) can chickpeas, drained and rinsed

4 large eggs

⅓ cup coconut oil, melted

⅓ cup honey

3 tablespoons unsweetened cocoa powder

1 tablespoon espresso powder (optional)

1 teaspoon baking powder

1 teaspoon baking soda

½ cup chocolate chips

1. Select Bake, Air Fry Fan, set temperature to 325°F (163°C) and set time to 20 minutes. Select Start/Stop to begin preheating. 2. Generously grease the baking pan with vegetable oil. 3. In a blender or food processor, combine the chickpeas, eggs, coconut oil, honey, cocoa powder, espresso powder (if using), baking powder, and baking soda. Blend or process until smooth. Transfer to the prepared pan and stir in the chocolate chips by hand. 4. Once preheated, place the pan on the bake position. It will be done until a toothpick inserted into the center comes out clean. 5. Let cool in the pan for 30 minutes before cutting into squares. 6. Serve immediately.

Blackberry Cobbler

Prep time: 15 minutes | Cook time: 25 to 30 minutes | Serves 6

3 cups fresh or frozen blackberries

1¾ cups sugar, divided

1 teaspoon vanilla extract

8 tablespoons (1 stick) butter, melted

1 cup self-rising flour

1 to 2 tablespoons oil

1. In a medium bowl, stir together the blackberries, 1 cup of sugar, and vanilla. 2. In another medium bowl, stir together the melted butter, remaining ¾ cup of sugar, and flour until a dough forms. 3. Spritz a baking pan with oil. Add the blackberry mixture. Crumble the flour mixture over the fruit. Cover the pan with aluminum foil. 4. Select Pizza, Air Fry Fan, set temperature to 350°F (177°C) and set time to 20 to 25 minutes. Press Start to begin preheating.5. Once preheated, place the pan on the pizza position. It will be done until the filling is thickened. 6. Uncover the pan and cook for 5 minutes more, depending on how juicy and browned you like your cobbler. Let sit for 5 minutes before serving.

Baked Brazilian Pineapple

Prep time: 10 minutes | Cook time: 10 minutes | Serves 4

½ cup brown sugar

2 teaspoons ground cinnamon

1 small pineapple, peeled, cored, and cut into spears

3 tablespoons unsalted butter, melted

1. Select Air Fry, set temperature to 400°F (204°C) and set time to 10 minutes. Select Start/Stop to begin preheating. 2. In a small bowl, mix the brown sugar and cinnamon until thoroughly combined. 3. Brush the pineapple spears with the melted butter. Sprinkle the cinnamon-sugar over the spears, pressing lightly to ensure it adheres well. 4. Place the spears in the baking pan in a single layer. You may have to do this in batches. Once preheated, place the pan on the air fry position. (If needed, cook for 6 to 8 minutes for the next batch, as the fryer will be preheated). Halfway through the cooking time, brush the spears with butter. 5. The pineapple spears are done when they are heated through and the sugar is bubbling. Serve hot.

Olive Oil Cake

Prep time: 10 minutes | Cook time: 30 minutes | Serves 8

2 cups blanched finely ground almond flour

5 large eggs, whisked

¾ cup extra-virgin olive oil

⅓ cup granular erythritol

1 teaspoon vanilla extract

1 teaspoon baking powder

1. Select Bake, Air Fry Fan, set temperature to 300°F (149°C) and set time to 30 minutes. Press Start to begin preheating. 2. In a large bowl, mix all ingredients. Pour batter into a baking dish that fits your air fryer oven. 3. Once preheated, place dish on bake position. The cake will be golden on top and firm in the center when done. 4. Let cake cool in dish 30 minutes before slicing and serving.

Maple-Pecan Tart with Sea Salt

Prep time: 15 minutes | Cook time: 25 minutes | Serves 8

Tart Crust:

Vegetable oil spray

⅓ cup (⅔ stick) butter, softened

¼ cup firmly packed brown sugar

1 cup all-purpose flour

¼ teaspoon kosher salt

Filling:

4 tablespoons (½ stick) butter,

diced

½ cup packed brown sugar

¼ cup pure maple syrup

¼ cup whole milk

¼ teaspoon pure vanilla extract   1½ cups finely chopped pecans   ¼ teaspoon flaked sea salt

1. For the crust: Select Bake, Air Fry Fan, set temperature to 350°F (177°C) and set time to 13 minutes. Press Start to begin preheating. Line a baking pan with foil, leaving a couple of inches of overhang. Spray the foil with vegetable oil spray. 2. In a medium bowl, combine the butter and brown sugar. Beat with an electric mixer on medium-low speed until light and fluffy. Add the flour and kosher salt and beat until the ingredients are well blended. Transfer the mixture (it will be crumbly) to the prepared pan. Press it evenly into the bottom of the pan. 3. Once preheated, place the pan on the bake position. When the crust has 5 minutes left to cook, start the filling. 4. For the filling: In a medium saucepan, combine the butter, brown sugar, maple syrup, and milk. Bring to a simmer, stirring occasionally. When it begins simmering, cook for 1 minute. Remove from the heat and stir in the vanilla and pecans. 5. Carefully pour the filling evenly over the crust, gently spreading with a rubber spatula so the nuts and liquid are evenly distributed. Set the air fryer oven to 350°F (177°C) for 12 minutes, or until mixture is bubbling. (The center should still be slightly jiggly, it will thicken as it cools.) 6. Remove the pan from the oven and sprinkle the tart with the sea salt. Allow to cool completely until room temperature. 7. Transfer the pan to the refrigerator to chill. When cold (the tart will be easier to cut), use the foil overhang to remove the tart from the pan and cut into 8 wedges. Serve at room temperature.

Pecan and Cherry Stuffed Apples

Prep time: 10 minutes | Cook time: 20 minutes | Serves 4

4 apples (about 1¼ pounds / 567 g)   1 tablespoon melted butter   Pinch salt
¼ cup chopped pecans   3 tablespoons brown sugar   Ice cream, for serving
⅓ cup dried tart cherries   ¼ teaspoon allspice

1. Cut off top ½ inch from each apple; reserve tops. With a melon baller, core through stem ends without breaking through the bottom. (Do not trim bases.) 2. Select Bake, Air Fry Fan, set temperature to 350°F (177°C) and set time to 20 to 25 minutes. Press Start to begin preheating. 3. Combine pecans, cherries, butter, brown sugar, allspice, and a pinch of salt. Stuff mixture into the hollow centers of the apples. Cover with apple tops. Put on the pizza rack. Once preheated, place the pan on the bake position. 4. Serve warm with ice cream.

Old-Fashioned Fudge Pie

Prep time: 15 minutes | Cook time: 25 to 30 minutes | Serves 8

1½ cups sugar   12 tablespoons (1½ sticks) butter,   ¼ cup confectioners' sugar
⅓ cup unsweetened cocoa powder   melted   (optional)
½ cup self-rising flour   1½ teaspoons vanilla extract
3 large eggs, unbeaten   1 (9-inch) unbaked piecrust

1. In a medium bowl, stir together the sugar, cocoa powder, and flour. Stir in the eggs and melted butter. Stir in the vanilla. 2. Select Pizza, Air Fry Fan, set temperature to 350°F (177°C) and set time to 25 to 30 minutes. Press Start to begin preheating. 3. Pour the chocolate filing into the crust. 4. Transfer crust to pizza rack. Once preheated, place the pan on the pizza position. Stir every 10 minutes, until a knife inserted into the middle comes out clean. Let sit for 5 minutes before dusting with confectioners' sugar (if using) to serve.

Rhubarb and Strawberry Crumble

Prep time: 10 minutes | Cook time: 12 to 17 minutes | Serves 6

1½ cups sliced fresh strawberries
¾ cup sliced rhubarb
⅓ cup granulated sugar
⅔ cup quick-cooking oatmeal
½ cup whole-wheat pastry flour, or all-purpose flour
¼ cup packed light brown sugar
½ teaspoon ground cinnamon
3 tablespoons unsalted butter, melted

1. Select Bake, Air Fry Fan, set temperature to 375°F (191°C) and set time to 17 minutes. Press Start to begin preheating. 2. In a baking pan, combine the strawberries, rhubarb, and granulated sugar. 3. In a medium bowl, stir together the oatmeal, flour, brown sugar, and cinnamon. Stir the melted butter into this mixture until crumbly. Sprinkle the crumble mixture over the fruit. 4. Once preheated, place the pan on the bake position. 5. After about 12 minutes, check the crumble. If the fruit is bubbling and the topping is golden brown, it is done. If not, resume cooking. 6. When the cooking is complete, serve warm.

Pecan Brownies

Prep time: 10 minutes | Cook time: 20 minutes | Serves 6

½ cup blanched finely ground almond flour
½ cup powdered erythritol
2 tablespoons unsweetened cocoa powder
½ teaspoon baking powder
¼ cup unsalted butter, softened
1 large egg
¼ cup chopped pecans
¼ cup low-carb, sugar-free chocolate chips

1. Select Bake, Air Fry Fan, set temperature to 300°F (149°C) and set time to 20 minutes. Press Start to begin preheating. 2. In a large bowl, mix almond flour, erythritol, cocoa powder, and baking powder. Stir in butter and egg. 3. Fold in pecans and chocolate chips. Scoop mixture into the baking pan. 4. Once preheated, place the pan on the bake position. 5. When fully cooked a toothpick inserted in center will come out clean. Allow 20 minutes to fully cool and firm up.

Air Fryer Apple Fritters

Prep time: 30 minutes | Cook time: 7 to 8 minutes | Serves 6

1 cup chopped, peeled Granny Smith apple
½ cup granulated sugar
1 teaspoon ground cinnamon
1 cup all-purpose flour
1 teaspoon baking powder
1 teaspoon salt
2 tablespoons milk
2 tablespoons butter, melted
1 large egg, beaten
Cooking spray
¼ cup confectioners' sugar (optional)

1. Mix together the apple, granulated sugar, and cinnamon in a small bowl. Allow to sit for 30 minutes. 2. Combine the flour, baking powder, and salt in a medium bowl. Add the milk, butter, and egg and stir to incorporate. 3. Pour the apple mixture into the bowl of flour mixture and stir with a spatula until a dough forms. 4. Make the fritters: On a clean work surface, divide the dough into 12 equal portions and shape into 1-inch balls. Flatten them into patties with your hands. 5. Select Bake, Air Fry Fan, set temperature to 350°F (177°C) and set time to 7 to 8 minutes. Select Start/Stop to begin preheating. Line the baking pan with parchment paper and spray it with cooking spray. 6. Transfer the apple fritters onto the parchment paper, evenly spaced but not too close together. Spray the fritters with cooking spray. 7. Once preheated, place the pan on the bake position. It will be done until lightly browned. Flip the fritters halfway through the cooking time. 8. Remove from the oven to a plate and serve with the confectioners' sugar

sprinkled on top, if desired.

Almond-Roasted Pears

Prep time: 10 minutes | Cook time: 15 to 20 minutes | Serves 4

Yogurt Topping:

1 container vanilla Greek yogurt (5 to 6 ounces / 142 to 170 g)

¼ teaspoon almond flavoring

2 whole pears

¼ cup crushed Biscoff cookies

(approx. 4 cookies)

1 tablespoon sliced almonds

1 tablespoon butter

1. Select Roast, Air Fry Fan, set temperature to 360°F (182°C) and set time to 15 to 20 minutes. Press Start to begin preheating. 2. Stir almond flavoring into yogurt and set aside while preparing pears. 3. Halve each pear and spoon out the core. 4. Place pear halves in baking pan. 5. Stir together the cookie crumbs and almonds. Place a quarter of this mixture into the hollow of each pear half. 6. Cut butter into 4 pieces and place one piece on top of crumb mixture in each pear. 7. Once preheated, place the pan on the roast position. It will be done until pears have cooked through but are still slightly firm. 8. Serve pears warm with a dollop of yogurt topping.

Breaded Bananas with Chocolate Topping

Prep time: 10 minutes | Cook time: 10 minutes | Serves 6

¼ cup cornstarch

¼ cup plain bread crumbs

1 large egg, beaten

3 bananas, halved crosswise

Cooking spray

Chocolate sauce, for serving

1. Select Bake, Air Fry Fan, set temperature to 350°F (177°C) and set time to 5 minutes. Press Start to begin preheating. 2. Place the cornstarch, bread crumbs, and egg in three separate bowls. 3. Roll the bananas in the cornstarch, then in the beaten egg, and finally in the bread crumbs to coat well. 4. Spritz the baking pan with the cooking spray. 5. Arrange the banana halves in the pan and mist them with the cooking spray. Once preheated, place the pan on the bake position. Flip the bananas and continue to cook for another 2 minutes. 6. Remove the bananas from the oven to a serving plate. Serve with the chocolate sauce drizzled over the top.

Chapter 10 Fast and Easy Everyday Favorites

Corn Fritters

Prep time: 15 minutes | Cook time: 8 minutes | Serves 6

1 cup self-rising flour

1 tablespoon sugar

1 teaspoon salt

1 large egg, lightly beaten

¼ cup buttermilk

¾ cup corn kernels

¼ cup minced onion

Cooking spray

1. Select Bake, Air Fry Fan, set temperature to 350°F (177°C) and set time to 4 minutes. Press Start to begin preheating. Line the baking pan with parchment paper. 2. In a medium bowl, whisk the flour, sugar, and salt until blended. Stir in the egg and buttermilk. Add the corn and minced onion. Mix well. Shape the corn fritter batter into 12 balls. 3. Place the fritters on the parchment and spritz with oil. Once preheated, place the pan on the bake position and cook. Flip the fritters, spritz them with oil, and bake for 4 minutes more until firm and lightly browned. 4. Serve immediately.

Spinach and Carrot Balls

Prep time: 10 minutes | Cook time: 10 minutes | Serves 4

2 slices toasted bread	½ onion, chopped	1 teaspoon salt
1 carrot, peeled and grated	1 egg, beaten	½ teaspoon black pepper
1 package fresh spinach, blanched and chopped	½ teaspoon garlic powder	1 tablespoon nutritional yeast
	1 teaspoon minced garlic	1 tablespoon flour

1. Select Air Fry, set temperature to 390°F (199°C) and set time to 10 minutes. Press Start to begin preheating. 2. In a food processor, pulse the toasted bread to form bread crumbs. Transfer into a shallow dish or bowl. 3. In a bowl, mix together all the other ingredients. 4. Use your hands to shape the mixture into small-sized balls. Roll the balls in the bread crumbs, ensuring to cover them well. 5. Once preheated, place the balls in baking pan on the air fry position. 6. Serve immediately.

Traditional Queso Fundido

Prep time: 10 minutes | Cook time: 25 minutes | Serves 4

4 ounces (113 g) fresh Mexican chorizo, casings removed	1 cup chopped tomato	Mozzarella cheese
1 medium onion, chopped	2 jalapeños, deseeded and diced	½ cup half-and-half
3 cloves garlic, minced	2 teaspoons ground cumin	Celery sticks or tortilla chips, for serving
	2 cups shredded Oaxaca or	

1. Select Roast, Air Fry Fan, set temperature to 400°F (204°C) and set time to 15 minutes. Press Start to begin preheating. 2. In a baking pan, combine the chorizo, onion, garlic, tomato, jalapeños, and cumin. Stir to combine. 3. Once preheated, place the pan on the roast position. Stir halfway through the cooking time to break up the sausage. 4. Add the cheese and half-and-half; stir to combine. Cook for 10 minutes more, or until the cheese has melted. 5. Serve with celery sticks or tortilla chips.

Cheesy Baked Grits

Prep time: 10 minutes | Cook time: 12 minutes | Serves 6

¾ cup hot water	1 large egg, beaten	½ to 1 teaspoon red pepper flakes
2 (1-ounce / 28-g) packages instant grits	1 tablespoon butter, melted	1 cup shredded Cheddar cheese or jalapeño Jack cheese
	2 cloves garlic, minced	

1. Select Bake, Air Fry Fan, set temperature to 400°F (204°C) and set time to 12 minutes. Press Start to begin preheating. 2. In a baking pan, combine the water, grits, egg, butter, garlic, and red pepper flakes. Stir until well combined. Stir in the shredded cheese. 3. Once preheated, place the pan on the bake position. It will be done until the grits are cooked through and a knife inserted near the center comes out clean. 4. Let stand for 5 minutes before serving.

Bacon Pinwheels

Prep time: 10 minutes | Cook time: 10 minutes | Makes 8 pinwheels

1 sheet puff pastry	¼ cup brown sugar	Ground black pepper, to taste
2 tablespoons maple syrup	8 slices bacon	Cooking spray

1. Select Air Fry, set temperature to 360°F (182°C) and set time to 10 minutes. Press Start to begin preheating. Spritz

the crisper tray with cooking spray. 2. Roll the puff pastry into a 10-inch square with a rolling pin on a clean work surface, then cut the pastry into 8 strips. 3. Brush the strips with maple syrup and sprinkle with sugar, leaving a 1-inch far end uncovered. 4. Arrange each slice of bacon on each strip, leaving a ⅛-inch length of bacon hang over the end close to you. Sprinkle with black pepper. 5. From the end close to you, roll the strips into pinwheels, then dab the uncovered end with water and seal the rolls. 6. Once preheated, arrange the pinwheels in the tray and spritz with cooking spray. 7. Once preheated, place the tray on the air fry position. It will be done until golden brown. Flip the pinwheels halfway through. 8. Serve immediately.

Air Fried Shishito Peppers

Prep time: 5 minutes | Cook time: 5 minutes | Serves 4

½ pound (227 g) shishito peppers (about 24)	1 tablespoon olive oil	Lemon wedges, for serving
	Coarse sea salt, to taste	Cooking spray

1. Select Air Fry, set temperature to 400°F (204°C) and set time to 5 minutes. Press Start to begin preheating. Spritz the crisper tray with cooking spray. 2. Toss the peppers with olive oil in a large bowl to coat well. 3. Arrange the peppers in the tray. 4. Once preheated, place the pan on the air fry position. It will be done until blistered and lightly charred. Shake the tray and sprinkle the peppers with salt halfway through the cooking time. 5. Transfer the peppers onto a plate and squeeze the lemon wedges on top before serving.

Crispy Green Tomatoes Slices

Prep time: 10 minutes | Cook time: 8 minutes | Makes 12 slices

½ cup all-purpose flour	1 cup panko	½ teaspoon ground black pepper
1 egg	2 green tomatoes, cut into	Cooking spray
½ cup buttermilk	¼-inch-thick slices, patted dry	
1 cup cornmeal	½ teaspoon salt	

1. Select Air Fry, set temperature to 400°F (204°C) and set time to 8 minutes. Press Start to begin preheating. Line the crisper tray with parchment paper. 2. Pour the flour in a bowl. Whisk the egg and buttermilk in a second bowl. Combine the cornmeal and panko in a third bowl. 3. Dredge the tomato slices in the bowl of flour first, then into the egg mixture, and then dunk the slices into the cornmeal mixture. Shake the excess off. 4. Transfer the well-coated tomato slices on the tray and sprinkle with salt and ground black pepper. 5. Spritz the tomato slices with cooking spray. Once preheated, place the tray on the air fry position. It will be done until crispy and lightly browned. Flip the slices halfway through the cooking time. 6. Serve immediately.

Cheesy Jalapeño Cornbread

Prep time: 10 minutes | Cook time: 20 minutes | Serves 8

⅔ cup cornmeal	½ teaspoon kosher salt	⅓ cup shredded sharp Cheddar cheese
⅓ cup all-purpose flour	1 tablespoon granulated sugar	
¾ teaspoon baking powder	¾ cup whole milk	Cooking spray
2 tablespoons buttery spread, melted	1 large egg, beaten	
	1 jalapeño pepper, thinly sliced	

1. Select Pizza, Air Fry Fan, set temperature to 300°F (149°C) and set time to 20 minutes. Press Start to begin preheating. Spritz the baking pan with cooking spray. 2. Combine all the ingredients in a large bowl. Stir to mix well.

Pour the mixture in a baking pan. 3. Once preheated, place the pan on the pizza position. It will be done until a toothpick inserted in the center of the bread comes out clean. 4. When the cooking is complete, remove the baking pan from the oven and allow the bread to cool for a few minutes before slicing to serve.

Garlicky Knots with Parsley

Prep time: 10 minutes | Cook time: 10 minutes | Makes 8 knots

1 teaspoon dried parsley

¼ cup melted butter

2 teaspoons garlic powder

1 (11-ounce / 312-g) tube refrigerated French bread dough, cut into 8 slices

1. Select Bake, Air Fry Fan, set temperature to 350°F (177°C) and set time to 5 minutes. Press Start to begin preheating. 2. Combine the parsley, butter, and garlic powder in a bowl. Stir to mix well. 3. Place the French bread dough slices on a clean work surface, then roll each slice into a 6-inch long rope. Tie the ropes into knots and arrange them on a plate. Brush the knots with butter mixture. 4. Transfer the knots into the crisper tray. You need to work in batches to avoid overcrowding. 5. Once preheated, place the tray on the bake position. Flip the knots halfway through the cooking time. The knots will be golden brown when done. 6. Serve immediately.

Classic Poutine

Prep time: 15 minutes | Cook time: 25 minutes | Serves 2

2 russet potatoes, scrubbed and cut into ½-inch sticks

2 teaspoons vegetable oil

2 tablespoons butter

¼ onion, minced

¼ teaspoon dried thyme

1 clove garlic, smashed

3 tablespoons all-purpose flour

1 teaspoon tomato paste

1½ cups beef stock

2 teaspoons Worcestershire sauce

Salt and freshly ground black pepper, to taste

⅔ cup chopped string cheese

1. Bring a pot of water to a boil, then put in the potato sticks and blanch for 4 minutes. 2. Select Air Fry, set temperature to 400°F (204°C) and set time to 25 minutes. Press Start to begin preheating. 3. Drain the potato sticks and rinse under running cold water, then pat dry with paper towels. 4. Transfer the sticks in a large bowl and drizzle with vegetable oil. Toss to coat well. 5. Place the potato sticks in crisper tray. Once preheated, place the tray on the air fry position. The sticks will be golden brown when done. Shake the tray at least three times during the frying. 6. Meanwhile, make the gravy: Heat the butter in a saucepan over medium heat until melted. 7. Add the onion, thyme, and garlic and sauté for 5 minutes or until the onion is translucent. 8. Add the flour and sauté for an additional 2 minutes. Pour in the tomato paste and beef stock and cook for 1 more minute or until lightly thickened. 9. Drizzle the gravy with Worcestershire sauce and sprinkle with salt and ground black pepper. Reduce the heat to low to keep the gravy warm until ready to serve. 10. Transfer the fried potato sticks onto a plate, then sprinkle with salt and ground black pepper. Scatter with string cheese and pour the gravy over. Serve warm.

South Carolina Shrimp and Corn Bake

Prep time: 10 minutes | Cook time: 18 minutes | Serves 2

1 ear corn, husk and silk removed, cut into 2-inch rounds

8 ounces (227 g) red potatoes, unpeeled, cut into 1-inch pieces

2 teaspoons Old Bay Seasoning, divided

2 teaspoons vegetable oil, divided

¼ teaspoon ground black pepper

8 ounces (227 g) large shrimps (about 12 shrimps), deveined

6 ounces (170 g) andouille or chorizo sausage, cut into 1-inch pieces

2 garlic cloves, minced

1 tablespoon chopped fresh parsley

1. Select Bake, Air Fry Fan, set temperature to 400°F (204°C) and set time to 12 minutes. Press Start to begin preheating. 2. Put the corn rounds and potatoes in a large bowl. Sprinkle with 1 teaspoon of Old Bay seasoning and drizzle with vegetable oil. Toss to coat well. 3. Transfer the corn rounds and potatoes on baking pan. 4. Once preheated, place the pan on the bake position. It will be done until soft and browned. Shake the pan halfway through the cooking time. 5. Meanwhile, cut slits into the shrimps but be careful not to cut them through. Combine the shrimps, sausage, remaining Old Bay seasoning, and remaining vegetable oil in the large bowl. Toss to coat well. 6. When the baking of the potatoes and corn rounds is complete, add the shrimps and sausage and bake for 6 more minutes or until the shrimps are opaque. Shake the pan halfway through the cooking time. 7. When the baking is finished, serve them on a plate and spread with parsley before serving.

Honey Bartlett Pears with Lemony Ricotta

Prep time: 10 minutes | Cook time: 8 minutes | Serves 4

2 large Bartlett pears, peeled, cut in half, cored	¼ teaspoon ground cardamom	1 teaspoon pure almond extract
3 tablespoons melted butter	3 tablespoons brown sugar	1 tablespoon honey, plus additional for drizzling
½ teaspoon ground ginger	½ cup whole-milk ricotta cheese	
	1 teaspoon pure lemon extract	

1. Select Bake, Air Fry Fan, set temperature to 375°F (191°C) and set time to 5 minutes. Press Start to begin preheating. 2. Toss the pears with butter, ginger, cardamom, and sugar in a large bowl. Toss to coat well. 3. Arrange the pears on pizza rack, cut side down. Once preheated, place the rack on the bake position. Then flip the pears and air fry for 3 more minutes or until the pears are soft and browned. 4. In the meantime, combine the remaining ingredients in a separate bowl. Whip for 1 minute with a hand mixer until the mixture is puffed. 5. Divide the mixture into four bowls, then put the pears over the mixture and drizzle with more honey to serve.

Air Fried Broccoli

Prep time: 5 minutes | Cook time: 6 minutes | Serves 1

4 egg yolks	2 cups coconut flower	2 cups broccoli florets
¼ cup butter, melted	Salt and pepper, to taste	

1. Select Air Fry, set temperature to 400°F (204°C) and set time to 6 minutes. Press Start to begin preheating. 2. In a bowl, whisk the egg yolks and melted butter together. Throw in the coconut flour, salt and pepper, then stir again to combine well. 3. Dip each broccoli floret into the mixture and place in the crisper tray. You may need to work in batches. Once preheated, place the tray on the air fry position. 4. Take care when removing them from the air fryer oven and serve immediately.

Beery and Crunchy Onion Rings

Prep time: 10 minutes | Cook time: 16 minutes | Serves 2 to 4

⅔ cup all-purpose flour	pepper	1 large Vidalia onion, peeled and sliced into ½-inch rings
1 teaspoon paprika	1 egg, beaten	Cooking spray
½ teaspoon baking soda	¾ cup beer	
1 teaspoon salt	1½ cups breadcrumbs	
½ teaspoon freshly ground black	1 tablespoons olive oil	

1. Select Air Fry, set temperature to 360°F (182°C) and set time to 16 minutes. Press Start to begin preheating. Spritz

the crisper tray with cooking spray. 2. Combine the flour, paprika, baking soda, salt, and ground black pepper in a bowl. Stir to mix well. 3. Combine the egg and beer in a separate bowl. Stir to mix well. 4. Make a well in the center of the flour mixture, then pour the egg mixture in the well. Stir to mix everything well. 5. Pour the breadcrumbs and olive oil in a shallow plate. Stir to mix well. 6. Dredge the onion rings gently into the flour and egg mixture, then shake the excess off and put into the plate of breadcrumbs. Flip to coat the both sides well. 7. Arrange the onion rings in the tray. Once preheated, place the tray on the air fry position. You may need to work in batches. Flip the rings and put the bottom rings to the top halfway through. It will be done until golden brown and crunchy. 8. Serve immediately.

Scalloped Veggie Mix

Prep time: 10 minutes | Cook time: 15 minutes | Serves 4

1 Yukon Gold potato, thinly sliced
1 small sweet potato, peeled and thinly sliced
1 medium carrot, thinly sliced
¼ cup minced onion
3 garlic cloves, minced
¾ cup 2 percent milk
2 tablespoons cornstarch
½ teaspoon dried thyme

1. Select Roast, Air Fry Fan, set temperature to 380°F (193°C) and set time to 15 minutes. Press Start to begin preheating. 2. In a baking pan, layer the potato, sweet potato, carrot, onion, and garlic. 3. In a small bowl, whisk the milk, cornstarch, and thyme until blended. Pour the milk mixture evenly over the vegetables in the pan. 4. Once preheated, place the pan on the roast position. Check the casserole—it should be golden brown on top, and the vegetables should be tender. 5. Serve immediately.

Easy Air Fried Edamame

Prep time: 5 minutes | Cook time: 7 minutes | Serves 6

1½ pounds (680 g) unshelled edamame
2 tablespoons olive oil
1 teaspoon sea salt

1. Select Air Fry, set temperature to 400°F (204°C) and set time to 7 minutes. Press Start to begin preheating. 2. Place the edamame in a large bowl, then drizzle with olive oil. Toss to coat well. 3. Transfer the edamame to the crisper tray. Once preheated, place the pan on the air fry position. Shake the tray at least three times during the cooking. It will be done until tender and warmed through. 4. Transfer the cooked edamame onto a plate and sprinkle with salt. Toss to combine well and set aside for 3 minutes to infuse before serving.

Golden Salmon and Carrot Croquettes

Prep time: 15 minutes | Cook time: 10 minutes | Serves 6

2 egg whites
1 cup almond flour
1 cup panko breadcrumbs
1 pound (454 g) chopped salmon fillet
⅔ cup grated carrots
2 tablespoons minced garlic cloves
½ cup chopped onion
2 tablespoons chopped chives
Cooking spray

1. Select roast, Air Fry Fan, set temperature to 350°F (177°C) and set time to 10 minutes. Press Start to begin preheating. Spritz the baking pan with cooking spray. 2. Whisk the egg whites in a bowl. Put the flour in a second bowl. Pour the breadcrumbs in a third bowl. Set aside. 3. Combine the salmon, carrots, garlic, onion, and chives in a large bowl. Stir to mix well. 4. Form the mixture into balls with your hands. Dredge the balls into the flour, then egg, and then breadcrumbs to coat well. 5. Arrange the salmon balls on the pan and spritz with cooking spray. 6. Once

preheated, place the pan on the roast position. It will be done until crispy and browned. Shake the pan halfway through. 7. Serve immediately.

Rosemary and Orange Roasted Chickpeas

Prep time: 5 minutes | Cook time: 10 to 12 minutes | Makes 4 cups

4 cups cooked chickpeas
2 tablespoons vegetable oil
1 teaspoon kosher salt
1 teaspoon cumin
1 teaspoon paprika
Zest of 1 orange
1 tablespoon chopped fresh rosemary

1. Select Roast, Air Fry Fan, set temperature to 400°F (204°C) and set time to 10 to 12 minutes. Press Start to begin preheating. 2. Make sure the chickpeas are completely dry prior to roasting. In a medium bowl, toss the chickpeas with oil, salt, cumin, and paprika. 3. Working in batches, spread the chickpeas in a single layer in the crisper tray. Once preheated, place the tray on the roast position. Shake once halfway through. 4. Return the warm chickpeas to the bowl and toss with the orange zest and rosemary. Allow to cool completely. 5. Serve.

Crispy Potato Chips with Lemony Cream Dip

Prep time: 20 minutes | Cook time: 15 minutes | Serves 2 to 4

2 large russet potatoes, sliced into ⅛-inch slices, rinsed
Sea salt and freshly ground black pepper, to taste
Cooking spray

Lemony Cream Dip:
½ cup sour cream
¼ teaspoon lemon juice
2 scallions, white part only, minced
1 tablespoon olive oil

¼ teaspoon salt
Freshly ground black pepper, to taste

1. Soak the potato slices in water for 10 minutes, then pat dry with paper towels. 2. Select Air Fry, set temperature to 300°F (149°C) and set time to 15 minutes. Press Start to begin preheating. 3. Transfer the potato slices in the crisper tray. Spritz the slices with cooking spray. You may need to work in batches to avoid overcrowding. 4. Once preheated, place the tray on the air fry position. It will be done until crispy and golden brown. Shake the tray periodically. Sprinkle with salt and ground black pepper in the last minute. 5. Meanwhile, combine the ingredients for the dip in a small bowl. Stir to mix well. 6. Serve the potato chips immediately with the dip.

Buttery Sweet Potatoes

Prep time: 5 minutes | Cook time: 10 minutes | Serves 4

2 tablespoons butter, melted
1 tablespoon light brown sugar
2 sweet potatoes, peeled and cut into ½-inch cubes
Cooking spray

1. Select Roast, Air Fry Fan, set temperature to 400°F (204°C) and set time to 5 minutes. Press Start to begin preheating. Line the baking pan with parchment paper. 2. In a medium bowl, stir together the melted butter and brown sugar until blended. Toss the sweet potatoes in the butter mixture until coated. 3. Place the sweet potatoes on the parchment and spritz with oil. 4. Once preheated, place the pan on the roast position. Shake the pan, spritz the sweet potatoes with oil, and cook for 5 minutes more until they're soft enough to cut with a fork. 5. Serve immediately.

Simple Air Fried Crispy Brussels Sprouts

Prep time: 5 minutes | Cook time: 20 minutes | Serves 4

¼ teaspoon salt

⅛ teaspoon ground black pepper

1 tablespoon extra-virgin olive oil

1 pound (454 g) Brussels sprouts, trimmed and halved

Lemon wedges, for garnish

1. Select Air Fry, set temperature to 350°F (177°C) and set time to 20 minutes. Press Start to begin preheating. 2. Combine the salt, black pepper, and olive oil in a large bowl. Stir to mix well. 3. Add the Brussels sprouts to the bowl of mixture and toss to coat well. 4. Arrange the Brussels sprouts in the crisper tray. Once preheated, place the tray on the air fry position. It will be done until lightly browned and wilted. Shake the tray two times during the air frying. 5. Transfer the cooked Brussels sprouts to a large plate and squeeze the lemon wedges on top to serve.

Purple Potato Chips with Rosemary

Prep time: 10 minutes | Cook time: 9 to 14 minutes | Serves 6

1 cup Greek yogurt

2 chipotle chiles, minced

2 tablespoons adobo sauce

1 teaspoon paprika

1 tablespoon lemon juice

10 purple fingerling potatoes

1 teaspoon olive oil

2 teaspoons minced fresh rosemary leaves

⅛ teaspoon cayenne pepper

¼ teaspoon coarse sea salt

1. Select Air Fry, set temperature to 400°F (204°C) and set time to 9 to 14 minutes. Press Start to begin preheating. 2. In a medium bowl, combine the yogurt, minced chiles, adobo sauce, paprika, and lemon juice. Mix well and refrigerate. 3. Wash the potatoes and dry them with paper towels. Slice the potatoes lengthwise, as thinly as possible. You can use a mandoline, a vegetable peeler, or a very sharp knife. 4. Combine the potato slices in a medium bowl and drizzle with the olive oil; toss to coat. Arrange the slices to crisper tray. 5. Once preheated, place the tray on the air fry position. You may need to work in batches. Shake gently halfway during cooking time. 6. Sprinkle the chips with the rosemary, cayenne pepper, and sea salt. Serve with the chipotle sauce for dipping.

Air Fried Tortilla Chips

Prep time: 5 minutes | Cook time: 10 minutes | Serves 4

4 six-inch corn tortillas, cut in half and slice into thirds

1 tablespoon canola oil

¼ teaspoon kosher salt

Cooking spray

1. Select Air Fry, set temperature to 360°F (182°C) and set time to 10 minutes. Press Start to begin preheating. Spritz the crisper tray with cooking spray. 2. On a clean work surface, brush the tortilla chips with canola oil, then transfer the chips in the tray. 3. Once preheated, place the tray on the air fry position. It will be done until crunchy and lightly browned. Shake the tray and sprinkle with salt halfway through the cooking time. 4. Transfer the chips onto a plate lined with paper towels. Serve immediately.

Lemony and Garlicky Asparagus

Prep time: 5 minutes | Cook time: 10 minutes | Makes 10 spears

10 spears asparagus (about ½ pound / 227 g in total), snap the ends off

1 tablespoon lemon juice

2 teaspoons minced garlic

½ teaspoon salt

¼ teaspoon ground black pepper

Cooking spray

1. Select Roast, Air Fry Fan, set temperature to 400°F (204°C) and set time to 10 minutes. Press Start to begin

preheating. 2. Put the asparagus spears in a large bowl. Drizzle with lemon juice and sprinkle with minced garlic, salt, and ground black pepper. Toss to coat well. 3. Transfer the asparagus in the crisper tray and spritz with cooking spray. Once preheated, place the tray on the roast position. Flip the asparagus halfway through. It will be done until wilted and soft. 4. Serve immediately.

Classic Latkes

Prep time: 15 minutes | Cook time: 10 minutes | Makes 4 latkes

1 egg

2 tablespoons all-purpose flour

2 medium potatoes, peeled and shredded, rinsed and drained

¼ teaspoon granulated garlic

½ teaspoon salt

Cooking spray

1. Select Pizza, Air Fry Fan, set temperature to 380°F (193°C) and set time to 10 minutes. Press Start to begin preheating. Spritz the baking pan with cooking spray. 2. Whisk together the egg, flour, potatoes, garlic, and salt in a large bowl. Stir to mix well. 3. Divide the mixture into four parts, then flatten them into four circles. Arrange the circles into the baking pan. Spritz the circles with cooking spray. 4. Once preheated, place the pan on the pizza position. Flip the latkes halfway through. It will be done until golden brown and crispy. 5. Serve immediately.

Baked Chorizo Scotch Eggs

Prep time: 5 minutes | Cook time: 15 to 20 minutes | Makes 4 eggs

1 pound (454 g) Mexican chorizo or other seasoned sausage meat

4 soft-boiled eggs plus 1 raw egg

1 tablespoon water

½ cup all-purpose flour

1 cup panko bread crumbs

Cooking spray

1. Divide the chorizo into 4 equal portions. Flatten each portion into a disc. Place a soft-boiled egg in the center of each disc. Wrap the chorizo around the egg, encasing it completely. Place the encased eggs on a plate and chill for at least 30 minutes. 2. Select Bake, Air Fry Fan, set temperature to 360°F (182°C) and set time to 10 minutes. Press Start to begin preheating. 3. Beat the raw egg with 1 tablespoon of water. Place the flour on a small plate and the panko on a second plate. Working with 1 egg at a time, roll the encased egg in the flour, then dip it in the egg mixture. Dredge the egg in the panko and place on a plate. Repeat with the remaining eggs. 4. Spray the eggs with oil and place in the baking pan. Once preheated, place the pan on the bake position. Turn and bake for an additional 5 to 10 minutes, or until browned and crisp on all sides. 5. Serve immediately.

Garlicky Zoodles

Prep time: 10 minutes | Cook time: 10 minutes | Serves 4

2 large zucchini, peeled and spiralized

2 large yellow summer squash, peeled and spiralized

1 tablespoon olive oil, divided

½ teaspoon kosher salt

1 garlic clove, whole

2 tablespoons fresh basil, chopped

Cooking spray

1. Select Roast, Air Fry Fan, set temperature to 360°F (182°C) and set time to 10 minutes. Press Start to begin preheating. Spritz the baking pan with cooking spray. 2. Combine the zucchini and summer squash with 1 teaspoon olive oil and salt in a large bowl. Toss to coat well. 3. Transfer the zucchini and summer squash in the pan and add the garlic. 4. Once preheated, place the pan on the roast position. Toss the spiralized zucchini and summer squash halfway through the cooking time. It will be done until tender and fragrant. 5. Transfer the cooked zucchini and summer squash onto a plate and set aside. 6. Remove the garlic from the baking pan and allow to cool for a few

minutes. Mince the garlic and combine with remaining olive oil in a small bowl. Stir to mix well. 7. Drizzle the spiralized zucchini and summer squash with garlic oil and sprinkle with basil. Toss to serve.

Beef Bratwursts

Prep time: 5 minutes | Cook time: 15 minutes | Serves 4

4 (3-ounce / 85-g) beef bratwursts

1. Select Air Fry, set temperature to 375°F (191°C) and set time to 15 minutes. Press Start to begin preheating. 2. Place the beef bratwursts on pizza rack and place the rack on the air fry position and cook, turning once halfway through. 3. Serve hot.

Simple Cheesy Shrimps

Prep time: 10 minutes | Cook time: 16 minutes | Serves 4 to 6

⅔ cup grated Parmesan cheese	1 teaspoon basil	shrimps, peeled and deveined
4 minced garlic cloves	1 teaspoon ground black pepper	Lemon wedges, for topping
1 teaspoon onion powder	2 tablespoons olive oil	Cooking spray
½ teaspoon oregano	2 pounds (907 g) cooked large	

1. Select Air Fry, set temperature to 350°F (177°C) and set time to 8 minutes. Press Start to begin preheating. Spritz the crisper tray with cooking spray. 2. Combine all the ingredients, except for the shrimps, in a large bowl. Stir to mix well. 3. Dunk the shrimps in the mixture and toss to coat well. Shake the excess off. 4. Once preheated, arrange the shrimps in the tray on the air fry position. Flip the shrimps halfway through. You may need to work in batches to avoid overcrowding. It will be done until opaque. 5. Transfer the cooked shrimps on a large plate and squeeze the lemon wedges over before serving.

Frico

Prep time: 5 minutes | Cook time: 5 minutes | Serves 2

1 cup shredded aged Manchego cheese	1 teaspoon all-purpose flour	¼ teaspoon cracked black pepper
	½ teaspoon cumin seeds	

1. Select Pizza, Air Fry Fan, set temperature to 375°F (191°C) and set time to 5 minutes. Press Start to begin preheating. Line the baking pan with parchment paper. 2. Combine the cheese and flour in a bowl. Stir to mix well. Spread the mixture in the pan into a 4-inch round. 3. Combine the cumin and black pepper in a small bowl. Stir to mix well. Sprinkle the cumin mixture over the cheese round. 4. Once preheated, place the pan on the pizza position. It will be done until the cheese is lightly browned and frothy. 5. Use tongs to transfer the cheese wafer onto a plate and slice to serve.

Air Fried Butternut Squash with Chopped Hazelnuts

Prep time: 10 minutes | Cook time: 20 minutes | Makes 3 cups

2 tablespoons whole hazelnuts	¼ teaspoon kosher salt	2 teaspoons olive oil
3 cups butternut squash, peeled, deseeded, and cubed	¼ teaspoon freshly ground black pepper	Cooking spray

1. Select Air Fry, set temperature to 300°F (149°C) and set time to 3 minutes. Press Start to begin preheating. Spritz the baking pan with cooking spray. 2. Arrange the hazelnuts in the pan. Once preheated, place the pan on the bake

position. It will be done until soft. 3. Chopped the hazelnuts roughly and transfer to a small bowl. Set aside. 4. Put the butternut squash in a large bowl, then sprinkle with salt and pepper and drizzle with olive oil. Toss to coat well. 5. Spritz the pizza rack with cooking spray. Transfer the squash in rack on air fry position. Set the temperature to 360°F (182°C) and set time to 20 minutes. Press Start. The squash will be soft when done. Shake the rack halfway through the frying time. 6. When the frying is complete, transfer the squash onto a plate and sprinkle with chopped hazelnuts before serving.

Simple Baked Green Beans

Prep time: 5 minutes | Cook time: 10 minutes | Makes 2 cups

- ½ teaspoon lemon pepper
- 2 teaspoons granulated garlic
- ½ teaspoon salt
- 1 tablespoon olive oil
- 2 cups fresh green beans, trimmed and snapped in half

1. Select Bake, Air Fry Fan, set temperature to 370°F (188°C) and set time to 10 minutes. Press Start to begin preheating. 2. Combine the lemon pepper, garlic, salt, and olive oil in a bowl. Stir to mix well. 3. Add the green beans to the bowl of mixture and toss to coat well. Transfer to baking pan. 4. Once preheated, place the pan on the bake position. It will be done until tender and crispy. Shake the pan halfway through to make sure the green beans are cooked evenly. 5. Serve immediately.

Easy Devils on Horseback

Prep time: 5 minutes | Cook time: 7 minutes | Serves 12

- 24 petite pitted prunes (4½ ounces / 128 g)
- ¼ cup crumbled blue cheese, divided
- 8 slices center-cut bacon, cut crosswise into thirds

1. Select Air Fry, set temperature to 400°F (204°C) and set time to 7 minutes. Press Start to begin preheating. 2. Halve the prunes lengthwise, but don't cut them all the way through. Place ½ teaspoon of cheese in the center of each prune. Wrap a piece of bacon around each prune and secure the bacon with a toothpick. 3. Working in batches, arrange a single layer of the prunes in the baking pan on air fry position once preheated. Flip halfway. The bacon will be cooked through and crisp when done. 4. Let cool slightly and serve warm.

Cheesy Potato Patties

Prep time: 5 minutes | Cook time: 10 minutes | Serves 8

- 2 pounds (907 g) white potatoes
- ½ cup finely chopped scallions
- ½ teaspoon freshly ground black pepper, or more to taste
- 1 tablespoon fine sea salt
- ½ teaspoon hot paprika
- 2 cups shredded Colby cheese
- ¼ cup canola oil
- 1 cup crushed crackers

1. Select Roast, Air Fry Fan, set temperature to 360°F (182°C) and set time to 10 minutes. Press Start to begin preheating. 2. Boil the potatoes until soft. Dry them off and peel them before mashing thoroughly, leaving no lumps. 3. Combine the mashed potatoes with scallions, pepper, salt, paprika, and cheese. 4. Mold the mixture into balls with your hands and press with your palm to flatten them into patties. 5. In a shallow dish, combine the canola oil and crushed crackers. Coat the patties in the crumb mixture. 6. Once preheated, place the patties in baking pan on the roast position. 7. Serve hot.

Crunchy Fried Okra

Prep time: 5 minutes | Cook time: 8 to 10 minutes | Serves 4

- 1 cup self-rising yellow cornmeal
- 1 teaspoon Italian-style seasoning
- 1 teaspoon paprika
- 1 teaspoon salt
- ½ teaspoon freshly ground black pepper
- 2 large eggs, beaten
- 2 cups okra slices
- Cooking spray

1. Select Air Fry, set temperature to 400°F (204°C) and set time to 4 minutes. Press Start to begin preheating. Line the crisper tray with parchment paper. 2. In a shallow bowl, whisk the cornmeal, Italian-style seasoning, paprika, salt, and pepper until blended. Place the beaten eggs in a second shallow bowl. 3. Add the okra to the beaten egg and stir to coat. Add the egg and okra mixture to the cornmeal mixture and stir until coated. 4. Place the okra on the parchment and spritz it with oil. 5. Once preheated, place the tray on the air fry position. Shake the tray, spritz the okra with oil, and air fry for 4 to 6 minutes more until lightly browned and crispy. 6. Serve immediately.

Sweet Corn and Carrot Fritters

Prep time: 10 minutes | Cook time: 8 to 11 minutes | Serves 4

- 1 medium-sized carrot, grated
- 1 yellow onion, finely chopped
- 4 ounces (113 g) canned sweet corn kernels, drained
- 1 teaspoon sea salt flakes
- 1 tablespoon chopped fresh cilantro
- 1 medium-sized egg, whisked
- 2 tablespoons plain milk
- 1 cup grated Parmesan cheese
- ¼ cup flour
- ⅓ teaspoon baking powder
- ⅓ teaspoon sugar
- Cooking spray

1. Select Roast, Air Fry Fan, set temperature to 350°F (177°C) and set time to 8 to 11 minutes. Press Start to begin preheating. 2. Place the grated carrot in a colander and press down to squeeze out any excess moisture. Dry it with a paper towel. 3. Combine the carrots with the remaining ingredients. 4. Mold 1 tablespoon of the mixture into a ball and press it down with your hand or a spoon to flatten it. Repeat until the rest of the mixture is used up. 5. Spritz the balls with cooking spray. Arrange in the baking pan, taking care not to overlap any balls. Once preheated, place the pan on the roast position. 6. Serve warm.

Easy Roasted Asparagus

Prep time: 5 minutes | Cook time: 6 minutes | Serves 4

- 1 pound (454 g) asparagus, trimmed and halved crosswise
- 1 teaspoon extra-virgin olive oil
- Salt and pepper, to taste
- Lemon wedges, for serving

1. Select Roast, Air Fry Fan, set temperature to 400°F (204°C) and set time to 6 to 8 minutes. Press Start to begin preheating. 2. Toss the asparagus with the oil, ⅛ teaspoon salt, and ⅛ teaspoon pepper in bowl. Transfer to the baking pan. 3. Once preheated, place the pan on the roast position and roast. It will be done until tender and bright green, tossing halfway through cooking. 4. Season with salt and pepper and serve with lemon wedges.

Baked Cheese Sandwich

Prep time: 5 minutes | Cook time: 8 minutes | Serves 2

- 2 tablespoons mayonnaise
- 4 thick slices sourdough bread
- 4 thick slices Brie cheese
- 8 slices hot capicola

1. Select Bake, Air Fry Fan, set temperature to 350°F (177°C) and set time to 8 minutes. Press Start to begin

preheating. 2. Spread the mayonnaise on one side of each slice of bread. Place 2 slices of bread on the pizza rack, mayonnaise-side down. 3. Place the slices of Brie and capicola on the bread and cover with the remaining two slices of bread, mayonnaise-side up. 4. Once preheated, place the rack on the bake position. It will be done until the cheese are melted. 5. Serve immediately.

Cheesy Chile Toast

Prep time: 5 minutes | Cook time: 5 minutes | Serves 1

2 tablespoons grated Parmesan cheese
2 tablespoons grated Mozzarella cheese
2 teaspoons salted butter, at room temperature
10 to 15 thin slices serrano chile or jalapeño
2 slices sourdough bread
½ teaspoon black pepper

1. Select Bake, Air Fry Fan, set temperature to 325°F (163°C) and set time to 5 minutes. Press Start to begin preheating. 2. In a small bowl, stir together the Parmesan, Mozzarella, butter, and chiles. 3. Spread half the mixture onto one side of each slice of bread. Sprinkle with the pepper. Place the slices, cheese-side up, on the pizza rack. Once preheated, place the rack on the back position. It will be done until the cheese are melted and start to brown slightly. 4. Serve immediately.

Spicy Air Fried Old Bay Shrimp

Prep time: 7 minutes | Cook time: 10 minutes | Makes 2 cups

½ teaspoon Old Bay Seasoning
1 teaspoon ground cayenne pepper
½ teaspoon paprika
1 tablespoon olive oil
⅛ teaspoon salt
½ pound (227 g) shrimps, peeled
and deveined
Juice of half a lemon

1. Select Air Fry, set temperature to 390°F (199°C) and set time to 10 minutes. Press Start to begin preheating. 2. Combine the Old Bay Seasoning, cayenne pepper, paprika, olive oil, and salt in a large bowl, then add the shrimps and toss to coat well. 3. Put the shrimps in the crisper tray. Once preheated, place the tray on the air fry position. It will be done opaque. Flip the shrimps halfway through. 4. Serve the shrimps with lemon juice on top.

Indian-Style Sweet Potato Fries

Prep time: 5 minutes | Cook time: 8 minutes | Makes 20 fries

Seasoning Mixture:
¾ teaspoon ground coriander
½ teaspoon garam masala
½ teaspoon garlic powder
½ teaspoon ground cumin
¼ teaspoon ground cayenne pepper
Fries:
2 large sweet potatoes, peeled
2 teaspoons olive oil

1. Select Air Fry, set temperature to 400°F (204°C) and set time to 8 minutes. Press Start to begin preheating. 2. In a small bowl, combine the coriander, garam masala, garlic powder, cumin, and cayenne pepper. 3. Slice the sweet potatoes into ¼-inch-thick fries. 4. In a large bowl, toss the sliced sweet potatoes with the olive oil and the seasoning mixture. 5. Transfer the seasoned sweet potatoes to the crisper tray. Once preheated, place the tray on the air fry position. It will be done until crispy. 6. Serve warm.

Beet Salad with Lemon Vinaigrette

Prep time: 10 minutes | Cook time: 12 to 15 minutes | Serves 4

6 medium red and golden beets, peeled and sliced
1 teaspoon olive oil
¼ teaspoon kosher salt
½ cup crumbled feta cheese
8 cups mixed greens

Cooking spray
Vinaigrette:
2 teaspoons olive oil
2 tablespoons chopped fresh chives
Juice of 1 lemon

1. Select Air Fry, set temperature to 360°F (182°C) and set time to 12 to 15 minutes. Press Start to begin preheating. 2. In a large bowl, toss the beets, olive oil, and kosher salt. 3. Spray the crisper tray with cooking spray, then place the beets in the tray. Once preheated, place the pan on the air fry position. It will be done until tender. 4. While the beets cook, make the vinaigrette in a large bowl by whisking together the olive oil, lemon juice, and chives. 5. Remove the beets from the oven, toss in the vinaigrette, and allow to cool for 5 minutes. Add the feta and serve on top of the mixed greens.

Southwest Corn and Bell Pepper Roast

Prep time: 10 minutes | Cook time: 10 minutes | Serves 4

For the Corn:
1½ cups thawed frozen corn kernels
1 cup mixed diced bell peppers
1 jalapeño, diced
1 cup diced yellow onion
½ teaspoon ancho chile powder
1 tablespoon fresh lemon juice
1 teaspoon ground cumin
½ teaspoon kosher salt
Cooking spray
For Serving:
¼ cup feta cheese
¼ cup chopped fresh cilantro
1 tablespoon fresh lemon juice

1. Select Roast, Air Fry Fan, set temperature to 375°F (191°C) and set time to 10 minutes. Press Start to begin preheating. Spritz the baking pan with cooking spray. 2. Combine the ingredients for the corn in a large bowl. Stir to mix well. 3. Pout the mixture into the pan. Once preheated, place the pan on the roast position. The corn and bell peppers will be soft when done. Shake the pan halfway through the cooking time. 4. Transfer them onto a large plate, then spread with feta cheese and cilantro. Drizzle with lemon juice and serve.

Herb-Roasted Veggies

Prep time: 10 minutes | Cook time: 14 to 18 minutes | Serves 4

1 red bell pepper, sliced
1 (8-ounce / 227-g) package sliced mushrooms
1 cup green beans, cut into 2-inch pieces
⅓ cup diced red onion
3 garlic cloves, sliced
1 teaspoon olive oil
½ teaspoon dried basil
½ teaspoon dried tarragon

1. Select Roast, Air Fry Fan, set temperature to 350°F (177°C) and set time to 14 to 18 minutes. Press Start to begin preheating. 2. In a medium bowl, mix the red bell pepper, mushrooms, green beans, red onion, and garlic. Drizzle with the olive oil. Toss to coat. 3. Add the herbs and toss again. 4. Place the vegetables in the baking pan. Once preheated, place the pan on the roasst position. It will be done until tender. Serve immediately.

Peppery Brown Rice Fritters

Prep time: 10 minutes | Cook time: 8 to 10 minutes | Serves 4

1 (10-ounce / 284-g) bag frozen cooked brown rice, thawed
1 egg
3 tablespoons brown rice flour
⅓ cup finely grated carrots
⅓ cup minced red bell pepper
2 tablespoons minced fresh basil
3 tablespoons grated Parmesan cheese
2 teaspoons olive oil

1. Select Air Fry, set temperature to 380°F (193°C) and set time to 8 to 10 minutes. Press Start to begin preheating. 2. In a small bowl, combine the thawed rice, egg, and flour and mix to blend. 3. Stir in the carrots, bell pepper, basil, and

Parmesan cheese. 4. Form the mixture into 8 fritters and drizzle with the olive oil. 5. Put the fritters carefully into the baking pan. Once preheated, place the pan on the air fry position. The fritters are golden brown and cooked through when done. 6. Serve immediately.

Appendix 1 Measurement Conversion Chart & Air Fryer Cooking Chart

MEASUREMENT CONVERSION CHART

VOLUME EQUIVALENTS (DRY)

US STANDARD	METRIC (APPROXIMATE)
1/8 teaspoon	0.5 mL
1/4 teaspoon	1 mL
1/2 teaspoon	2 mL
3/4 teaspoon	4 mL
1 teaspoon	5 mL
1 tablespoon	15 mL
1/4 cup	59 mL
1/2 cup	118 mL
3/4 cup	177 mL
1 cup	235 mL
2 cups	475 mL
3 cups	700 mL
4 cups	1 L

VOLUME EQUIVALENTS (LIQUID)

US STANDARD	US STANDARD (OUNCES)	METRIC (APPROXIMATE)
2 tablespoons	1 fl.oz.	30 mL
1/4 cup	2 fl.oz.	60 mL
1/2 cup	4 fl.oz.	120 mL
1 cup	8 fl.oz.	240 mL
1 1/2 cup	12 fl.oz.	355 mL
2 cups or 1 pint	16 fl.oz.	475 mL
4 cups or 1 quart	32 fl.oz.	1 L
1 gallon	128 fl.oz.	4 L

TEMPERATURES EQUIVALENTS

FAHRENHEIT(F)	CELSIUS(C) (APPROXIMATE)
225 °F	107 °C
250 °F	120 °C
275 °F	135 °C
300 °F	150 °C
325 °F	160 °C
350 °F	180 °C
375 °F	190 °C
400 °F	205 °C
425 °F	220 °C
450 °F	235 °C
475 °F	245 °C
500 °F	260 °C

WEIGHT EQUIVALENTS

US STANDARD	METRIC (APPROXIMATE)
1 ounce	28 g
2 ounces	57 g
5 ounces	142 g
10 ounces	284 g
15 ounces	425 g
16 ounces (1 pound)	455 g
1.5 pounds	680 g
2 pounds	907 g

Air Fryer Cooking Chart

Beef

Item	Temp (°F)	Time (mins)	Item	Temp (°F)	Time (mins)
Beef Eye Round Roast (4 lbs.)	400 °F	45 to 55	Meatballs (1-inch)	370 °F	7
Burger Patty (4 oz.)	370 °F	16 to 20	Meatballs (3-inch)	380 °F	10
Filet Mignon (8 oz.)	400 °F	18	Ribeye, bone-in (1-inch, 8 oz)	400 °F	10 to 15
Flank Steak (1.5 lbs.)	400 °F	12	Sirloin steaks (1-inch, 12 oz)	400 °F	9 to 14
Flank Steak (2 lbs.)	400 °F	20 to 28			

Chicken

Item	Temp (°F)	Time (mins)	Item	Temp (°F)	Time (mins)
Breasts, bone in (1 ¼ lb.)	370 °F	25	Legs, bone-in (1 ¾ lb.)	380 °F	30
Breasts, boneless (4 oz)	380 °F	12	Thighs, boneless (1 ½ lb.)	380 °F	18 to 20
Drumsticks (2 ½ lb.)	370 °F	20	Wings (2 lb.)	400 °F	12
Game Hen (halved 2 lb.)	390 °F	20	Whole Chicken	360 °F	75
Thighs, bone-in (2 lb.)	380 °F	22	Tenders	360 °F	8 to 10

Pork & Lamb

Item	Temp (°F)	Time (mins)	Item	Temp (°F)	Time (mins)
Bacon (regular)	400 °F	5 to 7	Pork Tenderloin	370 °F	15
Bacon (thick cut)	400 °F	6 to 10	Sausages	380 °F	15
Pork Loin (2 lb.)	360 °F	55	Lamb Loin Chops (1-inch thick)	400 °F	8 to 12
Pork Chops, bone in (1-inch, 6.5 oz)	400 °F	12	Rack of Lamb (1.5 – 2 lb.)	380 °F	22

Fish & Seafood

Item	Temp (°F)	Time (mins)	Item	Temp (°F)	Time (mins)
Calamari (8 oz)	400 °F	4	Tuna Steak	400 °F	7 to 10
Fish Fillet (1-inch, 8 oz)	400 °F	10	Scallops	400 °F	5 to 7
Salmon, fillet (6 oz)	380 °F	12	Shrimp	400 °F	5
Swordfish steak	400 °F	10			

Air Fryer Cooking Chart

Vegetables

INGREDIENT	AMOUNT	PREPARATION	OIL	TEMP	COOK TIME
Asparagus	2 bunches	Cut in half, trim stems	2 Tbsp	420°F	12-15 mins
Beets	1½ lbs	Peel, cut in ½-inch cubes	1 Tbsp	390°F	28-30 mins
Bell peppers (for roasting)	4 peppers	Cut in quarters, remove seeds	1 Tbsp	400°F	15-20 mins
Broccoli	1 large head	Cut in 1-2-inch florets	1 Tbsp	400°F	15-20 mins
Brussels sprouts	1 lb	Cut in half, remove stems	1 Tbsp	425°F	15-20 mins
Carrots	1 lb	Peel, cut in ¼-inch rounds	1 Tbsp	425°F	10-15 mins
Cauliflower	1 head	Cut in 1-2-inch florets	2 Tbsp	400°F	20-22 mins
Corn on the cob	7 ears	Whole ears, remove husks	1 Tbps	400°F	14-17 mins
Green beans	1 bag (12 oz)	Trim	1 Tbps	420°F	18-20 mins
Kale (for chips)	4 oz	Tear into pieces, remove stems	None	325°F	5-8 mins
Mushrooms	16 oz	Rinse, slice thinly	1 Tbps	390°F	25-30 mins
Potatoes, russet	1½ lbs	Cut in 1-inch wedges	1 Tbps	390°F	25-30 mins
Potatoes, russet	1 lb	Hand-cut fries, soak 30 mins in cold water, then pat dry	½ -3 Tbps	400°F	25-28 mins
Potatoes, sweet	1 lb	Hand-cut fries, soak 30 mins in cold water, then pat dry	1 Tbps	400°F	25-28 mins
Zucchini	1 lb	Cut in eighths lengthwise, then cut in half	1 Tbps	400°F	15-20 mins

Made in the USA
Middletown, DE
17 September 2022